3/72

JEWS IN
REMOTE CORNERS
OF THE WORLD

by IDA COWEN

PRENTICE-HALL, INC.
Englewood Cliffs, N.J.

Photographs on pages 33, 50, 166, 167, 214, 260 and 270
are from Hazel Greenwald's collection.
All other photographs are from the author's personal collection.

Cyrus Adler, *Jacob H. Schiff—His Life and Letters.* By permission of John M.
Schiff.
Louis Barish, Ed., *Rabbis in Uniform,* by Chaplain Simon and Lt. Gen. Styer. By
permission of Jonathan David, Publishers, N.Y.
Max Gordon, *Sir Isaac Isaacs, A Life of Service.* By permission of Heinemann,
Melbourne, 1963.
Rudyard Kipling, Departmental Ditties, Barrack Room Ballads. Doubleday &
Company, Inc., and Mrs. George Bambridge. '
Abraham Kotsuji, *From Tokyo to Jerusalem.* Bernard Geis Associates, N.Y.
Ernest Salmon, *Alexandre Salmon et sa femme Ariitaimai,* Société des Océanistes,
Musée de L'Homme, Paris.
Julius Stone, *Stand Up and Be Counted.* Permission by Professor Stone.
The author wishes to thank the editors of the following publications for permis-
sion to use material from her articles originally appearing in these periodicals:
The Chicago Jewish Forum. Winter, 68–69 issue.
Hadassah Magazine, issues of December, 1963; December, 1968; February,
1969; and April, 1969.
The Jerusalem Post, issues of July 1, 1962; February 14, 1967; March 6, 1967;
April 30, 1967; and August 16, 1967.
Jewish Chronicle, London, November 2, 1962 and October 13, 1967.
Jewish Heritage, published by B'nai B'rith's Commission on Adult Jewish
Education, 1640 Rhode Island Avenue, N.W., Washington, D.C. 20036.
Jewish Life, July-August, 1969 issue. Published by Union of Orthodox Jewish
Congregations of America.
Jewish Telegraphic Agency, Inc., Passover Feature, November 14, 1963.
Reconstructionist, April 17, 1964; February 28, 1969; and October 10, 1969.
The American Zionist, published by Zionist Organization of America, N.Y.

MRS. COWEN'S TRAVELS TO THE FAR-FLUNG JEWISH communities of the less well-known parts of the world are unique. Seldom has a woman ventured alone to these lands where an unaccompanied woman is a rarity, if not something of a scandal. And never to our knowledge did a traveler, in modern times, seek out her brothers and sisters for the sheer joy of establishing personal bonds with Jews, without the credentials generally in the possession of a visitor—such as the official documents carried by fund-raisers. With camera and notebook, and no ulterior motives, Mrs. Cowen followed in the tradition of ancient and medieval forebears, who exposed themselves to the hazards of the road so that they might say "Shalom" to Jews in isolated communities.

If she traveled without official credentials, it does not follow that she came unprepared. A long-time Zionist and a committed Jewess, she recognized that Jews constitute a *people,* united by a common tradition, a heritage of faith and fate, and that the sense of mutual responsibility would remain intense even among those who, for generations, had little or no contact with the outside world of Jewry. She knew, in other words, that they were her family, that she wished to be reunited with them, and that, most important of all, she would be received with warmth by the leaders of the communities she would reach—unannounced and uninvited. They would, she was certain, be as deeply interested in the news she might bring them of their fellow Jews as she was to learn of their history and their present situation.

And so it was—as the chapters of her book so vividly confirm. Wherever she introduced herself, she was able to move directly to the spokesmen of the communities; that is, as soon as they understood the genuine motives of her journey. And when she came at moments of festivity or celebration, she was introduced as a daughter of Israel, albeit speaking a strange tongue, dressing in the manner of the West, and (strangest of all) traveling alone.

Mrs. Cowen was probably more surprised than anyone to

find, upon her periodic trips back home, that Jews and others were fascinated to hear of her adventures and to view the pictures she had taken. And when, after including several of her accounts in *The Reconstructionist,* I suggested she try to find a publisher, since interest in her unusual reports would be widespread, she was modestly incredulous, until she did indeed submit her manuscript to the present publisher, who accepted it.

We certainly hope that our intuition will prove to have been correct, that many Jews and non-Jews will wish to read about these communities, some of them extremely ancient.

(RABBI) IRA EISENSTEIN

I HAVE HAD TWO MAIN INTERESTS THROUGHOUT MY life: one being travel, the other, people—especially the Jewish people, of whom I am a part. I combined these two interests by traveling to remote corners of the world—with the specific purpose of acquainting myself with Jewish life there. Twice I started out, alone, for the South Seas, the Pacific and Asia, to places (particularly the small places) where there were some surviving remnants of Jewish life, or where Jews had once lived.

I was intrigued. I wanted to know what had first brought the Jews to the faraway places. Was it a sense of adventure, a wish to "get away from it all," an escape from persecution, a search for gold, or a new field of trade?

And after the Jews did reach these far-off places, were they able to maintain themselves as a distinct group? How did they retain their group identity without being assimilated by the native population? What was life like for these Jews among such diverse peoples as the cannibals of Fiji, the Maoris of New Zealand, the convicts of Tasmania, the gold diggers of Ballarat, the aborigines of Malaysia, the temple monks of Bangkok, the Kuchis of Afghanistan, the Hindus of India and their rajahs, the Shiites of Iran?

This book is a record of my quest for Jews in thirty-six communities and the answers I found to these questions. Everywhere I went I was made to feel like "one of the family." Where English was not understood, I found the Hebrew language a common bond. My stay in each locality was long enough to permit me to share in the people's joys and in their sorrows.

I attended Bar Mitzvahs in Christchurch, in Manila and in New Delhi. I participated in Rosh Hashanah services in Hong Kong, broke Yom Kippur fast with the Jews of Bangkok, crowned the Queen of Beauty chosen at the Simhat Torah Ball in Calcutta. I watched Hanukkah lights being lit in Melbourne, joined Herat's Jews at their Purim feast, observed Seder nights in Izmir and I was among those paying final respects at the funeral of Afghanistan's last rabbi. Sadness, too, came with the thought that some of these communities, dwindling in numbers, would inevitably disappear from the Jewish world.

Through months of talking with people at their homes, at their places of business, at group meetings and at schools, through reading of early synagogue records, nineteenth-century newspapers and library records, came an understanding of the problems besetting small groups determined to maintain a Jewish way of life, far removed though they are from centers such as London and New York.

The path was eased for me over and over again. To give but a few examples: Savi Khafi of Singapore gave me letters of introduction to his family in Afghanistan (and presents for them); Harry Moses was waiting for me in Penang before my bags were even unpacked; Dolly Berman in Auckland aroused the entire New Zealand community to look after me; Farida Djemal of Bangkok suggested I call on her family in Beirut; and Raphael Cohen closed his shop in old Sidon in order to accompany me to points of Jewish interest there. So many people, everywhere, insisted that I take Shabbat or festival meals at a Jewish home and not at the hotel.

There are many people here in America to whom I want to acknowledge a debt of gratitude—particularly to Professor H. Louis Ginsberg and to Rabbi Max Schenk for their reading of the manuscript and their suggestions, to Rabbi Ira Eisenstein for his belief in me and for his encouragement, and to Hazel Greenwald for her warm offer of the use of a few of the photographs that she has taken around the world.

CONTENTS

• 1 •
TAHITI

◄§ ISLE OF PARADISE §►

TAHITI—JUST THE SOUND OF THE NAME OF THIS ISLE OF
Paradise—brings visions of swaying palms, balmy breezes, tranquil lagoons, coral atolls, beaches on the blue Pacific, the rich
green of plants, brilliant-hued hibiscus, poinsettia and bougainvillea, native huts of split bamboo with thatched roofs of
pandanus, on an island set 4,000 miles away from the workaday
world of the Pacific coast of the United States.

I found the vision a reality when in November of 1965 I arrived
at Hotel Tahiti in Papeete, the only town on this 33-mile-long
island. One sits in the open-air dining room, lulled by the breezes
on a terrace overlooking a calm lagoon, and is served by dark-
eyed, lustrous black-haired, cafe-au-lait-skinned Polynesian girls
wearing brightly colored print cotton sheaths, with a tiara—a
single sweet-scented flower behind one ear.

I began to realize the truth of the statement: "When it comes to
pleasure, Tahitians are all business." No wonder that entry visas
are now restricted to those holding a return ticket to their homes,
or to those having prepaid transportation for some other destina-

tion; else all the world's dreamers and beachcombers would end up in Tahiti.

Many have spoken of the charms of Tahiti's women. The crew sailing with Captain Samuel Wallis, the first Europeans to touch on the soil of this "Jewel of the Pacific," swore they had never seen handsomer women in their lives. And American whaler-author Herman Melville said, "Their physical beauty and amiable disposition harmonized completely with the softness of the clime."

But yet another feature had drawn me to this island paradise: The story of the English Jew, Alexander Salmon, who came to Tahiti about 130 years ago and married a princess and chieftainess of the Teva clan—a Tahitian daughter who fell in love with him.

What had brought Alexander Salmon from London to Tahiti, a distance of over 10,000 miles, long before the days when jet airflights brought the whole world so close? Was it a sense of adventure? Was it a desire to explore new horizons, such as the motives that had brought other Englishmen and Frenchmen?

The English navigator Captain Samuel Wallis received his sailing orders from King George III: "Whereas there is reason to believe that Land of great extent, hitherto unvisited by any European Power may be found in the Southern Hemisphere between Cape Horn and New Zealand . . . ." So Captain Wallis became the discoverer of Tahiti in 1766. He named this lovely island "George III Island" in honor of his king, the same monarch against whom the Americans were to rebel just ten short years later.

The year following Wallis's discovery of the island, Louis Antoine de Bougainville, commissioned by the French government to make a voyage of discovery around the world, also came to Tahiti. He gave a romantic description of this "island paradise—its balmy climate, the luxurious and plentiful fruit and the charms of its daughters."

And in 1768 English Lieutenant James Cook was put in command of an expedition on behalf of the London Royal Society of Geography. The official purpose of this trip on the 368-ton *Endeavour* was to make astronomical observations for the Society, but Lieutenant Cook also carried secret instructions:

> *You are also with the consent of the natives to take*
> *possession of convenient situations in the country*
> *[Tahiti] in the name of the King of Great Britain*
> *. . . you will also observe with accuracy the situa-*
> *tion of such islands as you may discover in the*
> *course of your voyage that have not hitherto been*
> *discovered by any Europeans and take possession*
> *for His Majesty.*

His route led him from England via the Madeira Islands, Rio de Janeiro, the Strait of Magellan, Cape Horn, and then west and north reaching Tahiti after 127 days at sea. It was Cook who gave the archipelago, of which Tahiti was the largest island, the name it holds to this day—the Society Islands, in honor of the London Royal Society of Geography.

Again and again Lieutenant Cook explored the Pacific, each time returning to Tahiti. By the time he began his third trip in July 1776—just one week after John Hancock had signed the Declaration of Independence—the newly promoted Captain Cook had established warm, friendly relations with the natives of Tahiti.

When nineteen-year-old Alexander Salmon set out on his travels some sixty years later, it was not for the purpose of discovering new lands for his king, nor was it a desire to escape from civilization, but rather the result of economic conditions within his own family.

Alexander Salmon was the son of an English Jew, John Salmon, who had fled his native France during the Revolution for he was suspect as having contributed financially to the flight of King Louis XVI to Varennes. In 1791 John Salmon escaped to London, where he joined a banking establishment started by a cousin. Ruined by the speculations of this relative, he moved his family to the town of Hastings in Sussex. There John Salmon began life over again as a merchant. Later, he was designated the rabbi for the small Jewish community.

The Salmon family, with four sons and four daughters, was one of distinction, culture and learning. In a portrait of her parents, artist daughter Rebecca portrays her father as a man of resolute determination and her mother as a delicate, charming beauty with large expressive eyes. Another daughter became a pianist and yet another distinguished herself as a contralto.

Fired with the desire to be totally independent, Alexander and two of his brothers renounced their hereditary rights to the family estate in favor of their sisters, and set off to make their own fortune. With fantasies of the fabulous wealth of an Eldorado they set off for California in 1839. It was a long and indirect ship route that lay ahead of them, for their course led them first to Boston, then all the way down the Atlantic rounding Cape Horn up the Pacific Coast, out to the Hawaiian Islands, north to Sitka and south to Vancouver—before reaching San Francisco.

At that time San Francisco was part of the Mexican province of California—a magnet for Russian fur traders, whalers, explorers, merchants and for those coming by covered wagon across the American continent.

It was in San Francisco that the Salmon brothers became acquainted with Captain George William Dunnett who sailed periodically from Sydney to San Francisco bringing cargoes to and from Hawaii and other Pacific islands. This time he had come with a cargo of oranges from Tahiti. Dunnett's tales of the fascinations of these far-off islands intrigued the young and fancy-free Alexander. And when Dunnett proposed that his new friend sail with him on the return to Tahiti, his main point of trade in Polynesia, it followed most naturally that Alexander Salmon set off on Dunnett's schooner for bewitching Tahiti.

Twenty-one-year-old Salmon landed in Tahiti in the spring of 1841, without fame or fortune. But by his handsome appearance, intelligence, gracious manners and knowledge of French, he made a deep impression on society, both European and the elite of the native group. Introduced to Queen Pomare IV, he was admitted to the intimate circle of her court.

It was there that he met twenty-year-old Princess Arrioehau, one of the most beautiful Tahitian women. She had great dignity of person, superior intelligence, a warm heart and irresistible charm of speech.

Her ancestry was also notable. On her paternal side she was the granddaughter of Chief Tati—adviser to the royal house—whose family had been spoken of in the journals of both Captain Wallis and Captain Cook. French Consul Moerenhaut said of Tati, "He is a most distinguished chief—handsome, tall, the most imposing and noble person one can see here. He lives more in a European manner than any of the others." Made welcome at Tati's home in the district of Papara, Moerenhaut was pleasantly surprised to find a good bed with canopy of mosquito netting, a table set impeccably and a tea service.

On her maternal side Princess Arrioehau was descended (as described by her daughter Marau in the latter's Memoirs):

> *According to the genealogy scrupulously transmitted from generation to generation, she was a direct descendant of Tetunae, authentic offspring of our creating gods, and the first sovereign of Tahiti.*

It was love at first sight. Forgotten were the princes with whom matchmaking arrangements had been under way ever since Arrioehau was fifteen years old. She declared she would have none other than Alexander Salmon and was ready to leave everything for his sake.

But an apparently insurmountable obstacle stood in the way of this union. This was a law passed under pressure of the missionaries who had followed in the wake of the navigators and explorers. According to this law, which came into effect only four years before Salmon's arrival, marriage between a foreigner and a native was forbidden.

Queen Pomare IV would not have Arrioehau, her adopted sister and inseparable friend, unhappy. So she found a way out of the impasse. By royal decree the law was abrogated for a period of three days, during which time Alexander Salmon was invested with the Tahitian title of Ariitaimai, "Prince who came from the Sea." Then Ariitaimai married Arrioehau, Princess de la Paix— Princess of Peace.

This happy marriage was to have a decisive influence upon Salmon's economic destiny and public life as well. He had come to Tahiti planning to become a trader, importing and exporting among the various islands. After his marriage, however, he was drawn into the sphere of agriculture, looking after his wife's inherited estates in several parts of Tahiti and on the island of Moorea. At Papara, twenty-four miles out of Papeete, Chief Tati had planted coconut groves. And Salmon introduced coffee on a large scale. Orange plantations yielded abundantly, and his old friend Dunnett now became one of his principal clients for the export of this fruit. Salmon introduced modern methods and the land yielded a good return.

When Salmon came to Tahiti, the islands were in a ferment of antagonism against the Protestant missionaries who had assumed more and more authority and were attempting to establish a British Protectorate over the country. In letters to Lord Palmerston, Salmon informed the British Foreign Secretary that some native chiefs had, under the advice of a French representative, already applied for the protection of the French government, and how much to the interest of England possession of the Society Islands would be.

His marriage to a princess of the Teva Clan, however, brought a decided change in Salmon's political outlook. Chief Tati, head of the Teva Clan, was a champion of French friendship. And the English missionaries, who had been hurt by Salmon's marriage, had put a ban on him. He reacted to their disfavor. Soon Salmon was devoting himself wholeheartedly to the cause of a French Protectorate over Tahiti, his adopted homeland.

An important obstacle to the acceptance of the French Protectorate was the opposition of Queen Pomare. Influenced by British Consul Pritchard, two French Catholic missionaries had been cruelly expelled by the authorities. This brought about French intervention demanding satisfaction and compensation. The French occupied Tahiti and set up an administration in Papeete. The Queen reversed herself and agreed to the setting up of the French Protectorate. Later she repudiated this agreement, exiled herself from Tahiti and took refuge in Raiatea on the Isles of Sous le Vent where anti-French feeling was strongly entrenched.

Aware of the close, affectionate relation between Ariitaimai (the name being applied to both husband and wife) and the Queen, and of the latter's attachment to Alexander Salmon (who was

*Great-grandson and namesake of the English Jew
who settled in Tahiti, present-day Alexander Salmon
acted as author's guide around the island of Tahiti.*

showing devotion to the cause of the French Protectorate), Governor Bruat asked the young English Jew and his wife to intercede with the Queen, putting a French warship at their disposal for the trip to Raiatea. The offer of the *Phaeton* was a mixed blessing, for the chiefs on that island had publicly declared that anyone debarking there from a French war vessel would do so under pain of death.

But Salmon did not let this danger stand in the way of his important mission. He and his wife proceeded to Raiatea, returning with some hope for reconciliation and the Queen's eventual return to Tahiti.

Negotiations dragged on—Tahitians never did like to do things in a hurry. Emissaries had to be sent by ship, and brought back the same way. The Queen was torn between her allegiance to England and her clan on one side, and her affection for the Salmons, the spokesmen for France; between the insistence and intrigues of her pro-British counsellors and the entreaties of Ariitaimai and her husband, who stayed for months at Raiatea.

Meanwhile the government could not function. No legislation could have any legal standing, for the Queen would not sign administrative acts. Despite the continuing insurrection, the French did not want to appear as if they were administering the country by "force majeure," something the press and the evangelical circles of England were stressing.

At one point of the negotiations—in January 1845—Governor Bruat suggested to the chiefs that they depose the Queen and replace her. Several times the crown was tendered to Princess Ariitaimai. Out of loyalty to the Queen and a sense of duty toward her family, Ariitaimai declined the proposal. Had she accepted the proffered crown, an English Jew would then have become the Royal Consort of Tahiti.

On yet another mission, Salmon appeared before an assemblage of 1,500 persons in the island of Huahine, sixty miles from Papeete. A letter giving a full report of this meeting is in the correspondence between Salmon and the governor, preserved in the government archives in Papeete. Included are the following passages:

SPEAKER FOR TAMATOA: *Salmon, what has brought you here?*
SALMON: *I bring you the conditions of peace.*
SPEAKER FOR TAMATOA: *Whose conditions are these, yours or someone else's?*
SALMON: *The conditions I bring are those of Bruat, the French governor.*

And after the presentation and discussion of the peace terms:

SPEAKER FOR TAMATOA: *Chiefs and Huiraa-tira, you have heard the conditions. What say you?*
ONE OF THE CHIEFS: *We have nothing more to say. We accept.*
SPEAKER FOR TAMATOA: *Salmon, the peace of God be with you for having brought us this good news, and the peace of God be with Bruat who has charged you with this mission of peace.*

After this, he asked all those who favored the peace to raise their right hands. Then as with one accord, all present—the entire assembly—raised their right hands. This acceptance was put in writing and Salmon signed it as a representative of the governor, who formally ratified it in April 1846.

After the successful conclusion of this mission, Alexander Salmon returned by whaleboat to report to the Queen. The parleys continued, for a treaty without Queen Pomare's signature was null and void. Salmon had asked Bruat to give the Queen assurance that her authority would be reestablished. In turn, Governor Bruat appealed to the Queen, "If you have any sentiment of pity for your children, your subjects and your country, return quickly."

Intimations of the Queen's change of heart came in a letter delivered secretly to Ariitaimai. Things began to move. Again the Salmons acted as intermediaries. The *Phaeton* was sent to Raiatea. The Queen and her suite, including the Salmons, began the return, sailing for Moorea and Ariitaimai's home on that island only twenty miles from Papeete.

The *Phaeton* continued on to Papeete, picking up Governor Bruat. The scene that followed is recorded by one of the Salmon children as she heard it told by her mother:

> *We did not have to wait long (in Moorea). The warship arrived with Bruat aboard. He landed and came to our home immediately. When he saw the Queen he bent down on his knee three times to pay her homage. She received him well and it was then that the question of the Protectorate was settled, for the Queen signed the treaty.*

The official ceremony of reconciliation took place in a Protestant church. Then the Queen, with Salmon at her side to translate the French documents, signed the act which endorsed the legislation that had been in force during her absence. Salmon was named secretary to the Queen so that he ". . . could have under surveillance the moves of people who might be hostile to the Protectorate."

On February 9, 1847, the Queen returned to Papeete and was received with royal honors, welcomed with the booming of cannons and an honor guard of soldiers. Thus the Princess of Peace and her Jewish husband had truly succeeded in bringing the return of peace to this Jewel of the Pacific.

That the French were grateful to Alexander Salmon for the role he had played in these events is clearly evident. Admiral Dupet-it-Thours, making payments, rewards and decorations to those who had helped the French, called Salmon and, pointing to a table with pen and paper on it, told him, "Write your conditions." Salmon returned the sheet of paper on which he had written the one word, "Nothing." Governor Bruat wrote him, " . . . You rendered us a service great enough during the establishment of the Protectorate to call for the government's generosity."

There was one thing, however, that Salmon did request—the honorary award of the French Legion of Honor—for, he said, "It has great prestige in the eyes of the natives in these faraway lands."

With the return of peace Alexander Salmon turned once again to his private affairs and to the needs of his growing family. Materially he found himself severely hit, for the large plantations at Papara had in the meanwhile been destroyed and the cattle killed or stolen. It was then that he reconsidered and asked indemnity for the losses he had sustained, and compensation for the expenses he had incurred in fulfilling the missions on behalf of the French government.

But by this time the French had assumed an ambivalent attitude. On the one hand they admired Alexander Salmon, but somehow they weren't altogether certain of his allegiance. Governor Bruat wrote, "Mr. Salmon is an English citizen of Jewish faith, married to a daughter of first cousins to the Queen; he is a young man, handsome and distinguished, refined, skillful—and ambitious." Later Commandant Pouget reported to Paris, "Salmon is a remarkable man, with a sure judgment, well educated and a hard worker with rare aptitudes—better versed in literature, jurisprudence, commerce and matters of public utility than most. . . . But if one is not careful, he will force us, out of weariness, to leave the country so that he can use his influence through his trade."

Paris honored neither Salmon's claim for indemnity nor his request for the award of the Legion of Honor. His pride was hurt and he felt that an injustice had been done. In 1858, although his financial position had improved in the period of economic expansion which followed the new peace in Tahiti, Salmon decided to carry his case to France.

Reaching Paris in July, he established himself at the Hotel Bristol on Place Vendome. He presented a letter from Queen Pomare to the director of the Ministry for Algeria and the Colonies for transmission to the Emperor. Then he wrote to the head of this Ministry—His Imperial Highness Prince Napoleon. He asked Lord Cowley, Ambassador of Great Britain to Paris, to intervene in his behalf. But nothing positive resulted.

He went on to London. There he appealed to the Foreign Office to convey his claim to the French government. This request was denied. Next he petitioned the Emperor of France. In December he addressed a letter to the Emperor's private secretary for transfer to the ruler. No response. Six months later, in June 1859, he sent a copy of the letter to Count Shaftesbury asking him to act as intermediary for its delivery to the Emperor. Finally he made the letter public under the heading: "Letter concerning the present state of Tahiti addressed to His Imperial Majesty Napoleon III." All to no avail.

The one bright interlude in this year of frustration and failure was Alexander Salmon's stay with his family in Hastings, England in the warm and intimate atmosphere of his old home, surrounded by his dear ones. After so many years abroad—in an island across the world—this reunion of son and brother with his family was indeed an emotional and happy time.

During the years communication between the family in England and in Tahiti had been maintained. On his marriage wedding gifts from Hastings had included a service of Sèvres and silver plates, flatware and a tea service. He would speak affectionately of "the old gentleman"—his rabbi father. Later he was to send two of his sons, Tati and Paea, to be educated in the same boarding school as their cousins (children of his sister Kate), not far from the grandparents in Hastings. During their five-year stay in England, Tati and Paea were spoiled by Aunt Rebecca, the artist of the family.

Life took on a more stable, contented tenor with his return home to Papeete in July 1859. Salmon became a partner in the firm of John Brander (husband of Salmon's daughter Titaua), who had made a fortune in pearl trading and had become the most important ship chandler in Tahiti. Again Alexander Salmon devoted himself to public service, becoming Honorary Consul for the United States, president of the Papeete Chamber of Commerce, president of the Papeete Lodge of Free Masons, vice-president of one of the courts and member of the Administrative Council.

A few years later, in 1865, when Brander was on an extended stay in Europe, Salmon directed the business. His reports to Brander on the state of their affairs form a 190-page journal that has been preserved in its entirety. It gives a vivid description of the economic state of the Protectorate as well as a picture of an important firm with extensive and diversified interests, not only in importing and exporting, but also in the cultivation on its own plantations of sugar cane and cotton.

In one letter dispatched in April by the schooner *Le Bremontier,* the following excerpts indicate this diversification of interests:

1. The *Hornet* arrived on the 24th at Anaa with 12 tons of oil; I hope to have 60 tons of oil for the *Sylph* in addition to 25,000 oranges; the *Ionia* and the *Samoa* arrived the same day.

2. Perhaps you could buy a second hand ship similar to the one that was used in the trading of fruit—from 120 to 160 tons.

3. Everyone's planting cotton.

4. As long as the American war continues, there is no hope for any change for the better in the cotton world.

5. You will also find a letter from Foster and Adams containing a purchase order for a sugar machine. They plant sugar cane on a large scale and depend on you to send the machine as you had promised before leaving.

6. I am buying for you the land of Teato, located at Pirae, as well as a magnificent lot close by.

7. There are some good pieces of land available at a cheap price.

And in July Salmon reported via letter sent by *L'Elise:*

> *I have now in the harbor the schooners Suerte, Favorite, Aorai, Eimeo, Anna Laurie, Sylph and Hornet without mentioning the chartered boats with their holds full of oil.*

The firm could afford itself such luxuries as spoken of in his August letter:

> *Should you decide to stay on longer, I would then send the Favorite to Payata [Panama] especially for you; you will then have the cabin to yourselves, plus the advantage of taking off whenever you wish.*

The Brander flotilla included a dozen schooners (of 120 to 160 tons) maintaining regular, active communications not only with Pacific Islands such as Fiji, Samoa, Rarotonga, New Caledonia, Independence, but also with New Zealand, Australia, Hawaii, San Francisco, Chile, Peru and Panama.

Throughout the correspondence there also runs the thread of the "pater familias" (Salmon fathered nine children). When Scotsman Brander visited with the family in Hastings, Salmon wrote him, "Tell the old gentleman that I'll write him regularly each month via Valparaiso." The journal is replete with steady reports on the health, growth and education of the children and grandchildren. All the children but one had been sent abroad for their education, either to Australia or to England, near their grandfather the rabbi, despite the fact that Salmon had by this time formally entered the Protestant Church.

Tomb of Pomare V, last king of Tahiti; his wife, Queen Marau, was a daughter of the English Jew Alexander Salmon.

In August 1866 Alexander Salmon died during a dysentery epidemic. Only forty-six years old at the time, he was mourned by the entire colony. Shops closed spontaneously, consular and ship flags in the harbor of Papeete were at half mast. Queen Pomare, the Imperial Commissioner, all the officials and a tremendous crowd—where all religions and nationalities were represented— followed the funeral procession. *Tirara to tatou metua i Taiti nei*—"Our father is dead. We have no longer a father in Tahiti," wept the natives.

Salmon's immediate family was affected very deeply by his death, particularly his seventh child Marau, who was only six years old when her father died. As preserved in the manuscripts, from which the quotations here have been made, and recorded by Marau's son Ernest Salmon, who was the first Tahitian to have made a career in the French magistracy (becoming Presiding Judge of the Court of Appeals in St. Denis on the island of Reunion), Marau recalls:

> *My father used to say that he preferred to see his daughters dead rather than married to Tahitian*

*princes, as he predicted only evil from their brutal
instincts and their deplorable education.*

The father's advice had been followed: Two daughters married
Scotsmen, one wed a Frenchman, and another married an American Civil War hero who became United States Consul in Papeete.
But Marau was different. She married Prince Ariiaue, who later
became Pomare V, last king of Tahiti. Marau's Memoirs continue:

> *Queen Pomare wanted me for her son and heir. It
> was the traditional policy of the Pomares. Of a
> race foreign to the country, they felt the need to
> marry into our family so that our ancestral titles
> and authority would legitimize somewhat the usur-
> pation that circumstances and the support of the
> missionaries had allowed them. My mother, not
> wishing to hurt her adopted sister by a clear re-
> fusal, left the decision to a family council which
> ended by yielding to the Queen's wishes. And that
> is how, without even being consulted, I found my-
> self engaged to the future king of Tahiti, then thir-
> ty-six years old while I was barely fifteen. . . .
> My fiance had superb presence and had traveled to
> Valparaiso and to San Francisco, but he remained
> very Tahitian and all his desires were indulged. I
> regret to be obliged to say that he would get drunk,
> a failing common among his people; the respon-
> sibility for which rests with the Europeans who en-
> couraged this amongst those of our people in
> whose good graces they wished to be.*

And so they were married in the palace. Old customs were
revived for the occasion. Chiefs, magnificently dressed in Polynesian ponchos ornamented with floating ribbons, delivered dis-
courses of glorification; ancient tunes were chanted; natives
brought precious wedding gifts.

The marriage was not a success and they separated. When
Queen Pomare IV died after a reign of half a century, history
repeated itself—for now it was Alexander Salmon's daughter
Marau whom the chiefs (whose consent was required for the
nomination of a king or queen), wished to name as successor to
the throne. And again Princess Ariitaimai, remaining faithful to

the line laid down by Tati, refused. So Prince Ariiaue became King Pomare V on condition that he send away his mistresses and resume life with Marau.

A few years later, Pomare V, upon the promise of a large sum of money, abdicated the throne. Down came the flag of the Protectorate and up went the flag of France. Tahiti, by the Act of Annexation of 1880, became part of France.

Some time later, when Marau traveled to France incognito as Mrs. Salmon, her visit caused a furor. *L'Illustration* and the *Graphic* of London devoted articles to her visit: "Queen Marau is a young woman twenty-five years old, tall and handsome with an oval face, big languid eyes, a straight nose, well marked lips and two long plaits." Paris fashion was influenced by her Tahitian mode of dress. At theatres the presidential box was put at her disposal. Sarah Bernhardt, whose performance in *Dame aux Camélias* Marau attended, sent a photograph with the inscription: "To the Very Gracious Queen Marau, from another subject."

During my visit in Papeete, young Alexander Salmon, who told me he was so named because of his resemblance to his forebear, and his cousins—although Christian by faith—acknowledge their descent from the scion of the house of an English Jewish banker and rabbi.

• 2 •
FIJI

⋅⋅§ JEWS IN CANNIBAL LAND §⋅⋅

L'HAYIM I SAID, RAISING MY WINE GLASS AT CLAUDE ISRA-
el's dinner table in Suva, capital city of the Fiji Islands. My hosts
looked at me without understanding. After sixty years spent in an
area once familiar to the world as the Cannibal Islands, set 5,600
miles from California across the Pacific, the toast "L'hayim" had
lost all meaning for Claude Israel and his wife.

I had flown the Pacific to see for myself what remained of a
once prosperous community of Jews trading in the Fiji Islands, a
sort of way station between America and Australia. It's fortunate,
I thought, as the jet taxied to a stop at Nandi Airport, that this was
1965 and not a hundred years ago when cannibalism was still
being practiced here. At that time strangers were not encouraged
to visit. An old Fijian proverb held that "people with salt water in
their eyes" must be killed! So woe betide the shipwrecked person
who reached the shores of these unfriendly islands.

In those days members of the warrior caste, as a mark of
triumph, ate the bodies of enemies fallen in battle. A set ritual and
ceremony covered every step in the procedure. Today at the Suva

Museum one can see the special three-pronged cannibal fork used for such occasions. Eating human flesh was acceptable, but etiquette demanded that such viands never be eaten with one's fingers.

But times had changed, and I set out confidently on the 135-mile automobile trip from Nandi, on the west coast, to Suva on the east coast of Viti Levu, principal island of the Fiji group which totals 300 islands.

The countryside was peaceful: small villages, sugar cane fields, children carrying lunchpails on their way to school. There were very few Fijians to be seen, as most of the inhabitants are Indians, descendants of those who had been brought to the Fiji Islands as indentured laborers in these same sugar cane fields, at the close of the nineteenth century.

After Korolevu the countryside grew wilder. Roads were rough-going through the lush tropical jungle area. Rubber, bamboo, banyan and coconut trees grew high. Brilliant-hued flowers and the mynah birds added their own beauty. Yoked oxen were seen plowing the small fields. Villages were infrequent, and the native Fijians were of the Melanesian Negroid race.

Stopping at villages along the way, I was invited in by friendly women, barefoot, but clad in blouse and sulu, the ankle-length skirt. Their huts were of bamboo framework with thatched walls and roof. Plaited bamboo separated the sleeping quarters from the living area. Straw mats were spread on the floor, and atop those an eating mat. Occasionally there was a picture of Christ hanging on the wall, a reminder that missionaries had braved the danger of cannibalism to spread their faith here over 135 years ago.

When I arrived in Suva I walked along Victoria Parade, the main street facing the waters of the Pacific. It was here that Jews had had their business establishments. Among them were the Hort brothers, Abraham and Alfred, sons of the founding father of the Wellington congregation in New Zealand. The Horts had operated a fleet of sailing vessels trading among the islands of Fiji, Tahiti and New Zealand. Then there were the Marks brothers, Henry and Gabriel, of Melbourne. Among other Jewish business men were the Brodziaks, Lazarus, Joske, Benjamin,

Library in capital city of Fiji, enlarged during term of office of Sir Henry Marks, Jewish Mayor of Suva.

Samuel and Levy. Some of them had branched out into the smaller islands of the Fijis and built up chain stores of significance.

Today the shops along Victoria Parade are run by Indians or Chinese. Further down the street I came to a white-washed, columned building surrounded by a spacious lawn bearing the inscription:

ADDITIONS TO THE
CARNEGIE LIBRARY
BUILDINGS
COMMENCED
SEPTEMBER 1ST, 1929
HENRY MARKS, C.B.E.
MAYOR

This was the Henry Marks of Melbourne who had come to Fiji as a young man and had opened a store in Suva, trading under the name of Henry Marks & Co. Being successful, he opened branches in all the country districts. In 1920 he amalgamated with the Morris Hedstrom firm which, under the latter name, grew to be the wealthiest merchant house in all of the South Sea Islands.

But Henry Marks was more than a successful businessman. He played a prominent role in civic life, becoming known as the uncrowned king of Fiji. During World War I he raised a contingent of a hundred Fijians for transport service in France, personally contributing £5000 for their equipment. His firm also donated a large sum for the same cause.

Henry Marks was Mayor of Suva and bore the title of C.B.E. (Commander, Order of the British Empire). On the occasion of his golden wedding anniversary, the British monarch further honored Marks by conferring a knighthood upon him.

Henry Marks brought over several relatives from Australia to join him in the business. Among these was brother Gabriel, who became the leading force in keeping the spark of Judaism alive in Fiji. Religious services were held in his home. It was both a personal and community tragedy when Gabriel Marks and his wife were drowned when the *Emperor of Ireland,* a ship on which they had sailed for a trip to England, sank in the St. Lawrence River.

Whatever organized Jewish life there had been in Suva died with the loss of Gabriel Marks. Public worship ceased, and ritual objects, for which there were no further use, were sent to New Zealand. Today in Suva Park there stands a water fountain, given to the people of the city by Henry Marks in memory of his brother.

I retraced my steps along Victoria Parade, passing the policeman directing traffic in scalloped, knee-length white sulu skirt and elbow-high white gloves. Soon I reached the large open-air, canvas-topped marketplace where sari-clad Indian women shoppers made a brilliant sight amid the lush-colored tropical vegetables. Just beyond the marketplace I boarded a bus for the short ride to the community cemetery.

The city of the dead in Suva serves the needs of a polyglot population. In addition to the two main groups (Indians and Fijians), natives from the neighboring island groups, Europeans and Chinese, rest in this cemetery. I passed the sections serving each of these sectors before reaching the Jewish quarter on a hilltop. I came to an impressive yet simple tombstone, a palm tree at its head and a sweet-smelling cinnamon tree at its foot, bearing the inscription:

IN MEMORY OF
HENRY MARKS
KNIGHT BACHELOR
COMMANDER OF THE MOST EXCELLENT
ORDER OF THE BRITISH EMPIRE
JUSTICE OF THE PEACE
WHO DIED ON 4TH JUNE 1938
AGED 77 YEARS

Nearby, surrounded by trees and overlooking Suva harbor, was a rain-blackened tombstone with the inscription in Hebrew and English letters:

IN LOVING MEMORY OF
PHILLIP SAMUEL SOLOMON
BORN IN ESSEX 1ST OCT. 1830
DEPARTED THIS LIFE AT SUVA, FIJI
23RD MARCH 1897

ERECTED BY HIS MANY FRIENDS AS TRIBUTE
OF THE ESTEEM IN WHICH HE WAS HELD BY
THEM AND AS A MEMENTO OF HIS KIND-
HEARTEDNESS AND PHILANTHROPY

This was the resting place of the Honorable P. S. Solomon who had been active in synagogue affairs in Sydney and minister to the congregation of Auckland before coming to Fiji to become editor of the *Fiji Times*, Queen's Counsel, Acting Attorney General and member of the Fiji Legislative Council.

Remembered also was Isaac Solomon Fernandez, Australian Jew who had been manager of one of the Brodziak stores at Nausori. His wife raised this memorial:

IN LOVING MEMORY
OF MY DEARLY BELOVED HUSBAND
ISAAC SOLOMON FERNANDEZ
DIED 10TH NOV.   30TH MARCHESHVAN 5692

The Hebrew lettering said that Isaac Solomon was the son of Solomon Jochanan the priest.

Tombstone of Hon. Phillip Samuel Solomon, Queen's Counsel, Acting Attorney, member of Fiji Legislative Council, in Jewish cemetery overlooking Suva harbor.

But what of Fiji's Jews today? Back in town, again on Victoria Parade, I dropped in at the Jewelry and Watch Shop run by H. D. Thaw, a man whom I could have identified in any crowd as a European Jew. Mr. Thaw had been brought to Fiji from Berlin under the sponsorship of Sam Levy (a local Jew) just before the outbreak of World War II. Taken into Mr. Levy's jewelry business, Thaw did very well, particularly during the war period when American troops were stationed in Fiji. To use the Fijian idiom, Mr. Thaw is now "very financial."

Noel Levy (brother of the Sam Levy who had sponsored the entry of Mr. Thaw and others during the Hitler era) denied being a Jew. "Yes, our name is Levy, but we're not Jews," said Mrs. Levy.

The one household in Suva where people were proud to acknowledge themselves as Jews was that of my hosts, the Israels. Claude Israel was born in Melbourne, the grandson of a man who had migrated from Poland to England before coming "down under" to New Zealand. At the age of sixteen he joined Uncle

Henry Marks in the Fijis. At that time all the large commercial establishments were still in Jewish hands. "There were incidents of cannibalism when I first came here," Claude Israel told me. Head of Rotary and active in Masonic work, Mr. Israel's card carried the initials M.B.E. and J.P. He speaks both the Hindustani and Fijian languages. Now eighty, Mr. Israel has retired from his post as Managing Director of C. Sullivan & Co., which represents Columbia Pictures and various manufacturers in the Fiji Islands.

Mrs. Israel, the former Doris Abraham of Melbourne (before her marriage over fifty years ago), is the personification of the Biblical "Ayshet Hayil" (Woman of Valor). For years she worked with her husband in the business. During World War II she operated a canteen for the 50,000 American soldiers stationed in Fiji.

Claude and Doris Israel are part and parcel of the capital of this British Crown Colony. When Queen Elizabeth and the Duke of Edinburgh paid a visit to Suva, it was the Israels' son Mark, a member of the Suva City Council, who welcomed Her Majesty to the capital.

When the Israels invited me to take "pot luck" with them, how could I withstand the temptation when I heard that the *pièce de résistance* was to be matzoh balls. The mere thought of matzoh balls in Cannibal Land was irresistible. Proudly, Mr. Israel showed me the container of "Kosher L'Pesach Matzoh," imported from Australia and made under the supervision of the Beit Din of Sydney.

As we sat around the table in the lovely home high on a hill rising above Suva Harbor, my hosts summoned up Jewish memories out of the past. "What is the name of that song which comes near the close of services in the synagogue?" asked Mr. Israel, as he started to hum a tune which I easily identified as "Adon Olam." Mrs. Israel was proud of the fact that recently, when someone had sent her a Rosh Hashanah card, she had recalled enough to be able to wish the sender "well over the fast" of Yom Kippur.

These Jews have forgotten the meaning of "L'Hayim" (to life)—and I am afraid there is not much hope of life for a Jewish community in the foreseeable future in the Fiji Islands.

• 3 •
NEW ZEALAND

THE FIRST Jewish wedding in New Zealand was about to take place in 1841 in Kororareka, that town notorious for its many saloons, grogshops, lawless adventurers, escaped Australian convicts, whalers and wild brawls. Such requisites as a "ketubah" (marriage contract) were not available then in the "Wild West" setting of Kororareka, in the northern part of New Zealand.

The bride, Rosetta (widow of a ship's captain), had with her the ketubah of her first marriage in England. So it was carefully copied, letter for letter, dot for dot, on the reverse side of the original. The name of the groom, David Nathan, was substituted and the correct date and place noted. Performing the ceremony was Israel Joseph, the business partner of the groom. Two hundred officers of the British fleet, then in port, attended the wedding reception.

White people had just begun to drift in to New Zealand, a two-island Pacific Ocean country slightly smaller than Colorado, set halfway between the equator and the South Pole, about 1,200 miles to the southeast of Australia. The first known inhabitants were the Maoris, far-voyaging, brown Polynesians who first touched these shores back in the ninth century. The lure of the land stayed with these people, and their descendants returned in the fourteenth century to settle permanently, coming from the Society Islands, a distance of 1,650 miles, in catamarans, large canoes with masts and sails.

The Maoris established a communal society, everyone sharing what was possessed by the group as a whole. They dressed in feather cloaks and clothing made of flax fiber, they used green-stone adzes, were adept in woodcarving and lived happily in their "Gift of the Sea," as they named their land.

Three centuries later rumors spread around the world—then in a fever of exploration—that there was a large island in the Pacific that was full of gold and inhabited by Jews. The Dutch East India Company sent Abel Tasman to investigate. His party, in 1642, was the first white group actually to see the shores of these islands. But the natives frightened the "palefaces" off, and Tasman forbore from landing on what he named Statenland, later to be renamed by the East India Company as Nieuw Zeeland, for a Dutch province of that name.

About a century and a quarter later, in 1769, indefatigable English Captain Cook landed in New Zealand and English interest was aroused in the land of the Maoris and the possibilities for trade in that part of the world. By the beginning of the nineteenth century, whaling ships, missionaries and traders began coming.

Among the early arrivals was Joseph Barrow Montefiore (cousin of Sir Moses Montefiore). He arrived from Australia in 1830, developed good relations with the natives and learned to speak their language. Chartering a vessel, he sailed around North Island, making several excursions into the interior. Reporting to a committee of the House of Lords in London some years later, Mr. Montefiore said, "When I was at Kawhia Harbor I obtained a grant of land from a chief under condition that I should establish a mercantile establishment there. I did not purchase it—it was given to me." This was at a time when individuals, including missionaries, were making land purchases in New Zealand for a fraction of the actual value of the land.

The following year, his cousin John Israel Montefiore set up a trading station on the waterfront at the Bay of Islands on the east coast. In the same year, Joel Samuel Polack—artist, writer, explorer—reached New Zealand and began as a trader and merchant at Kororareka, later recording his New Zealand experience in two books. Both John Israel Montefiore and Polack were linked with the early days of the Jewish community at Auckland.

Glowing reports about New Zealand reached England. Joseph Barrow Montefiore said:

> *It is a perfect paradise. I think so highly of the country that although when I went out to New South Wales [Australia] His Majesty granted me 5000 acres of land, I would readily have changed it for 1000 acres in New Zealand.*

It was a scenic wonderland, a land of mountain peaks, spouting geysers, bubbling mud, lakes and fjords. It was a land rich in economic possibilities, for the waters surrounding it abounded in whales and seals. Kauri timber, hemp and flax grew on the land. All this at a time when poverty was rife in England. The New Zealand Land Company, a joint stock association, was set up in London offering land in New Zealand at £1 an acre.

Interest in the shares soared, and in July 1839 subscribers met in an auction room in London to draw lots for priorities in the selection of lots in a land almost 12,000 miles distant. Sir Isaac Lyon Goldsmith, first Jewish baronet in England and a director of the New Zealand Land Company encouraged Jews to emigrate from poverty-stricken England to the new land of hope.

Two months later a small sailing vessel set out for New Zealand, arriving there in January 1840. During the year that followed, four more small sailing ships made the long voyage from England to New Zealand. Soon the number of whites on the island had grown to a thousand, and speculation in land prices was running high.

Then, as in so many other places, the flag followed trade. The

British government sent Captain William Hobson to arrange for the annexation of New Zealand, on the strength of Captain Cook's discovery and the number of English settlers already in the land.

This was carried through, not by conquest, but by treaty—the Treaty of Waitangi, signed in February 1840 by 512 Maori chiefs (either in writing, or by mark or by sketch of the pattern of the chief's face tattoo) and by Captain Hobson, now commissioned Consul and Lieutenant-Governor of New Zealand. The terms of the treaty were:

> *Article 1. The Chiefs of the Confederation of the United Tribes of New Zealand, and the separate and independent Chiefs . . . cede to Her Majesty the Queen of England, all the rights and powers of Sovereignty which the said Chiefs respectively exercise or possess.*

> *Article 2. Her Majesty the Queen of England confirms and guarantees to the Chiefs and Tribes of New Zealand . . . the full and undisturbed possession of their Lands . . . and other properties . . . so long as it is their wish and desire to retain the same; but the Chiefs . . . yield to Her Majesty the exclusive right of preemption over such lands as the proprietors thereof may be disposed to alienate . . .*

> *Article 3. In consideration thereof, Her Majesty the Queen of England extends to the Natives of New Zealand Her Royal Protection, and imparts to them all the Rights and Privileges of British subjects.*

Because of Kororareka's bad reputation and its location near the extreme north of the island, Hobson chose a new, as yet undeveloped site further south, to be the capital and named it Auckland. As soon as this was done, many transferred their activities to the new capital. Among these was David Nathan, who became the founding father of the Jewish community in Auckland.

David Nathan's grandfather, of a Dutch Orthodox family, had moved to London. A rich cousin there started off every young member of the family with some business training and sent them out to the colonies with a stake of £100. While still in London, David Nathan bought some acreage in New Zealand. At the age of twenty-four he set up a store on the seashore at Kororareka. Transferring to Auckland, he opened his "Commercial House" on what is now the corner of Shortland Crescent and High Street. It was while on a business trip to Kororareka that he married Rosetta Aarons, using that Double Ketubah in what was the first Jewish wedding in New Zealand.

Everything David Nathan touched turned to gold. Starting with the export of kauri gum (a resinous product of the tall kauri tree, used for making varnish), the firm soon handled half of the country's entire yield of that product. Gradually the firm enlarged its sphere of activities to include wine and spirits, groceries, general merchandise, pianos, a brewery, an ostrich farm, marine insurance and shipping. David Nathan also became a commission agent and auctioneer, at a time when being an auctioneer meant one was a man of good standing in the community.

Jewish religious services were held at first in David Nathan's home, until he fitted up a room at his warehouse for Sabbath and festival prayers. In 1855 a one-story wooden building in Emily Place was leased and later bought for use as a synagogue for the community, which by then numbered almost a hundred. For twenty years David Nathan was president of the congregation, and in 1884 he laid the foundation stone of an enlarged synagogue for the needs of the 375 Jews then in Auckland. Erected on Princes Street and Bowen Crescent, it remained in continual use until 1968.

Privileged membership in the Beth Israel Congregation, giving a person the right to vote, was "lost by any member marrying out of the faith or who violated the covenant of Abraham or didn't have his daughter named in the synagogue." These stipulations intimated the religious problems Auckland and other pioneering groups faced when single young men settled in a strange land.

The Chief Rabbi of the British Empire* was sympathetic. Although no Beit Din existed on the island, temporary courts were established to handle cases of desired conversion to the Jewish faith. All requests approved by these courts were sent on for authorization to the Chief Rabbi.

During the early years the Maoris had rebelled against the whites, opposing land sales to Europeans. As a mark of disaffection they turned away from Christianity, to which the missionaries had converted them, and adopted a new religion. Believing themselves to be Jews, their new faith was a mixture of belief in the Jewish Bible (they observed the Sabbath in preference to Sunday), some paganism and cannibalism. In war they cut off the heads of enemies, drank the blood and ate the eyes as a sign of victory over the defeated one. Newspapers of the world at one time gave accounts of how one Jew, Captain Levy, managed to save the life of the Christian missionary Grace, only because of the good will that existed between the Maoris and Captain Levy—a Jew.

The Jews played an important role in the general life of the city. Philip Aaron Philips, while serving as the first mayor, had local law changed so that Auckland's market day would be on Friday instead of on the customary Saturday. Henry Isaacs was the second mayor and Sir Ernest Davis was a three-time mayor of Auckland. David Nathan, Charles Davis and Henry Keesing were commissioners on the first Harbor Board.

But there was one Jew who belonged not only to Auckland, but to all of New Zealand, a man who was the virtual ruler of the country for an entire decade: Sir Julius Vogel, known as the Disraeli of New Zealand. Born in London in 1835, two years before Queen Victoria came to the throne, he died a few years after her death. Julius Vogel was orphaned at an early age and lived with his grandfather. While yet a teen-ager he set out alone for Australia when gold was discovered there, reaching Mel-

*The official designation is: Chief Rabbi of the United Hebrew Congregations of the British Empire. Since 1953, the title has been Chief Rabbi of the United Hebrew Congregations of the Bristish Commonwealth. The terms are used interchangeably according to the appropriate dates.

bourne when he was only seventeen years old. Assaying gold and other early ventures proved unprofitable. But success in journalism came when he was twenty-one.

He went on to New Zealand when gold was found around Dunedin in South Island and started a newspaper there. He found his true niche in life, however, when he was elected to the Provincial Assembly. From then on politics was his consuming passion. He moved on to the capital city, Auckland. Although a member of various ministries and Prime Minister on two different occasions, Julius Vogel preferred to pull the strings of power while keeping himself out of sight.

A visionary, he called for a large loan on the London money market to build railroads in New Zealand; he urged a national lottery for disposition of large areas of land; he sponsored a Government Life Insurance Act; he initiated a government mail service between New Zealand and England via San Francisco; he fought for the rights of women.

Audacious, he pressed a plan to make New Zealand the headquarters of a South Sea Empire, the trading center for all the Pacific communities. The plan called for the produce of the various Pacific Islands to be brought to New Zealand where all manufacturing would be done, and finished products then shipped back to the islands.

Vogel's dream of empire called for the annexation of Samoa. At one time he had a steamer waiting in Auckland harbor "with a landing force of a police sergeant and four constables and a single brass gun" ready to go to Samoa with a minister for the island. But the British government would not accede to his plan.

Self-confident, ambitious, versatile, he became Sir Julius Vogel when England honored him with the K.C.M.G. (Knight Commander, Order of St. Michael and St. George). The last years of his life were spent in England.

An important element in the stable development of Auckland's Jewish community was the fact that its rabbis remained for long periods. First there was the Reverend Moses Elkin who served for fifteen years from 1864 to 1879. For much of this time his effort was to strengthen observance of the Sabbath. Reverend Elkin wrote in the *Australian Israelite* of November 1873, "The love of

God was exchanged for that of Mammon. To remove this temptation has been my great endeavor."

Then came the Reverend Samuel Aaron Goldstein, who ministered to the community for over half a century from 1880 until his death in the early 1930s. He is remembered with affection as a saintly person with great knowledge, a man of culture who devoted his life to the congregation.

Since 1931 the community has been led by Reverend Alexander Astor. Russian-born and a student at Jews' College in England, Reverend Astor was the Senior Jewish Chaplain to the New Zealand forces in World War II. This was the period when local Jewry went all out to aid German and Austrian Jewish "alien" internees who had been sent from England to Australia and New Zealand. Funds were collected and Reverend Astor signed affidavits admitting the refugees from Nazi Europe, so that today half of Auckland's Jews are of Central European origin.

This was in the tradition of Auckland's Jewry showing its kinship with Jews around the world. It appealed to the Czars on behalf of Russian Jews and contributed to the relief of Jews in Jerusalem and other places in Palestine, as well as to the support of the Beth El Synagogue in San Francisco. To mark the centennial of Sir Moses Montefiore in 1884 an illuminated address enclosed in New Zealand timber was sent to him.

Lawrence David Nathan, great-grandson of the first David Nathan, was head of the community when I came to New Zealand in 1965. With great pride Mr. Nathan showed me the Double Ketubah used at the wedding of his ancestor. Now framed in glass, so one can see both marriage contracts, the ketubah holds a place of importance in the head office of L.D. Nathan & Co.

The office itself is a far cry from the tent store on the seashore, set up by the founder of the Nathan company. But reminders of those early days are maintained, for New Zealanders take delight in their achievements here. Samples of kaori gum, first acquisition of the Nathan clan, are on display, as well as some Maori artifacts including a cannibal knife. A portrait of the first David Nathan overlooks today's office. Head of the Nathan family, wounded at the Libyan front in World War II, in which he was mentioned in dispatches, Lawrence David Nathan not only head-

*Auckland, N.Z.—Synagogue of the Auckland He-
brew Congregation on Princes St. and Bowen Crescent, in use from 1885 to 1968.*

ed the wide commercial interests of L.D. Nathan & Co., but
has also acted as chairman of the Auckland Harbor Board and
chairman of Consolidated Hotels. As a Nathan had been in every
generation, he was the president of the Auckland Hebrew Congregation.

Notwithstanding the fact that Auckland is New Zealand's busiest commercial center, with one-third of the country's trade
passing over its wharves, life in this subtropical city is relaxed.
People live in homes, not in apartments, and many have a
weekend home near the ocean. Many people own a little boat or
yacht. New Zealanders are sports-loving—participating in bowling, boating, horse racing, skiing and cricket playing. There are
not very many wealthy families, nor are there many who are very
poor. This is a welfare state and everyone is looked after from the
cradle to the grave.

A Jew in Auckland belongs to the synagogue as a matter of
course. At every service the rabbi is ceremoniously garbed in
black robe, black shirt and reversed white collar. Pews are like
high-backed stalls. The Sunday school has volunteer teachers and
youth services are held. A B'nai B'rith group exists and also the
Habonim Youth Group, some of whose members look ahead to

life in Israel. Women have their special groups as elsewhere—Wizo, Union of Jewish Women and the Synagogue Women's Guild.

The Auckland Hebrew Congregation, to which the large majority of the families belong, is Orthodox and under the aegis of the Chief Rabbi of the British Commonwealth. But nearly everyone rides to synagogue on the Sabbath. Only about ten of the families associated with this Orthodox synagogue are strict observers of the Sabbath and live near enough to the synagogue to walk to services.

In 1955 a small group broke away and organized a Liberal congregation holding prayer services at a rented store until they were able to arrange better quarters. Now grown to number almost one hundred families, they have built an architecturally modern Temple Shalom on Manakau Road. Affiliated with the World Union for Progressive Judaism, it conducts weekly Sabbath services and has a full roster of activities including a religious school for the children and a class in Hebrew for the adults. Leader of Temple Shalom since 1969 has been Jerusalem-born Rabbi Samuel H. Tov Lev. A graduate of the Hebrew University, he received his ordination after attending the Liberal College of Rabbinical Studies in Paris.

Resentment against the breakaway group was very strong on the part of those attached to the Orthodox synagogue, but in recent reports I have received, there has been indication of an improving relationship between the two wings of Jewry in this pleasant, relaxed community of fifteen hundred Jews.

⊸§ WINDY WELLINGTON §⊷

Short, wiry Sid Braham reeled off his boxing honors—flyweight fighter in London, bantamweight champion of Auckland, life member of the Wellington Boxing Association—as we talked in New Zealand's only kosher butcher shop, where the ex-boxer, wearing his all-enveloping butcher's apron, assisted his son-in-law.

From Auckland I had gone to windy Wellington, where this kosher butcher shop is located. Near the southern tip of New Zealand's North Island, Wellington's winding streets and red-

Wellington, N.Z.—Only kosher butcher shop in the country; on the right, Sid Braham, former bantam-weight boxing champion of Auckland, assistant to his son-in-law, the butcher.

roofed buildings climb the terraced hillsides from the harbor of Port Nicholson.

Almost a century and a half ago white men had touched here when two English vessels, the *Rosanna* and the *Lambton,* left a party of men on shore to collect flax and timber. The captain of the *Rosanna* named the harbor Port Nicholson after the harbor master of Sydney, Australia, whence they had come.

Actual settlement was not thought of until 1839, when the New Zealand Land Company sent an advance party to choose a site for the company's first planned settlement in this part of the island. They named the chosen site Wellington, in honor of the first Duke of Wellington, who had lent his support to the company. There now stands on the shore a memorial to the city's pioneer white settlers, erected on the centennial of their arrival. In the form of a sailing vessel marked with the dates 1840–1940, it contains a roster of "Pioneer Settlers of New Zealand." I found included in this list the names of two Jews, Benjamin Levy and Solomon Levy.

Other early Jewish arrivals were Moses and Jacob Joseph,

Wellington, N.Z.—Memorial marking centenary of arrival of pioneer white settlers in 1840; roster of Aurora includes names of Benjamin Levy and Solomon Levy.

C. Cohen and Morris Asher. Nathaniel Levin began trading on Lambton Quay under the name of Levin & Co., which soon had a ship, the *Wellington* built in Glasgow for the firm's use. Its brigantine *Rover's Pride* traded with Tahiti, and one of its ships sailed as far as California after the gold strike of 1849. Twenty-year-old Abraham Hort, Jr. and his brother Alfred left London and its poverty to seek their fortune "down under." They, too, established trading connections between New Zealand and the islands of Fiji and Samoa.

As always in a pioneering place, there was a dearth of women, so Sir Isaac Lyon Goldsmith, a director of the New Zealand Land Company, encouraged girls living in a London Jewish orphanage to go out to New Zealand. The first Jewish marriage in Wellington, in June 1842, was that of Benjamin Levy to eighteen-year-old Esther Solomon, one of the girls who had made the trip from the orphanage.

Then there came to Wellington a Jew who was searching for

something more than financial success. Already a man of comfortable means and of high position in the Duke's Place Synagogue in London, Abraham Hort, Sr. started out with his family (wife, five daughters and son-in-law) to join his two sons, Abraham and Alfred, who had preceded him. Armed with a letter from Dr. Solomon Herschell, then Chief Rabbi of Great Britain, "bearing his signature and official seal, expressive of his unqualified approval of all I might here undertake," Abraham Hort came to Wellington with the express intention of organizing a Jewish congregation.

The trip itself was not an easy undertaking for an Orthodox family. Leaving England in September 1842, it was not until four months later that they completed the 12,000-mile voyage, reaching Wellington on the *Prince of Wales* on January 3, 1843.

Abraham Hort's letters from Wellington, published in the *Voice of Jacob,* a London fortnightly periodical, give an invaluable record of the fledgling group and of this forceful, human dynamo, Abraham Hort. Within four days of his arrival he conducted a Sabbath service of thankfulness, and nine days thereafter he applied to the government for a grant of land for a Jewish synagogue and cemetery.

In a letter written January 21, 1843, to the *Voice of Jacob,* he recorded those beginning days:

> *The whole time I was on board ship I did not diverge in the slightest degree from any observance. . . . The young man David Isaacs whom I took with me in a religious capacity has conducted himself quite satisfactorily on the ship* Prince of Wales. *It redounds both to his credit and to that of the public institution (Neveh Zedek) in which he was reared . . . . On Saturday the 7th instant the one immediately succeeding my arrival I had the delight of convoking the first Hebrew congregation ever assembled in these colonies for the purpose of rendering thanks to Almighty God for having graciously protected us through the perils of the voyage . . . .*
> *In addition to the* Gomel *I offered up a prayer in*

*English which I composed for the solemn occasion,
as being better understood by those present, consisting independently of my whole family, of nine
males who appeared rejoiced at the opportunity
afforded them for the performance of divine worship according to our own ritual.*

*Neither in respect to provision have I found any
difficulty, my young man having already killed 2
oxen, a calf, 3 sheep and a lamb of which the meat
is excellent.*

A few months later, in May 1843, he wrote:

*I imagine it will not be wholly uninteresting to
your readers to know how we have celebrated the
Passover in these remote and until very lately,
completely uncivilized regions. We were supplied,
in addition to what I carried with me from London, with most excellent matzos from Sydney. We
congregated on the evenings of the first and seventh days, and on the first and two last days of the
festival about 24 souls male and female. On the
first and second nights all my family with the addition of Mr. Levien, Mr. Joseph and Mr. Isaacs
(the young man whom I brought with me) assembled at my house to the Seder and the whole party
with the exception of my daughter and son-in-law
Mr. and Mrs. Solomon Mocatta, who were at their
own house Hol Hamoed, took all their meals with
me during the entire week. . . . Before Kriath
Hatorah [Reading of the Law] I delivered lectures. . . . It is my aim to guide our little community on perfectly orthodox principles.*

Other developments are registered in various letters of June 1843:

*The government has already granted me an acre of
land for a cemetery. . . . Although the residents
here will not shut up after service on the second
day of the Festival [Shavuot], two have already by
my exhortation and out of respect to me closed on
Sabbaths. . . . On Friday there will be a Brit Mil-*

lah. . . . Mr. Isaacs will be Mohel and perform the
first operation of the kind here; of course I am to
be godfather. . . . I have just returned from the
Brit. Mr. Isaacs is a first rate Mohel; . . . all went
on exactly as in a well-regulated Kehillah.

Abraham Hort's "young man," nineteen-year-old David Isaacs, acted as Wellington's mohel, shohet and hazzan, but actually earned his living as a shoemaker.

At first services were held in the parlor of Mr. J. Levien. When Abraham Hort built his home on Abel Smith Street, provision was made for constructing a gallery over a large room in order to accommodate the women at religious services. By 1848 the community numbered twenty-eight.

When in 1859, sixteen years after his arrival, Abraham Hort returned to England with his wife and two daughters, he left behind a community and a congregation he had welded together, a community that recognized his achievements with a public dinner and an illuminated address of thanks for what he had accomplished for Jewish life.

It is the irony of fate, however, that he also left behind a daughter who married Sir Francis Dillon Bell—a prominent Christian, member of the cabinet and Agent-General for New Zealand—a daughter who herself later was baptized; and two sons, Abraham, Jr. and Alfred, both of whom also married out of the faith in the islands to which their commercial activities had taken them.

The group in Wellington remained small, and services were held in the home of Joseph Nathan or in Jacob Joseph's drawing room on Lambton Quay. One of the congregants recalled these home services:

The Reading Desk in the center of the room was
five feet high with a sloping top which used to lift
up and in it were kept the large volumes from
which the prayers were read. There was no Sefer
Torah. . . . The bottom portion of the desk was a
spacious boxlike drawer in which books and tal-
aisim [prayer shawls] were kept.

When these homes were outgrown, space in the Masonic Hall was rented. Not until 1868, three years after Wellington had been made New Zealand's capital, did the Jewish community, then numbering over a hundred, achieve its aim of purchasing ground for the construction of a synagogue on the street called The Terrace high above Lambton Quay. In January 1870 a consecration service was held for Congregation Beth El in the new 32-by-52-foot wooden building. Unto this day, however, everyone speaks of "The Terrace" when the Beth El Congregation is meant.

This first service was led by Reverend David Isaacs, the same "young man" whom Abraham Hort had brought along in the early days. Reverend Isaacs took as the text for his first sermon in the new house of worship, "How goodly are thy tents, O Jacob, thy tabernacles, O Israel" (Numbers 24:5). The congregation's continued closeness with the Mother Country was contained in the "Declaration of Trust" made by the leaders at the consecration:

> *Provided always that no person whatsoever shall at any time hereafter be permitted to preach or expound God's Holy Word or to perform any of the usual acts of religious worship upon the said piece of ground and hereditaments who shall maintain and promulgate or teach any doctrine or preach contrary to what is contained in the Pentateuch as expounded and explained by the Chief Rabbi in London in England.*

Reverend Isaacs was a bachelor, so he was not retained as minister for long. In 1876 they chose the man who remained as minister at The Terrace for over half a century. This was Dutch-born Reverend Herman Van Staveren, a legend in Wellington to this day. Ordained at Jews' College in London, he came to New Zealand when he was twenty-seven years old, married and with an infant daughter. Tall, dark, handsome, and with a flowing beard, his was an independent spirit brooking no direction or interference from a board of trustees.

His family grew: There were four sons and nine daughters. I visited with two of the Van Staveren "girls" (as they are spoken of in the community), one in her seventies, the other in her eighties, in the old family home that still retains the walnut dining-room table with room for seventeen around it.

There never was much money in the family, Reverend Van Staveren receiving a salary of £6 when he first came—and ending up over fifty years later with a weekly stipend of no more than £8. So "hand-me-downs" were the natural thing within the family, and one son became a "commercial traveler" at the age of twelve. But somehow money was found for music, dancing and elocution lessons for the children, and on Fridays each one would receive a bag of boiled sweets.

The Van Staverens recalled family outings to the theater. Children then were admitted free if accompanied by a parent. So the rabbi would purchase one ticket and would be followed into the theater by a long procession of children—free of charge.

Many are the legends about Reverend Van Staveren, who was not only the rabbi, but also the shohet and the mohel. Dressed in frock coat and high hat, he would ride his horse Yankel to and from the slaughter house, urging Yankel on in Hebrew.

During this half century when Reverend Van Staveren was the spiritual leader, the community grew in numbers, and the wooden synagogue was replaced with a larger brick building constructed on the same site. All activities continued to center around the synagogue.

Walk about windy Wellington now and you come upon names honoring Jews who left their mark on the life of this city. In one quiet corner I came to a spot where Lipman Street ran into Levy Street, both streets named for Mr. Lipman Levy who, among his other civic roles, had chaired the Chamber of Commerce. Another street name honored Sir Julius Vogel, one-time Prime Minister of the country.

The town of Levin, between Wellington and Rotorua, which publicizes that "Levin Welcomes Industry," is named for William Hort Levin, whose father was the founder of Levin & Co. and whose mother was a daughter of Abraham Hort. "Willie," as he was known, was a director of the Wellington and Manawatu Railway which passed through this junction town. He was also first chairman of Wellington's Harbor Board, president of its Chamber of Commerce and held political office as well.

Many other Jews served in the House of Representatives, in

various ministries and as councillors. It is said that New Zealand's Labor Party came into existence after gatherings and discussions in a tailor shop operated by a Wellington Jew. Sir Michael Myers (G.C.M.G.), a brilliant lawyer, was appointed Chief Justice and became the first New Zealand-born judge to sit on the Judicial Court of the Privy Council.

During this time the make-up of the Jewish community had changed. To the original 100 percent all-English group had been added Russian Jews escaping from the pogroms of the 1880s, an "invasion" which had been feared by local workers, alarmed at the possibility of losing their jobs. At the turn of the century, when there were 500 Jews in Wellington, the English Jews had control of communal affairs, the Russian Jews still being spoken of as foreigners.

In the decade between 1931–1941, Central European refugees to the number of 1,100 had settled in New Zealand, most of these being professionals.

Two tablets in the entrance foyer of The Terrace bring World War II history close. One reads:

IN SACRED MEMORY OF THE HEROIC GHETTO
FIGHTERS AGAINST TYRANNY
AND THE 6 MILLION JEWISH MARTYRS
WHO PERISHED DURING 1933–1945

The other plaque erected by American Jewish servicemen at American bases in New Zealand honors the memory of the rabbi who succeeded Reverend Van Staveren in 1930—Rabbi Solomon Katz, Russian-born graduate of the Jewish Theological Seminary of America, in New York:

IN GRATEFUL TRIBUTE
TO THE MEMORY OF
RABBI SOLOMON KATZ
WELLINGTON
HEBREW CONGREGATION
BY THE JEWISH MEN
OF THE 2ND MARINE DIVISION U.S.M.C.
WHOM HE SERVED WITH KINDLY
DEVOTION

I found The Terrace a busy place on Sunday. In the morning a Hebrew school with an attendance of 150 was in session. Some of the Post-Bar Mitzvah group stayed on for the afternoon get-together of the Habonim Zionist Youth group, with its membership of 120. The rabbi at the time [1965] was East-European-born Reverend T. Silberman, who came to Wellington after service in Scotland. He was happy that these teenagers were spending all of Sunday under the roof of The Terrace, no matter whether they spent their time praying, singing, eating, dancing or holding discussions.

A Liberal congregation, started in 1959, held services conducted by dedicated Lay Minister Edward Kranz, who had studied for the rabbinate in his youth in Germany. Temple Sinai, the Liberal synagogue, already had a religious school with Post-Bar Mitzvah and Bat Mitzvah groups functioning.

On the one hand, the great majority of Wellington's Orthodox Jews use their automobiles to reach The Terrace for Sabbath services; and on the other hand, most of Temple Sinai's men wear yarmulkes at services.

The question of conversion separates the Orthodox from the Liberals. Rabbi Silberman told me he was averse to conversions altogether, requiring a period of four years of study and testing for any applicant who wished to accept Judaism. The Liberals grant admission to the Jewish faith after one year's study and testing by an Australian Liberal rabbi.

One project of which the entire community is proud is its Home for the Aged, at Eventide Village, twelve miles out of the city, overlooking wide lawns and mountains. Indoors there are cheerful drapes and rugs, ramps in place of stairs, built-in furniture and individual galleys for making tea. "It's like a hotel," said one resident.

The story behind this Home for the Aged recalls other facets of Jewish history in the twentieth century. Max and Annie Deckston had emigrated from Poland and sought a free life for themselves in New Zealand. Hard-working people, they saved a considerable sum of money and in 1929 they returned for a visit to their old home in Poland. On their return to Wellington, this childless couple established an orphanage to which Polish Jewish children could be brought. By 1937, twenty-five children had been brought to this haven in Wellington. Both Mr. and Mrs. Deckston died, in 1938 and 1939, and their estate was left to the Deckston Hebrew Institute, as the orphanage was known.

When World War II broke out, Jewish world leadership felt that children being saved from the holocaust should begin life anew in Israel, so an institution for saving European children was not needed anymore in Wellington. But the fund was still available. So in 1949 the New Zealand Parliament passed the Deckston Hebrew Trust Act, extending its beneficiaries to include aged or any religious, educational or social organization of the Jewish community. And the Deckston wing at Eventide (operated by the Methodist Social Service Trust) was built, with the Jewish community taking care of the domestic requirements and general welfare of the residents.

Although Jews in New Zealand form only one-fifth of one percent of the total population, the Wellington community is warm-hearted and outgoing, rich in activities for both young and mature people. Particularly impressive to me was the participation of the younger generation in such communal activities as student teaching at the Hebrew school and the youth minyan that held religious services at a home where a death had occurred the previous week.

꧁ BAR MITZVAH IN CHRISTCHURCH ꧂

Bar Mitzvah in Christchurch—that is in Christchurch, New Zealand, was a moving experience. Actually, Christchurch, in the South Island of New Zealand, is the most English city outside of England. Its gardens are beautiful as only English gardens can be. Its Avon River flows gently through the town. From my hotel windows I could see young people dawdling during their lunch hours on the banks of the Avon. The cathedral is the heart of the city. Ask direction to any point in Christchurch, and inevitably comes the reply, "Go down to the cathedral. From there . . . ." All transportation radiates from the square surrounding the cathedral.

Christchurch's synagogue is on Gloucester Street and the rabbi lives on Worcester Street. Among other streets that remind one of England are Oxford and Cambridge streets, as well as Dorset, Salisbury and Chester streets.

Hotel Clarendon spoiled me with morning tea brought to my bedside in fine English bone china. At mealtime in the dining room I was faced with a full array of silver including, in English fashion, both spoon and fork for dessert. And the waitresses were as stiffly starched as nurses once were.

It is no accident that this city is so English, or that it is named Christchurch. Back in the 1830s an English bishop had discussed the possibility of encouraging colonization of New Zealand on a religious basis; of organizing a Church of England settlement here. New Zealand, so named by Captain Cook in the eighteenth century, had by 1830 attracted only five hundred white people— chiefly traders, whalers and adventurers. It was John Robert Godley who began the actual work looking towards the organization of this Church of England community-to-be. Of the fifty-two original members who were to pioneer in the distant country, seventeen had studied at the college with which Godley was associated, Christchurch College at Oxford. It was therefore resolved that the name of the new province was to be Canterbury, and the name of its chief town (as yet just an idea in their heads) was to be Christchurch. Later, Queen Victoria gave the project her blessing and declared Christchurch a city.

Along with the early pioneers came the Jewish merchant Louis Edward Nathan. Other Jews followed. In 1863, even before the foundation stone of Christchurch's cathedral had been laid, the Jews asked for and received a government grant of £300 towards the building of a synagogue. This was in keeping with the local custom of offering government grants for all houses of worship, serving any denominational group of Christchurch's settlers.

A wooden shul (synagogue) was built. Necessary religious articles were culled from all parts of the world. A Scroll of the Law was obtained in London; mezuzot, ketubot and a shofar came from Melbourne; a lulav from Sydney. The etrog was imported from the Holy Land. The community was not a wealthy one and could not, at the beginning, afford a paid reader or minister. Mr. Henry Jones, first salaried minister, received a weekly salary of £1/12/6. A congregational rule said that the lowest acceptable offer one could make when "shnodering" for synagogue honors was to be a shilling.

In 1865 the gold rush on the western coast of New Zealand started. The fever hit Christchurch's thirty-five Jewish families. Soon so many had left for Hokitika in the goldmining area that barely a minyan was left for Sabbath services.

Within five years, the gold rush had run its course. Back came the men, bringing with them the Baghdadi Jew, Reverend Isaac Zachariah, who had been minister to the Jews in the gold fields. He became Christchurch's next reader and shohet at the munificent salary of £2 a week. The story goes that Reverend Zachariah wrote his parents that he had been appointed minister in Christchurch. Upon hearing this name, his parents assumed that their son had converted to Christianity and broke off all contact with him.

Things began to look brighter for the Jewish community and soon talk started of the need for a new and larger synagogue. Subscribers to the fund numbered four hundred, including many Christian neighbors. In 1881 the new synagogue was consecrated.

Christchurch's Jewry felt itself a part of world Jewry. At the close of World War I, they contributed £500 for the relief of Polish, Romanian and Russian Jews; £175 for the relief of refugees from Palestine; and pledged to raise £200 for the Zionist cause.

Again, during the Hitler period, a Jewish Welfare Society was organized to channel aid for European Jews. Twenty-five German-Jewish families came to live in Christchurch. Clothing and food were sent to refugee camps in Europe.

Upon my arrival at Hotel Clarendon on the Avon I found an invitation to attend the Bar Mitzvah service of Stephen Hollander, whose mother was president of the local Union of Jewish Women. So on Sabbath morning I crossed the Avon River and walked up one block to Gloucester Street to reach the synagogue, which just a few years previously had celebrated a hundred years of existence, commencing in the wooden shul of the 1860s. If you're new in town and ask to be directed to the Christchurch Synagogue, you may find some difficulty in getting the desired information. Locally the synagogue is known as the Canterbury Hebrew Congregation, taking its name from the province in which it is located. And perhaps Canterbury Hebrew Congregation sounds better to the Jewish ear than does Christchurch Synagogue.

Stephen was nervously pacing up and down in front of the synagogue as I turned into Gloucester Street. Indoors, the women made a gay picture in their light dresses, colored petal hats and white gloves. It was November and "down under" in New Zealand late spring reigned at the time.

Promptly at ten o'clock the service started—not with the Shaharit (the Morning Service), but with the ceremony of taking the Sefer Torah from the Ark for the reading of the weekly portion. Stephen chanted the entire section for all who were called up to the reading of the Torah that day, concluding with the Maftir and the Haftorah. His father, Eber Hollander, Board member of the synagogue, had done the same when, as a youth, he had become Bar Mitzvah, and the son wished to follow in his father's footsteps. After the return of the Scroll to the Ark, Stephen recited the Ten Commandments in Hebrew and in English.

In place of a kiddush at the synagogue, the Hollanders invited the entire Jewish community for a reception at their home—an all-day affair. And a real home happening it was. Everything on the table had been prepared at home, including the festive and traditional hallah. Even the trout and salmon which were served that day had been caught by fisherman Eber Hollander.

The toast was offered by the president of the congregation, and responded to by the rabbi, the parents and the Bar Mitzvah himself. In his response, Mr. Hollander said, "Stephen never gave up cricket and tennis while preparing for his Bar Mitzvah." A good old-fashioned songfest with people gathered round the piano concluded the warm festivities. Bar Mitzvah celebrations do not occur frequently in this community of sixty families. Two years earlier there had been such an event, and another had been observed seven months before Stephen's. The next such occasion was scheduled for eighteen months hence.

Among those at the reception was a man who had come to New Zealand as a child in a sailing vessel that was seven weeks at sea between England and the colony; Adele Morris, who was born on the gold coast of western New Zealand, to which her grandfather had emigrated from England; and a man who, of all his family, remained the only practicing Jew. All his brothers and sisters had "married out" (the New Zealand term for intermarriage)—a frequent occurrence in small communities.

The Masur family had trekked from Hitler Germany to Eritrea, then to Uganda and Kenya, leaving each of these countries in turn as independence came to them—followed by unsettled conditions. Finally the Masurs took root in Christchurch.

Also taking root in this quiet corner of the world was a Canadian family that left the hustle and bustle of Western life in search of a serene place in which to raise its young children. Joseph Bercusson had "been in fur linings" ever since he was eighteen years old. At the age of forty-four he and two former competitors united to form the Universal Bercusson Fur Lining Company on the condition that they dissolve the firm within five years.

"Making money is the easiest thing. Living is more important," said Elizabeth Bercusson, anxious that her husband be with the children while they were growing up, and be more to them than just the money-maker of the family. True to the agreement, the Universal Bercusson Fur Lining Company was dissolved at the end of five years, and the family came to live in tranquil Christchurch.

Here they live in an old mansion, with wood-paneled walls and a fine curved banister down which the children can slide. On the acre of grounds are stables and maids' quarters not in use anymore. The former hen house, however, is in use as a playhouse for the children.

Serving as Christchurch's minister was English-born Rabbi Joseph Wolman. His first pastorate had been at Cork, Ireland. When General Douglas MacArthur, in retreating from the Philippines, turned Australia's Brisbane into a garrison city, the rabbi served there as Army chaplain. The Wolmans took the American soldiers to their hearts. One year seventy soldiers celebrated the Passover Seder at the large Wolman home, the chaplain himself nailing down the boards which served as seats for the occasion. And the soldiers begged, "Mamma, let me come and stand in your kitchen." Well, one of them is still close to the family, for he married one of the Wolman daughters. Today, in Christchurch, highly respected Rabbi Wolman accepts no fees for wedding, funeral or Bar Mitzvah services.

Jews of Christchurch have time to be friendly and neighborly. There was the case of the Melbourne couple touring New Zealand in jeans, sweaters and sandals. By the time they reached this city, they decided to get married. Rabbi Wolman contacted Melbourne to assure himself that they were Jewish. Then Christchurch went into action. The bride was outfitted in a white dress and veil. A minyan was gotten together, and two couples were unterfuehrers. A feast was prepared and a gift given to the couple.

In time of sorrow, too, the Jews in Christchurch are understanding and helpful, taking turns in the watch over a deceased person until time for burial.

When a death occurred among a tiny group of Jews remaining now in Hokitika, two hundred miles away, two busloads of people went out from Christchurch, in order that the mourners in Hokitika would have the solace of a minyan for services.

Gradations in the social ladder do not seem to matter in this democratic country. Simply and unaffectedly people said, "My father was a 'shuster' in England. Things didn't go well, so he tried his luck in New Zealand," or "My father became a 'shneider' here."

Life is good in quiet, peaceful Christchurch.

LOOKOUT ON ANTARCTICA—DUNEDIN

"There is nothing between us and Antarctica but the waters of the Pacific," said my hostess as we looked out across the water from the garden of her hilltop house in Dunedin, near the southern tip of New Zealand's South Island. Known as the Edinburgh of the south, started by the Church of Scotland and

Newly constructed synagogue with eight pews for the sixteen Jewish families in Dunedin, N.Z., the most southern congregation in the world, looking out on Antarctica.

boasting a statue of Robert Burns in the center of town, Dunedin is also the site of the most southern Jewish congregation in the world.

I met one of Dunedin's Jewish sons, Peter Salinger, twenty-one, leader of the local Torah study group. Among the 4,000 students of Dunedin's University and New Zealand's only Medical School, there were eighteen Jewish students. Ten or twelve of these were meeting regularly, for the second year on Sunday evenings, bringing their Bibles for study and discussion. But Peter felt frustrated. "The group is so small. We're still studying the Book of Genesis. I know we should go on to something else—but what?"

Alone in a dwindling Jewish community of sixty persons, where there was no rabbi, no Hillel chapter, no program material available, small wonder young Peter felt troubled and frustrated.

At the Moray Place Synagogue I sat all alone in the silent structure late in 1965. Sold to the adjacent Y.M.C.A., the impressive place of worship was soon to be torn down. There were mute reminders of other days when Jewry had flourished here. Lions embroidered in gold metallic thread embellished the green velvet curtain in front of the Ark. An organ stood undisturbed and dusty to one side. Seats for 110 men were made of carved wood. The stairs leading to the women's gallery were decorated with a Magen David (Star of David) at each step.

The Reading Desk still retained a card with the prayer for the royal family of an earlier day:

Our most gracious Sovereign Lady Queen Victoria
Albert Edward the Prince of Wales
and all the Royal Family

Another card on the Reading Desk gave the outline for performing the marriage ceremony. The order, a traditional one, had been:

1. *Afternoon service and Kaddish*
2. *Writ of Halitzah explained to brothers of the groom*
3. *Groom signs the Ketubah*
4. *M'kabel Kinyan—Groom holds the talit of the officiating minister while the latter asks the following questions:*
   MINISTER: *Will you hereby undertake the solemn responsibility of maintaining this woman who is about to become your lawful wedded wife in a just and lawful manner?*
   GROOM: *I will*
   MINISTER: *And have you any objections to urge against this Ketubah made by you to her K'dat Moshe v'Yisrael [according to the laws of Moses and Israel]?*
   GROOM: *None*
   MINISTER: *Then hold this firmly binding as a Writ of Possession*
5. *Couple then led under the canopy for the ceremony*

Contents of the small desks in front of the pews told the story of Jews who had come to Dunedin from various countries. Desks No. 15 and 43 held prayer books published in London. Left in desk No. 57 was a Frankfort-am-Main prayer book. A Yiddish-

Hebrew Book of Supplications published in Wilno, Lithuania, remained in desk No. 39.

I fingered the pages of the old Correspondence Books of the Dunedin Hebrew Congregation, the brown ink on its thin rice paper now faded. Honorary Secretary L. Mendelsohn had written with big flourishes and curlicues; C. I. Levien wrote in a beautiful slanting script with heavy down strokes. The face of the community came to life as I read.

One problem in a community such as this, to which men came alone from distant lands, was that occasionally the bonds with wives waiting back home were broken. Evidence of this I read in the letter sent by Henry Hart, president of the Congregation in 1866, to a man named Jacob:

> *Letter received from your wife of Spitalfield, London, in which she expresses great anxiety in your behalf as she has not heard from you for more than two years. I deem it my duty to make you acquainted with above facts so that you may as in duty bound at once communicate with your wife and thereby alleviate the distress of mind she is laboring under.*

The said Jacob had in the meanwhile moved on from Dunedin to the gold fields at Hokitika and the letter was delivered to him there by a "party who knew him," according to word sent back to the waiting wife in London.

But other problems—such as questions of intermarriage and conversion, insufficient funds, the choice of a rabbi, the religious education of the children, conformity to religious observance—all perplexed Dunedin a century ago just as they do communities around the world today.

In December 1874 Chief Rabbi of the British Empire, Dr. Nathan Adler, was asked:

> *Kindly give your opinion as to whether committee would be justified in letting seats in the synagogue to gentlemen who are married contrary to the laws of Judaism. The bylaws in force will not allow of gentlemen so circumstanced to become members of the congregation and it is the opinion of some that*

they may pay for and occupy seats without being accorded any other privilege.

Then, as now, it was most often the women who sought conversion to Judaism, before or after marriage to a Jewish man. Mr. Ottolanguin, who inquired in December 1891 about the conversion of his wife and daughters was informed:

> *It is necessary for them to possess a fair knowledge of the Jewish festivals and fasts, the creeds and commandments (not necessarily by heart), the blessings, at least the first two lines of Shema Yisrael in Hebrew and English, the rules as to kosher food. They will have to appear before the Melbourne Beit Din.*

And in another instance in October 1899, Mr. Palek received this reply regarding his wife's conversion:

> *If she undergoes instruction in the language and laws of our Faith and leads the life of a Jewess and Jewish wife during ensuing twelve months . . . submitting herself to the Committee for examination at the end of that time—the Committee will be prepared to give the matter their serious consideration.*

But the "serious consideration" of the Synagogue Committee was not sufficient, as Mrs. Alice Maud Montague discovered the following year, on her request for admission to the Jewish faith. The Committee sent on a favorable report to the Beit Din in Melbourne. Three months later Mrs. Montague was informed that her application (after meeting approval with the Beit Din) was being forwarded to the Chief Rabbi in London.

The problems involved with spiritual leadership, as seen in the following communication to the Chief Rabbi Dr. Adler written in 1867, have a familiar sound:

> *Our congregation consists of 60 members, half of whom are married. . . . In consequence of debt incurred in building the synagogue, which has not yet been liquidated, we have not up to the present time been able to support a paid minister.*

In November of the same year Reverend Jacob Levy of Geelong, Australia, was appointed minister. His duties were spelled out very clearly in this message:

> *It has been agreed to engage you as Reader,*
> *Shohet and Collector to this congregation at £150*
> *per annum—subject to the following conditions:*
>
> 1. *That you shall attend and open the synagogue*
>   *on all proper occasions and perform divine*
>   *service according to the regulations of Rev. Dr.*
>   *Adler.*
> 2. *You shall perform all marriage and funeral*
>   *services and not demand any fees for the same.*
> 3. *You shall when required attend such places as*
>   *the President or Committee may approve there*
>   *to act as Shohet.*
> 4. *You shall collect all monies due to the congre-*
>   *gation and hand over same to the secretary at*
>   *least once a week.*
> 5. *You shall perform circumcisions to members'*
>   *children and not demand a fee exceeding*
>   *£2. 2.0*
> 6. *You shall do such other services as is consis-*
>   *tent with the office of Reader, Shohet, Col-*
>   *lector.*
> 7. *And lastly that you shall have the use of the*
>   *room under the synagogue (during the pleasure*
>   *of the Committee) as a school for teaching He-*
>   *brew and shall make such maximum charge as*
>   *the Committee may approve.*

Within a few years, Reverend Levy was asked to resign, and again the community went in search of a minister. They were now willing to double the salary, but the qualifications demanded were also increased, as seen in letters sent to London:

> *Our congregation numbers now about 45 members.*
> *The children are greatly in want of instruction in*
> *Hebrew and the tenets of our faith. We would*
> *guarantee £300 a year—which would be a heavy*
> *tax upon so small a community but we are willing*
> *to make the sacrifice. . . . such minister not to*

*make any charge for circumcision, marriage or any
other rite or to receive any donations offered in the
synagogue and to give gratuitous instruction in
Hebrew to children of members of the synagogue
. . . to be a moderate good English scholar and not
over 45 years of age.*

Dunedin's interest in the Jewish education of its children was
deep. That it was well ahead of the times in meeting the problem
of training for the Bar Mitzvah ceremony is clear from a resolu-
tion passed in 1896:

*The minister shall not be empowered to commence
teaching boys their portion of the Law until they
produce a certificate from the master of the school
showing they are grounded in the rudiments of Hebrew and therefore qualified for Bar Mitzvah.*

The community's ministers were asked to cope with the problem of laxity in observance of the Sabbath and of kashrut by the
members. Reverend L.J. Harrison received this petition in 1893:

*The minister's attention be drawn to the indiffer-
ence shown by the community as regards Sabbath
observance and that he be requested to personally
interview the members.*

Ten years later Rev. Adolf T. Chodowski was asked: "To interview members who do not obtain their meat from the Kosher
Butcher and endeavour to induce them to become customers."

There was one aspect of community life, however, in which
Dunedin's Jews performed the required duties faithfully and
voluntarily. This was the service rendered by the Hevrah Kaddisha, the group of men and women that assisted if there was a
death. At one time, it was recorded, the chairman sent notices to
sixteen women about the need for more shrouds. Fifteen women
immediately responded. Chairman Hyman exhorted his people in
1899:

*The discharge of the sacred duties should be ap-
proached with the greatest decorum and a deep
religious feeling. One member should remain with
the body during the day and two during the night*

until internment. . . . During the watch, time
should be occupied in reading prayers.

Although far from the large centers of Jewish life, Dunedin maintained links with world Jewry. In 1899 Reverend Chodowski was requested "to write to the *Otago Daily Times* dealing with the question"—the question then being a blood libel which had been made in Vienna. And when Theodor Herzl, founder of modern Zionism, died in 1904, a collection was made in aid of the Herzl National Memorial Fund.

In those days Dunedin was the largest Jewish community in New Zealand. A good indicator of the community population might well have been the size of the order for matzoh, which was distributed among the members. In 1865 one hundred pounds of matzoh were ordered. In 1892 the amount required was 655 pounds and in 1901—the last order to be recorded—the order was for 800 pounds.

When New Zealand's gold rush subsided, the Jewish population of Dunedin dwindled. I found this Lookout on Antarctica composed of sixteen families (only five of which had children) and six single adults.

Although small in number, the qualitative level of the group was high. More than half of the men were in the medical field, most of them at the university. Among them was a research endocrinologist, a microbiologist, a thoracic surgeon, an orthopedic surgeon, an eye-ear-nose-and-throat specialist, a general practitioner, two veterinary surgeons and a medical researcher. Only two of the Jews were in business, one of these the managing director of a chain of stores. A pharmacist, an engineer, an accountant, a teacher and a civil servant concluded the roll.

Many doctors have come to and have gone from Dunedin. The Hitler period brought more than twenty men from Germany and Vienna who studied and qualified at the medical school here (the only one in the country) for the practice of medicine in New Zealand. Most came without means, so the Jewish Philanthropic Society (actually the congregation) paid their fees at the university and gave any needed help. The majority of these physicians

have moved on to practice in other cities and have repaid the
community for the help given.

A newcomer to Dunedin from Germany in the 1930s in yet
another field is Ernest Hirsh, who acts as the community's lay
spiritual leader. Services are held once a month, on the first
Sabbath of each month, in the newly constructed small synagogue on Dundas Street. A modern structure, it has eight pews
and an Ark with doors of polished wood set into a granite wall.

Room is set aside in this new synagogue for a religious school.
At weekly sessions, the children's ties with Jewry are kept firm
through the study of Jewish history, holidays and the Hebrew
language. End-of-the-school-year ceremonies—at Hanukkah time
in this "down under" city—means distribution of prizes, with
every child receiving some sort of an award.

What does the future hold in store for this younger generation?
Will these children, when grown, find an incentive for staying in
Dunedin? Will they go on to larger centers of Jewish life to search
for marriage partners? Or will they intermarry with the majority
population and bring Jewish history in this "Lookout on Antarctica" to a close?

• 4 •
AUSTRALIA

◂§ FROM CONVICTS TO CORONATION IN SYDNEY COVE §▸

THE LONDON COURT'S VERDICT WAS "GUILTY," THE SEN-
tence "Death." The crime: "Feloniously stealing on 30th December 1782, eight silver teaspoons." This was a death sentence
decreed for John Harris but later commuted to "Fourteen Years'
Transportation."

At about the same time twenty-year-old Esther Abrahams,
whose crime was shoplifting, was indicted for "Feloniously
stealing 24 yards of black lace." She was found guilty and
sentenced to "Transportation" for seven years.

John Harris and Esther Abrahams were transported to the new
British penal colony set up in New South Wales on the east coast
of Australia. They arrived in 1788 aboard a vessel of the First
Fleet that reached Sydney Cove after an eight-month voyage,
along with 700 other convicts and 300 free men.

Both John Harris and Esther Abrahams were Jews, as were
some others similarly deported to Australia. Years before, many
Jews had left Eastern Europe in the wake of persecution and had
emigrated to England. Reaching that country at a time of econom-

ic depression and having no skills, some had turned to a life of petty crime.

John Lara, descendant of a Spanish-Jewish family, was indicted for stealing a tankard worth £5, found guilty and sentenced to death. He was one of a convicted group that accepted "Royal Mercy upon condition of being transported to New South Wales for the term of their respective natural lives." Lara was shipped off with the Second Fleet. He was among the fortunate, surviving a voyage during which sixty-eight convicts died.

And there was fourteen-year-old Joseph Samuel, sentenced for stealing bed linen, a silk cloak and two silver tablespoons—all valued at seventy shillings. None of the witnesses who appeared at his trial were positive in their identification of the youth, who was alleged to have assisted two adult housebreakers who were not apprehended. Young Joseph stated that at the time of the robbery he was at the home of the man to whom he was apprenticed. His master, however, was not called as a witness at the trial and the youth was found guilty and sentenced to seven years' transportation.

What befell these four Jews—John Harris, Esther Abrahams, John Lara and Joseph Samuel—in the penal colony? We are indebted to Dr. G. F. J. Bergman, in papers read before the Australian Jewish Historical Society, for the answers.

John Harris, in his new surroundings, proposed setting up a night watch, and was selected from among the convicts to be the guard. He was probably Australia's first policeman. In one of the proceedings recorded in 1789 "a widow complained that two gentlemen tried to climb through her window into her house." The men were taken into custody by Harris "as he was going on his duty of the watch." Called as a witness, he was sworn on the Old Testament. Seven years later he received unconditional emancipation "in consideration of good services as principal of the night watch," at Norfolk Island in Tasmania to which new convict settlement he had been transferred from the penal colony on Australia's mainland.

Aboard the ship *Lady Penrhyn,* on which Esther Abrahams had been transported, was 1st Lieutenant of Marines George Johnston, who had seen service in the American War of Independence and was then under orders to form a garrison at the penal settlement. A romance between the two developed; she became his mistress and was never treated as an ordinary convict. Years later they were married.

During his career in Australia, George Johnston served as Lieutenant Governor of the colony for a period of six months and was commissioned Lieutenant Colonel. In the 1828 census, Esther Abrahams was listed as a "free settler."

When John Lara reached the colony he was assigned to labor on a farm. In 1794 he received a conditional pardon and a fifty-acre grant of land. Later he was awarded a full pardon for "good conduct and faithful discharge of his duty as a Principal of the Night Watch," a post in which he had succeeded John Harris. Lara received further grants of land, was successful in business and participated in civic life.

Then he overextended himself and went bankrupt. At the age of seventy-six he went to a debtor's prison for an obligation contracted by his wife. Upon his release (the debt having been paid by a family member), he once more became successful in his business ventures. He died at ninety, and was buried in the Jewish cemetery.

And what of Joseph Samuel? Two years after his arrival in the colony, he was in trouble again. Taken into custody for robbery and murder of a constable, he admitted the robbery but denied the murder. He was found guilty and sentenced to death by hanging. According to the practice of the times, he was taken to the gallows by a horse-drawn cart. Then the cart was to be driven ahead and the prisoner left dangling from the gallows.

However, as the cart drove away, the rope broke and Samuel fell to the ground. The procedure was repeated. A new rope was applied and the cart pressed forward. Again the rope unraveled and the prisoner's feet dragged on the ground. A third time a new rope was prepared. The cart drove away, and for the third time the rope snapped. This time a reprieve was given. The governor commuted the sentence to life imprisonment, saying, "It would seem there has been Divine intervention." And so Joseph Samuel became "The Man They Couldn't Hang."

By 1817 there were about twenty young Jewish men in Sydney—all Londoners, all convicts or former convicts. Although not too familiar with Jewish religious practice, they formed a Hevrah Kaddisha.

Possibilities of trade brought "free settlers," men who came of their own volition, seeking economic advancement. The first Jewish free settler was said to have been Barnett Levey, who came in 1821. Another one of the tribe of Levi was Walter Levi, well supplied with money, who became a trader, importer and shipping agent.

As trade and production improved, more free settlers were attracted. By 1828, when a census showed 120 Jews living in Sydney, the composition of the group had changed. From an aggregation of convicts, the number now included only forty-two convicts, ten more who had been pardoned and seventeen ticket-of-leave men (probationers working on their own). All the rest were free men—such as the Cohens and the Levis—who had chosen to take up life in the new colony. The chief occupation of the Jews, both free and freed, was trading or innkeeping.

The number of Jews in the colony at that time probably was larger than the 120 given in the official census figures. Among convicts who declared themselves of "No Religion" were Robert Cohen, Jacob Cohen and others with Jewish-sounding names. Indeed, some of these men subsequently became seat holders in the synagogue or were buried in the Jewish cemetery.

For those who came unmarried, there was the problem of finding a marriage partner. As few single Jewish women in England ventured forth to the rough pioneering colony, the alternative for the Jewish men was intermarriage. Some of the women then adopted their Jewish husbands' religion.

In 1832, when there were 345 Jews in Sydney, a congregation was formally organized. Among the "Laws and Rules for the Management and Regulation of the Sydney Synagogue" one reads the following: 1) The form of service is to be the same as read by the German Jews in England. 2) Membership is barred to "all persons marrying contrary to the Judaical Marriage Rites, violating the Laws of Brit Milah or neglecting to have their daughters named agreeably to the prescribed Hebrew Ritual." 3) Illegitimate or baptized persons are barred. 4) Any member refusing a Mitzvah or any committeeman attending service "not attired in a decent and respectable manner" is to forfeit a guinea for each offence. 5) No one is to be married without the written permission of the President who would "nominate a worthy and competent person to officiate." 6) It is requested that "No conversation take place during Service and that all will use their utmost efforts to preserve order and decorum."

In that same year, 1832, the first Jewish marriage in Australia was celebrated. The groom was Moses Joseph and his bride was Rosetta Nathan.

Three years later, the number of Jews desiring to attend services on High Holydays had outgrown the room generously offered by Phillip Joseph Cohen in his dwelling on George Street. Larger quarters were acquired in a building at No. 4 Bridge Street. In 1838 The Reverend M. E. Rose came from England to serve as hazzan, shohet and mohel, with accreditation from Chief Rabbi Solomon Herschell.

The community continued to grow and expand. Within a few years, in 1841, a site on York Street was purchased for construction of a larger synagogue, which was dedicated in 1844. Joseph Fowles in his pamphlet about Sydney, published in 1848, said:

> *At length the Hebrews became so numerous and respectable a portion of the community that it was thought necessary to erect a new Synagogue. Subscription lists were opened, to which many names belonging to various denominations of Christians were added, displaying a liberality rarely to be met with even in England. . . . And the present chaste and classic edifice was erected.*

The "so numerous" Jewish community of Sydney actually numbered only 600 at the time. The "chaste and classic edifice" was 72 by 32 feet and 35 feet high, built in a "pure Egyptian Order." That it was considered highly ornamental to this street was not surprising, for York Street at that time was the main thoroughfare leading to the markets, especially busy on Saturday mornings, and in the vicinity were the taverns Erin-Go-Bragh and the Harp of Erin.

The new synagogue, named Beit Israel, was consecrated in

1844 and the local newspaper, *The Herald,* reported on April 3:

> *Yesterday the New Synagogue was consecrated according to the Hebrew Rites in the presence of a congregation comprising nearly all the Jews in Sydney and a considerable number of Christians. . . . The interior is very handsomely fitted up; along the sides are three rows of open-backed pews; at the eastern end is the ark. It is lighted by two large gas chandeliers suspended from the ceiling, and by four lamps placed on ornamental pyramids alongside the ark.*

In addition to the presence of Christian neighbors at the service, the general feeling of goodwill that existed in the colony is also supported by the fact that of the 266 subscribers to the building fund *before* the consecration took place, 120 were Christians.

Transportation of convicts to New South Wales ceased about this time, but prospects for a continuing and developing Jewish life seemed promising. The Anglo-Jewish publication, *Voice of Jacob,* reported that in Sydney in 1845:

> *S. Benjamin imported four palm branches which he presented to the synagogue [for Sukkot]. The myrtle, citron and willows were of colonial growth. The shamash built a tabernacle at his residence. Religious fervor with which it was attended all served to demonstrate the progress of Judaism at the Antipodes. . . . At Simhat Torah, the Bridegrooms of the Law (Hatan Torah and Hatan Breshit) gave a sumptuous feast to the heads of families.*

Reverend Herman Hoelzel, a European-trained minister who could preach in English came to Sydney in 1855. Communal activities continued to develop, and the Hebrew Philanthropic and Orphan Society, a Jewish Library and a Literary Society were established.

Then as has happened elsewhere, a schism developed. In 1859 some members seceded and organized their own New Synagogue on Macquarie Street. In a preamble to their rules, this congregation stated:

> ... *that it asserts its right to decide upon all affairs which may concern themselves on their own responsibility, and without reference to any clerical authority whatever; and though they will at all times be most happy to listen to the advice of eminent men learned in our holy Religion, still whether upon a religious or any other subject, the decision of the congregation properly assembled must be considered decisive and acted upon.*

Three years later came the minister who was successful in healing the breach and reuniting the congregation. This was London-born Reverend Alexander Barnard Davis, who had had colonial experience in Kingston, Jamaica. He was destined to stay for more than forty years.

With the growth of the community, by now increased to 1,100, the need for larger synagogue quarters was once more felt. A plot of land between Elizabeth and Castlereagh streets was put up for sale by the government, and the community thought it would be a favorable location.

Interestingly enough it was the government itself that played a role in uniting the two congregations. There was an involved question as to which group was entitled to compensation for the sale of certain properties. It was then that the government Ministry concerned with the matter invited both congregations to jointly nominate trustees for the eventual erection of a new synagogue with these Trust Funds.

In February 1871 the tract facing Hyde Park was bought at an auction sale and held for the community as a whole. Plans were drawn and the foundation stone laid in the name of both congregations. The York Street premises were sold and for a while the two congregations worshipped together at the Macquarie Street Synagogue.

The new synagogue, named the Great Synagogue, was dedicated in March 1878 "in the presence of a large assemblage of the most influential citizens of all denominations." The tradition that all people participating in congregational administration "should be themselves observant Jews personally devoted to the Ritual of the Synagogue" was maintained.

During this era, a time of religious fervor, the *Australian Israelite* recorded that "The contributions at the synagogue during the holiday season by those called up to *aliyah* reminded the writer of the 1851–1852 golden-era period—they were so liberal and handsome." When in 1885 the synagogue was free of all liabilities the system of shnodering during the reading of the Torah was discontinued.

Life for the Jews continued in an even tenor in Sydney, and the community steadily grew in numbers. In 1881 there were 2,480 Jews; by 1891 there were 4,425, and by the turn of the century 5,137 Jews had made Sydney their home. In 1928 Sydney Jewry numbered almost ten thousand. A local Beit Din was organized with the approval of the Chief Rabbi of the British Empire, Joseph Herman Hertz. And to cement their ties with World Jewry funds were raised for needy Jews in Russia, in Poland and in Belgium.

When in 1901 the Commonwealth of Australia was inaugurated, the Governor General ruled that the Chief Minister of the Great Synagogue should be given the same recognition as the heads of various churches at levees and other official gatherings.

Other Jews were honored for service to the general community. There was Sir Saul Samuel, K.C.M.G., who was Colonial Treasurer in four ministries and Postmaster General in three other ministries. Upon his resignation from the post of Agent General, in which he represented the colony in England, he was made a baronet.

The Honorable Henry Emanuel Cohen served in two ministries before becoming Justice in the Supreme Court of New South Wales; John Jacob Cohen was Speaker of the Legislative Assembly; J. F. Josephson was Lord Mayor, as was Ernest S. Marks. At one time the Legislative Assembly had to suspend deliberations for a day when the Speaker and the Deputy Speaker—both of whom were Jews—were away in observance of Yom Kippur. George Judah Cohen was a founder of the Commercial Banking Company and of the Stock Exchange of Sydney. More recently

Sydney Einfeld, native-born son of a Galician cantor, has served in Parliament.

Jewish education in Sydney (now a community of over 28,000 Jews), meant Sunday School classes at the synagogues, or religious instruction within the public schools, in accord with the Education Act of 1880, which gave all denominations the "Right to Enter" public schools to teach religion once a week. There were two small Jewish Day Schools, the King David, with eighty pupils and the Moriah College (classes ranging from Primary through Secondary School) with 250 pupils, most of whom were in the elementary grades.

Following a meeting in 1937 with Melbourne's Liberal Rabbi Herman M. Saenger, a group of about twenty-five people declared themselves ready to form a Liberal congregation in Sydney. In September 1939, simultaneously with the outbreak of World War II, Rabbi Max Schenk of New York landed in Sydney to take up the post of spiritual leader of this group. Within ten days of his arrival, High Holyday services were held in the St. James Hall of the Church of England. Despite war conditions, blackouts, children's evacuation and military call-ups, membership in the Liberal group continued to grow. Within eighteen months of Rabbi Schenk's arrival, the cornerstone was laid for Temple Emanuel with a seating capacity of 725. For the High Holydays of 1942, the City Conservatorium of Music was rented for the congregation, which by then topped 900 members and had an attendance of 1,200 at the services. Men wore hats during worship and holidays were observed for two days as in Orthodox synagogues.

Deeply involved in community affairs, Rabbi Schenk and his wife (presently National President of American Hadassah) both took an active part in Zionist work at a time when some Australian Jews felt themselves so "British" they would not criticize England for its policy in Palestine. In 1945 Rabbi Schenk became President of the Zionist Federation of Australia and New Zealand.

When in 1949 he decided to return to the United States, Temple Emanuel had grown to a membership of 1,400. Since 1949, German-born Rabbi Rudolph Brasch has been leader of Temple Emanuel.

For the last thirty years the Great Synagogue, Sydney's leading Orthodox house of worship, has been headed by Jerusalem-born Rabbi Israel Porush who trained at Berlin's Rabbinical Seminary. Since 1940, when he arrived in Sydney, he has also been Chairman of the Beit Din, has been actively concerned in all branches of community life and a lecturer at Sydney University.

The "order and decorum" rule written into the regulations of the first synagogue has become the hallmark of the present-day Sydney Jewish community. During Sabbath services at the Great Synagogue, as men ascend to the Reading of the Torah, they bow to the congregation's officers, wearing high silk hats and seated in special pews on either side of the pulpit. When the Torah is carried around the synagogue at the conclusion of the reading, all bow deeply in deference to the Scroll of the Law.

And there was "order and decorum" at the sessions I attended of the Executive Council of Australian Jewry in Sydney on the day following my arrival in November 1965. Sessions started promptly at the announced hour, there was no interruption of speakers and no walking about during speeches. All in all, a spirit of great formality prevailed.

Sydney Jewry retains an air of English formality even though the proportion of British Jews within the city has steadily decreased. In the early years of the colony—before 1851—fully 90 percent of Sydney's Jews were British born. Synagogue members were then reminded, according to a report of the Synagogue Committee, that "As British Jews it is necessary we should not throw off the connection which binds us to our Mother Country and that, having no spiritual guide of our own, we should place ourselves under the protection of the Chief Rabbi of England."

Within a century all this has changed. By 1954 only 12 percent of Sydney's Jewry were born in the United Kingdom, 24 percent were natives of Central Europe, 14 percent came from Eastern Europe and a New South Wales Association of Sephardim had already been organized to look after the needs of immigrant Oriental Jews. More recently Jews from Egypt, India and Singapore have settled in Sydney. Currently there are over 500 families in the local Sephardi community.

Rabbi of the Sephardim is Calcutta-born Simon Silas, who attended both the Manchester Talmudical College and the Ponyevezher Yeshiva in Israel's Bnei Brak, where he added a knowledge of Yiddish to his other learning. The Eastern Jews' Association was headed by Meyer Musleah, member of an Iraqi family that had lived in Calcutta for six generations.

With the increase in the size of the community came a decline in mixed marriages. But even at that, 14 percent of the Jewish men and 8 percent of the women in New South Wales were married to Christians, according to the 1961 census figures. This means that the rate of intermarriage in New South Wales was twice as high as that in Melbourne.

An Australian event with overtones of British form is the Coronation Ball, held annually since 1939. For three months each year all fund-raising activities of organizations such as the Wizo, the Council of Jewish Women and youth groups are dedicated to the Jewish National Fund.

Groups or chapters around the country choose a candidate in whose honor funds are raised through various projects during these three months. The candidate in whose name the largest sum has been raised is then crowned Queen at the Coronation Ball.

The Coronation Ball that I attended—*the* big event of the year—with the women in long formal gowns, was held at the swank Chevron Hotel in Sydney. Down the red-carpeted length of the ballroom and through a bower of flowers glided the reigning Queen, wearing a white gown with blue sash and tiara. Curtsying to the reception committee, which included the Israeli Consul, she took her seat on the dais. She was followed by the current year's candidates, each wearing a blue-sashed white gown. Sealed envelopes were then opened and the amounts raised in honor of each candidate announced. Crowned Queen at the ball that year was Polish-born Giza Gryf.

Jews at the Coronation Ball came from many locales. Back in 1828 when there were only over a hundred Jews in Sydney, the majority had lived in what is now the "downtown" area, between Castlereagh and Sussex streets, though a few resided near the Circular Quay approach to the Harbor Bridge. Then Barnett Levey, distinguished as the first free Jew to settle in Sydney, made himself famous for another first—he built his home on land he had acquired five miles to the east and called it Waverley, after the novels of his favorite author, Sir Walter Scott.

It is to the eastern suburbs of Waverley, Woolahra and Randwick that the trend of Jewish settlement has been ever since. When the 1961 census was taken, almost 60 percent of Sydney's 23,000 Jews were living in these eastern suburbs, and only 6 percent remained in the downtown areas or had established themselves in the newly fashionable sections within the city, such as Potts Point or Elizabeth Bay.

Sophisticated Sydney—with its world-famous harbor, its skyscrapers, its luxury apartments and Coronation Balls—is a far cry from the primitive aboriginal Sydney Cove to which the First Fleet in 1788 ferried prisoners and free men from England.

◄§ MELBOURNE
VICTORIAN GRANDE DAME §►

Melbourne, after Sydney, seemed a "Victorian *Grande Dame*"—a dignified quiet city of stately buildings, fine shops, attractive arcades, tree-lined streets and parks. Its "Little Streets"—Little Collins Street and Little Bourke Street— originally envisaged as the rear entrances to palatial town houses that were to be built on the main streets, now house many of the city's business establishments.

I attended Sabbath morning services at the city's cathedral synagogue, the Toorak Synagogue, with its impressive dome and marble steps leading to the pulpit. A teenager was assisting in the details of the Reading of the Torah. The youth wore the Mount Scopus College uniform: sky-blue visored cap, school tie and dark blue blazer with the school emblem—the Lion of Judah holding a Scroll of the Law, and the inscription of the school motto "Be Strong and of Good Courage." Clearly it gave one status to be known as a student at the community's Mount Scopus College.

Another day, in another part of the city, I came across an enraptured group of middle-aged men in an ecstatic circle dance. These were Lubavitsher Hasidim expressing their joy on the anniversary of the liberation from solitary confinement and death sentence imposed upon their "Alter Rebbe" Shneur Zalman in a Leningrad prison in 1798.

Domed synagogues, school ties, sports fields, Lubavitsher yeshiva—the Melbourne Jewish community has come a long way since its start over a century and a quarter ago. It was in 1835 that Joseph Solomon, nephew of Judah Solomon of Hobart fame, was one of a party of three white men and six aborigines who came with John Batman from Van Diemen's Land to the south to explore the possibilities of the rich grazing land of Victoria.

Batman bought the rights to a tract of land at the head of Port Phillip Bay from the chief of an aboriginal tribe who put his signature (a mark) on a document, transferring the land for £200 worth of knives, tomahawks, blankets, mirrors, flannel shirts and flour. Other men followed Batman. Finally, the population having grown to 224, an official administrator—Captain William Lonsdale—chose the site of the authorized settlement, where Melbourne now stands. Crown land was sold by public auction, the government auctioneer standing on a fallen log selling half-acre lots for £35 each.

Early Melbourne was a village of primitive huts in a forest of gum, wattle and oak trees. Kangaroos and wild dogs roamed the settlement. Duels and shootings were not uncommon. Convicts were brought in from other parts of the colony of New South Wales to work on the roads and the public buildings. About a thousand convicts were brought in directly from England, it being agreed that they were not to return to the homeland until their terms had expired.

Prisoners who had completed their terms elsewhere in the colony came here to start life anew as free men. They became tavern keepers, shopkeepers, small merchants. The majority of them opened drapery or clothing shops.

Among the small number of Jews who had come was the free settler Michael Cashmore. Son of a London goldsmith, he sailed for Australia at the age of twenty-one to strike out in business for himself. After four years in Sydney he left for Port Phillip in 1840 aboard the *Bright Planet* with four trunks and twenty-two cases full of wares intended for sale at the drapery shop he proposed to open at the corner of Elizabeth Street and Great William Street (later known as Collins Street).

The premises of his London and Manchester Warehouse (the name of his establishment) was distinguished by the postal address "Number 1 Melbourne," a fact recorded on a brass plate on the building now occupying the site. Soon the intersection itself became known as Cashmore's Corner. Imaginative and original, he made his mark upon the settlement. Within a month of signing the lease for the premises, he was already advertising in a manner unique for those times:

> *Economy being the order of the day*
> *Thither to Cashmore's quickly bend your way.*
> *Plenty you'll there behold to please the eyes,*
> *At prices low that must create surprise.*
> *The assortment is the best that can be found,*
> *Seek Melbourne through, seek Melbourne round.*

In September of the following year, when there were fifty-seven Jews in Melbourne, a meeting was held at the home of Edward and Isaac Hart at which the Jewish Congregational Society was organized, with 26-year-old Michael Cashmore as President. High Holyday services were held at the Port Phillip Hotel in Flinders Street with newly arrived Asher Hyman Hart, another magnetic, energetic leader, acting as Honorary Reader of the service.

Not until six years later, Melbourne having in the interim passed through a period of deep economic depression, was the foundation stone of the synagogue placed on an acre of land granted by the government on Bourke Street between Elizabeth and Queen streets. In 1848, the community then numbering one hundred, the synagogue named Shearit Yisrael was consecrated. Soon Reverend Moses Rintel, born in Scotland of Polish parentage and educated in the East European tradition, became the spiritual leader of the small community.

In the same year that the synagogue was dedicated, the Melbourne Jewish Philanthropic Society was organized at the Old Rainbow Tavern, its purpose being to grant relief in case of sickness or misfortune, and to provide homes for the poor, the aged and the infirm. Later it opened an immigrants' hostel and extended aid to discharged Jewish prisoners by supplying them with clothing and funds with which to start life over again.

Then came the era of gold fever. One nugget of California gold was displayed in H. J. Hart's Jewelry shop. The precious metal having been found in New South Wales, a local Gold Committee offered a reward of 200 guineas to anyone discovering a profitable gold mine near Melbourne.

And gold was found. The result was inevitable. Thousands came from far and near. During the hectic days of the gold rush, Americans also came. Some of these became bartenders at a hotel. Dressed like the traditional "Uncle Sam" figure, they introduced mint juleps and planter's punch to Australia. Bourke Street became the starting point for Clark's Union Line of Coaches to the gold fields in the northern part of the colony. The immigrants poured in, the fit and the unfit, the skilled and the unskilled. By 1854 the population of Melbourne had grown to 80,000.

The Philanthropic Society pleaded with the London Jewish Emigration Society, which was assisting those who desired to emigrate to other countries, to direct only those with skills or those accustomed to manual work to come to Victoria, which by this time had officially become a separate colony, distinct from the mother colony of New South Wales.

Another request was that, in any case, the supported emigrants be British-born Jews only. If not Sephardim, they should be Ashkenazim "who had been born in England and who would have reached the Sephardi standard and level."

The gold finds were extravagantly successful. To mark their thankfulness for the gold yield, a Victorian Gold Subscription Committee was formed in June 1852 (only seventeen years after the first Jew had reached Melbourne) with the purpose of presenting a kiddush cup—made of the gold mined in Victoria—to the Chief Rabbi of the British Empire, Reverend Dr. Nathan M. Adler. Within a month, over forty ounces of gold bullion had been subscribed for this purpose and shipped to England under consignment to a committee in London that was appointed to carry out the project.

The cup was formed by C. F. Hancock and stood ten inches high. The *Jewish Chronicle* of July 22, 1853—described the cup:

From circular foot, with chased border, springs a
tree which expands into and supports the cup.
From the body of the cup hang festoons of flowers,
and the cover is embossed with wreaths of laurel.

. . . The outer surface of the cup was divided into four compartments on two of which are chased medallions of the "Lion and the Lamb" and the "Chalice and Open Bible"; the other two are occupied by the inscription in Hebrew and English: This cup made from gold, the produce of the mines of Victoria, is presented to the Reverend Dr. Nathan Marcus Adler, Chief Rabbi of the British Jews as a token of the high esteem in which he is held by his brethren in this colony and to mark their sense of his indefatigable exertions in the holy cause of religion and education.

In the presentation address made at the residence of Reverend Adler, Elias Davis of the London committee said as reported in the *Jewish Chronicle* of August 12, 1853:

Reverend Sir: The Jewish inhabitants of the colony of Victoria respectfully desire to express the feelings of veneration and respect they entertain towards you and avail themselves of this opportunity of returning you their unfeigned thanks for the kindly affection you express for them and for the anxiety you display to hear of their welfare both spiritual and temporal. They have not remained in ignorance (although residing at this remote distance) of the great good rendered by you to the causes of religion and education.

They have every confidence in your power and will to promote the spiritual and temporal happiness of their brethren both at home and abroad; and their humble prayer is that you may long be spared to continue your exertions in this good and holy cause, and while they express this, their earnest wish, they respectfully request your acceptance of the accompanying "Sanctification Cup" (manufactured from the produce of the colony) as a slight token of the esteem and respect they entertain for you and to mark their sense of the untiring zeal and perseverance evidenced by you in all that concerns the welfare of the Jews generally.

Trusting they may long retain your paternal

watchfulness, they beg to subscribe themselves,
Reverend Sir, yours in the bonds of our holy faith.
  For and on behalf of the Jews of the colony of
Victoria,
  Angel Ellis
  Honorary Secretary to the Subscription
Committee

In his formal letter of acceptance of the Kiddush Cup, Rev. Adler said:

> *To the Jewish inhabitants of the colony of Victo-*
> *ria—Gentlemen. . . . I perceive in this distin-*
> *guished mark of attention this higher motive,*
> *namely that amidst the first dazzling of plenty and*
> *affluence you have not lost sight of "people and*
> *father's house" . . . [you] have looked back to*
> *those with whom you are linked by the same ori-*
> *gin, history and religious belief . . . and that you*
> *will contrive to use those blessings for the strength-*
> *ening of our holy faith, by the furtherance of the*
> *social, moral and religious condition of your*
> *colony. . . .*

A link of quite another sort was forged between London and the young pioneers in Australia. This was done by a London woman reformer, a Roman Catholic known as the emigrants' friend—Mrs. Caroline Chisholm—who encouraged Jewish girls to make the trek to the Australian colony where there was a scarcity of Jewish young women. In a public address before a Jewish audience in London she said: "Emigration to be effectual must be respectably conducted. If you send young women to Australia, send them so that they may take a respectable position in society." And one London newspaper announced:

> *Maidens, we are pleased to learn that Mrs. Chis-*
> *holm is about to take in her own ship, the* Caroline
> Chisholm, *no less than twenty young maiden Jew-*
> *esses resolved to migrate to Australia for the most*
> *noble and most human of purposes. These dam-*
> *sels, should matrimony be their fate, have every*
> *hope that they should be enabled to win their*

*gold-digging husbands from an unceasing pursuit
of the root of all evil.*

Rabbi Jacob Sapphir, in Australia in the 1850's on his missions to gather funds for the poor of Jerusalem reported that a large number of women had come out of Ireland, where "seven women take hold of one man." In Australia they served as domestics and housekeepers, and eventually some became wives of the men.

All this brought about the question of conversion of women who wished to accept the faith of their Jewish husbands. At first the Melbourne congregation ruled, "No application for conversion to the Jewish faith would be received by this congregation." But life itself forced a change. So few Jewish young women emigrated to the colony, it was decided to refer the entire matter to the Chief Rabbi. It was then ruled that as there was no Beit Din and no mikveh in the colony, no conversions could take place in Australia. Anyone desirous of accepting the Jewish faith would have to apply in person in London.

When a Beit Din was later established in Melbourne (the first one outside of London), it was authorized to proselytize—but only after receiving such authority from the Chief Rabbi. The *Australian Israelite* in May 1874 commented editorially:

> *The Bourke Street Synagogue has always been thoroughly opposed to the indiscriminate making of proselytes and under its auspices not a single case has been made, except with special authority of the Chief Rabbi. . . . Dr. Adler has placed it on record that he himself is opposed to proselytization. . . . But occasionally cases crop up where it would be an injustice, nay, a positive wrong not to permit it.*

To discourage marrying out of the faith, the synagogue established two types of membership—privileged and non-privileged. No man who had married a non-Jewish woman or who was "living openly in a state of concubinage" could be a privileged member (being one conferred certain rights in the synagogue and also gave social status).

Another problem that beset the young community about twenty years after the gold rush era had started came to be known as the "Battle of the Synagogues." The leader of the first synagogue, Reverend Moses Rintel, who had come to Melbourne when he was twenty-five years old, was well versed in scholarship, strong-willed and adamant in his views—even in cases where he disagreed with the opinion of the Chief Rabbi. After differences between himself and the congregation, Reverend Rintel resigned and in 1857 established a second congregation. This new group—the East Melbourne Hebrew Congregation—was in an area to which many of the non-British immigrants had gravitated. Disagreements continued between Reverend Rintel and Reverend Ornstein, who had succeeded him as rabbi of Shearit Yisrael, the Bourke Street Synagogue.

But it was also a matter of background, of English versus "foreign" Jews. When first settled, 90 percent of Melbourne Jewry came from England, and what was accepted as proper in England became the accepted way of life in Australia. The gold rush era had brought an influx of Jews from Continental Europe, who were called "foreign" Jews by the earlier arrivals. The *Australian Israelite* remarked:

> *It is time that among Jews the heed given to all*
> *differences of nationality be abolished. It may be*
> *true that at the present era, continental Jews are, as*
> *a rule, more intimately acquainted with Hebrew*
> *lore, and perhaps more scrupulous in their regard*
> *to our ancient rites and ceremonies than their*
> *English co-religionists.*

Alarmed by the laxity in observance of rites, a Sabbath Observance Association had been formed, which recommended that the synagogues render ineligible to office any member who publicly violated the Sabbath. The Bourke Street Synagogue refused to do this.

But it was this first synagogue, the Bourke Street Synagogue, that sent out a call for the reunification of the two groups. For a year and a half meetings were held. When one congregation said

"Amalgamation impracticable," the other group simultaneously favored amalgamation. At another time, each one reversed its own previous stand. Matters got so involved it was impossible to know which group wanted what! A joint conference took place, with both congregations represented. Nothing was accomplished. Each congregation pursued its own course.

In the meantime the community continued to grow. By 1861 there were 1,796 Jews in Melbourne and by 1881 this number had increased to 3,343. From the center around Bourke Street, Collins Street and Elizabeth Street, Jews began moving out to the south and to the east.

Economic conditions improved. Small drapery shops became large retail stores; small dealers became heads of large merchant houses. Among the immigrants from Germany were the merchants and jewelers; those from Eastern Europe were the tailors, some of whom became textile manufacturers; Romanians were generally the fruiterers.

Business advertisements in the early 1871 issues of the *Australian Israelite* included the following:

Levy & Bros. & Co.——Great Bourke St.
Importers of British, Foreign and American Merchandise
Edward Cohen & Co.——Little Collins St.
Fine teas, brandies, candles, champagne
Feldheim, Jacobs & Co.——Queen St.
Cutlery, saddlery, ironmongery
D. Rosenthal——Little Collins St.
Wholesale Jeweler & Importer—General Merchandise
P. Falk & Co.——Little Collins St.
Tobacco—Patent Medicines—Saddlery
Levi & Davis——Russell St.
Fresh sausages
C.J. Hughes——Collins St.
Caterer & Confectioner
Victor Hoelsken——Swanson St.
Kosher preparation of every class of Wedding Breakfast, Dinners and Other Entertainments

Monument to the six million who died in Hitler's Europe—Jewish cemetery in Melbourne, Australia.

Many changes have taken place in the century since these advertisements appeared on Page One of the newspaper. Melbourne is no longer a pioneer town of primitive huts. It has become the stately Grande Dame of Victoria. But in one respect it remains the same: Melbourne is a first-generation immigrant city.

When after World War I, quota laws cut down the number of Eastern European immigrants admitted to the United States, many turned to Australia. Then came the Hitler period, at the beginning of which Melbourne's Jewry numbered 8,904.

At the Evian Conference, convened by the United States in July 1938 (with thirty-two nations represented) to consider the problem of European refugee migration, Australia made the only constructive proposal. It offered to accept 15,000 refugees over a period of three years.

Thus began Australia's greatest wave of Jewish immigration. The Australian Jewish Welfare Society, set up to sponsor and handle the immigrant settlement, tried to direct the newcomers to work on "station" properties (sheep ranches) or to start their own dairy or poultry farms. But very few of the new arrivals had any skills in these directions.

Less than half of the 15,000 had actually arrived in Australia when World War II broke out. The war put a new face on matters. German and Austrian Jews were "enemy aliens" and were not admitted. After the war immigration was resumed.

For one period, from mid-1946 to the end of 1947, large numbers of refugees from Shanghai, DP's, or concentration camp survivors were admitted in a special category—the "Close Relative" scheme—whereby Australian Jews' relatives who had survived the horrors of the war were given special landing permits. Since 1933 the Melbourne Jewish population has almost quadrupled, and now numbers 33,000. Said one Polish-born Jew, "For immigrants Australia is a Gan Eden. This is a Heaven-blessed land."

Leo Fink, a native of Bialystok, is one member of the 30 percent of Melbourne Jewry born in Eastern Europe. When he and his three brothers decided to leave Europe, they chose Australia for, said Leo Fink, "I saw an ad in the Australian press offering £2 a week for domestic help. Another country was offering only bed and board for the same work. I realized that life in Australia must be of a higher standard, so we came here." The four Fink brothers first went into farming, then turned to metropolitan Melbourne, where they began spinning and weaving carpets.

They are still together in that business with over 800 employees, but Leo Fink devotes most of his time and energy to communal work. President of the Overseas Relief Fund (later combined with the Australian Jewish Welfare Society), he remained president of the combined organization until a few years ago. "Of course we wanted to bring refugees for humane reasons; but we also had our own personal reasons for wanting more and more Jews here. We wanted the Jewish communities of this continent to stay alive," said Leo Fink.

Assimilation was then prevalent in the country. In the 1933 Australian census, 21 percent of the Jewish men and 11 percent of the Jewish women reported that they were married to non-Jews. Taking into account that stating one's religious affiliation was not a required part of the census form, and that there is no exact knowledge of the number who had been converted to or out of the

Jewish faith, it can be assumed that the actual number of intermarriages must have been considerably larger than that indicated in these census figures.

"We are concerned about the future of our children as Jews," continued Leo Fink. So the survivors of the camps, and those who returned from Russia to Poland at the end of the war, and Jews from Hungary—all were brought over. The American Joint Distribution Committee and the HIAS helped defray the costs of transportation. Boats were met, hostels built to accommodate the newcomers, jobs secured, interest-free loans procured for buying the tools of trade or to help in purchasing homes. Landsmanschaften (associations uniting immigrants from one place) sprang up and served as a social group anchor.

Included among the newcomers was one group that had survived Buchenwald. Young (between the ages of sixteen and twenty-one), they had learned to exist by their wits, by trickery or by other forms of delinquency. They, too, were taken in and today are respected members of the community.

All this effort has borne fruit. The 1961 census showed that the state of Victoria had the lowest rate of mixed marriage of all the Australian states. This time only 8 percent of Jewish men and 4 percent of Jewish women reported having married non-Jewish partners.

As Melbourne grew in numbers, it spread out into the suburbs. A century ago 62 percent of the Jews lived within the limits of the City of Melbourne, most of them in Carlton. Today only 5 percent live within city limits. The rest have fanned out to the north, to the west, to the east; but chiefly to the southeastern suburbs of Prahran, St. Kilda, Caulfield, Malvern and Brighton. Over 60 percent of today's Jewish community live within these five suburbs. And the suburbs of Moorabbin, Kew and Camberwell claim another 20 percent of the total Melbourne Jewish population.

The nineteenth-century "Battle of the Synagogues" (between Bourke Street Synagogue and the East Melbourne Hebrew Congregation) seems now to have been an exercise in futility. Today eighteen Orthodox synagogues and three Liberal temples minister to the augmented Jewry. Though I did find some who walked miles to attend Sabbath services at the old Carlton Synagogue, most people attend places of worship closer to their new homes.

Today Melbourne Jewry is a vigorous, lively community. As Bernard Gottlieb of the American J.D.C. said at a meeting of the Victorian Jewish Board of Deputies (on which all groups are represented), "Melbourne has a plethora of organizations." The Welfare Society supplies immigration and social services of a modern advanced nature. Units of the B'nai B'rith, the Council of Jewish Women, Hillel, a Free Loan Society, Philanthropic and Benevolent Societies, the Y.M.H.A., and a full spectrum of Zionist and youth organizations all function. Cultural groups include theatre and dance troupes; book clubs and debating societies exist, as do two Jewish newspapers.

Unusual, however, is the attention given here to sports within the Jewish fold. AJAX—Associated Judean Athletic Clubs—has under its banner clubs and teams participating in badminton, cricket, squash rackets, basketball, football, boxing, fencing, gymnastics, hockey, judo, swimming, wrestling, table tennis, bowling and weight-lifting.

The Bialystoker Center, outstanding among the twenty-one Landsmanschaften, is housed in an old mansion that has paneled rooms, high carved ceilings and leaded windows. The Bialystoker brought in 500 families from their native city and its surroundings. The center has fifteen rooms and was used as a hospital during the war. During the height of immigration, it was used as a hostel and housed as many as seventy people at a time.

Melbourne takes great pride in its Mount Scopus College (classes ranging from sub-primary through secondary school) set up in the historic year of 1948, and owned by the Victorian Jewish Board of Deputies. To have a certain status in the community, one's children must attend this Jewish Day School. Situated on Burwood Highway, its physical plant provides the most modern in educational equipment. To give but two small examples: Every primary classroom has access to its own outdoor terrace, to which the children can take their chairs on hot days, and classrooms have one-way windows in the doors so that one may look in without disturbing the pupils.

Driving from the highway I noted a football field, tennis courts, basketball courts, hockey and baseball grounds—all part of the school's thirty-seven acres of sports fields. A cadet corps and prefects to regulate student activity are also part of the school.

Of the week's thirty-nine learning periods, ten are devoted to Jewish studies, the average time allotment being five hours weekly. Attendance at morning services is optional. All Jewish subjects, except Hebrew language, can be studied either in Hebrew or English.

"Speech Night," marking the close of the school year, is held in December (this being "down under") at Melbourne's Town Hall. When I attended it was a formal affair, the boys in their school uniforms, and the girls in white dresses with white gloves and black patent-leather shoes. The school staff wore their academic robes. Three flags were in procession at the start of the exercises—the Australian, the Jewish and the school flags. The commencement address and the distribution of prizes were made by a man introduced as an "Old Boy," a graduate of six years ago. The statement in an address by one of the graduating students, "Our school has instilled in us what it means to be part of the Jewish people," brought forth great applause.

The Lubavitsher movement operates a yeshiva at Hotham and East St. Kilda streets. Here too the boys, two-thirds of them still in the primary grades, wear a school uniform—dark blue visored cap, light blue shirt, grey sweater and shorts. Classes for the girls are at Beit Rivkah, another building in the same compound.

The boys' school day is a long one, from 8:50 in the morning to 5:00 in the afternoon. The first two hours in the morning and the final hour of each day are devoted to Jewish studies. Minhah (the Afternoon Service) is recited during the lunch hour.

Although classrooms at the yeshiva are bare and scantily furnished, the kindergarten is a bright, airy, cheerful room fully equipped, and with an outdoor playground. Kindergartners painting at easels are garbed in artists' smocks and yarmulkes.

Principal of this yeshiva is Rabbi Yitzhak Groner. He is a big, broad-shouldered man with thick black beard, a picture of motion and energy. December being school year's end, pupils were coming in and out of his office to get their year-end report cards; a

Young artists in smocks and yarmulkes in kindergarten of Lubavitsher Yeshiva in Melbourne, Australia.

woman telephoned to inquire whether she could fry fish in a "fleishige" electric frying pan; another mother came in offering to look after four of his children so that he could get away for a week's holiday—all this while we were trying to talk.

A true follower of the Lubavitsher Rebbe, Rabbi Groner has served the movement in his native United States and in Cuba, Central America, the West Indies, South America, London, Paris, Japan, Singapore and now in Australia. The Rebbe's requests are carried out implicitly and unquestioningly. Once Rabbi Groner was directed to leave books on Jewish subjects in the Fiji Islands. His airplane landed at the Nandi Airport in those islands at 4:00 o'clock in the morning. Undaunted, he searched for a Jewish-sounding name in a telephone book, telephoned Mrs. Israel at that hour, and the books were left for placement in Suva, capital of the Fiji Islands (a story I heard from Mrs. Israel).

Not all the pupils at the Melbourne Lubavitsher Yeshiva come from families allied to that movement. "There are only about ten families in the city who are really Lubavitsher," said Rabbi Groner, "and half of our pupils come from families that desecrate the Sabbath. Yet they want their children to get the kind of Jewish education that we provide."

The kind of education offered in this school is described proudly in the Melbourne Lubavitsher Yeshiva College Annual

Preparing for kibbutz life in Israel at Toolomba, Australia, 113 miles north of Melbourne. (see p. 117)

Report:

> *Many of our first matriculation class have completed an intensive study of 400 pages of the Gemara and Commentaries, which are the key to all Jewish learning. The knowledge of the Hebrew language is in itself insufficient. This must be supplemented with Humash, Rashi, Shulhan Arukh, Jewish Ethics, Philosophy, and above all—an appreciation of Jewish values and the desire to fulfill Mitzvot.*

Other Jewish Day Schools are the Zionist-sponsored Bialik College at Shakespeare Grove in Hawthorn (in a residence once the home of a German consul—an imposing building with high ceilings, curved balustrades, lawns and playgrounds); the Mizrahi Yavneh College in Caulfield; the Orthodox Adass Israel School and the Moriah College affiliated with the Elwood Congregation. Altogether about 40 percent of Melbourne's Jewish children attend Jewish Day Schools.

The United Jewish Education Board of Australia has a three-pronged program: part-time after-school centers that provide Hebrew language instruction; religious classes within the secular state schools; and correspondence courses for children in isolated areas in the Pacific.

The Zionist Council and the synagogues conduct Hebrew classes, lectures and seminars for adults. All in all, Melbourne is a community of intense educational involvement.

Many of Melbourne's Jews have been concerned with the general life of the city. Among these were Edward Cohen and Benjamin Benjamin, both of whom were Mayors of the city; Simon Isaacs, who was Judge of the Supreme Court and Trevor G. Rapke, who was Advocate General of the Royal Australian Navy.

Two local Jews have carved special niches in the pantheon of Australian heroes: One was Sir John Monash, son of a German-Jewish family who was, according to Britain's wartime Prime Minister, David Lloyd George, "The most resourceful general in the whole of the British army" although not a soldier by profession; the other was Sir Isaac Isaacs, son of a Polish tailor, who became the first Australian-born Governor General of the Commonwealth of Australia.

Born in 1865 Lieutenant General Sir John Monash was the son of German immigrants, drawn to Melbourne during the gold rush era. The Monash family moved out to the "bush," to the country towns where the father, Louis Monash, ran a general store.

The mother returned to the big city to give her children the opportunity of a good education. Son John entered Melbourne University at the age of sixteen, "with a vast and undisciplined appetite for knowledge." Because the family was in financial need, he had to leave before graduation, getting his degrees in engineering and law at a later date. (A consulting engineer, he pioneered the use of reinforced concrete.)

He enlisted at an early age as a private in the Victorian Rifles. When World War I broke out, 49-year-old Monash was appointed Commander of the 4th Infantry Brigade of the Australian Imperial Force. After heavy fighting in Gallipoli, he was sent to the French front. As Commander of the 3rd Australian Division, he was promoted to the rank of Major General and served in the Armentieres section. In May 1918, then Commander of the Australian Army Corps, he developed the tactical strategy which paved the way for the final victorious Allied offensive of the war.

In August of that year, King George V knighted General Monash, it being the first time in nearly two centuries that a British King had knighted a commander on the field.

Everyone delighted to do him honor. He returned from the war as a K.C.B. (Knight Commander of the Bath) and G.C.M.G. (Knight Grand Cross of the Order of St. Michael and St. George). France bestowed upon him a Croix de Guerre and made him an officer in its Legion of Honor. Belgium, too, gave him the Croix de Guerre and made him a Grand Officer in the Belgian Order of the Crown. From America he received the Distinguished Service Medal.

Upon his return to civilian life, General Monash became the general manager of the State Electricity Commission. It was now, too, that he participated actively in Jewish communal life as member of the Board of St. Kilda's Synagogue and as president of the Zionist Federation of Australia. When he died in 1931, at the age of sixty-six, he received a military funeral and world-wide tributes.

Monash University in his hometown is named in his memory, and an equestrian statue of Sir John, a tribute of the people of the state of Victoria, stands near the Shrine of Remembrance. An Australian publication said of him, "Monash was Australia's greatest son, brilliant in war, brilliant in peace, a scholar amongst scholars, a lover of the arts."

Melbourne Jewry's other world-famous figure was the son of skilled tailor Alfred Isaacs, who had emigrated to London from his native Mlava in Poland. Hearing of the Australian gold strikes, he and his young wife, an English Jewess, decided to try their luck in the island continent. They set out on the ship *Queen of the East* and going via the Cape of Good Hope reached Melbourne in 1854. The following year their son Isaac was born in the family dwelling behind his father's tailor shop on Elizabeth Street near Flinders Street. Gold having been reported in the country towns of Yackandandah and later at Beechworth, Alfred Isaacs moved his tailor shop, and his family, to these smaller communities.

When twenty years old, Isaac Isaacs returned to Melbourne to study law. Law practice followed and participation in public affairs—as a member of the Victorian Legislative Assembly, as Solicitor General, then Attorney General. At all times he was, in his own words, "For the maintenance of even-handed justice to all—rich and poor, titled and obscure," and he drafted much social legislation.

He was also leader of the Victorian delegation to the convention for the Federation of the Australian colonies. At a dinner marking his election to the Federal or Commonwealth Parliament, Isaac Isaacs had his father, the Polish-born tailor, sit at his right hand.

Appointed a Justice on the High Court (corresponding to the Supreme Court of the United States), he served for nearly a quarter of a century. During this time he was the first member of the High Court to be appointed Privy Councillor, traveling to London for his investiture by King George V at Buckingham Palace.

A Sydney newspaper said of him, "Short and slight, Sir Isaac's features are of a delicate mold and express the strong humanity which has on some occasions been passionately shown in his judgments." Elevation to the post of Chief Justice of the High Court which followed might normally have been the crowning achievement of one's life—but not in the life of Sir Isaac.

When in 1930 it was felt that an Australian citizen should act as Governor General of the country, only two men were considered for the post. Both were native sons of Melbourne Jewry—Sir John Monash and Sir Isaac Isaacs. Monash was ill at the time. It was then that Sir Isaac was recommended to and appointed by King George V to represent the British Crown in Australia.

Describing the pageantry of the day on which the 75-year-old Sir Isaac took the oath of office, Max Gordon, in his biography of the Governor General *Sir Isaac Isaacs—A Life of Service* says:

> *Sir Isaac was dressed in full court uniform of a*
> *Privy Councillor, with plumed cocked hat and*
> *sword at his side. . . . Drawn up by the side of the*
> *avenue was a guard of honor of Light Horsemen,*
> *with pennoned lances and fluttering emu plumes in*
> *their famous hats. Sir Isaac finished the inspection*

*[and] stepped into the State carriage, drawn by
four horses ridden by bewigged and powdered pos-
tillions. Outriders in top hats rode ahead; two
coachmen sat behind the carriage. The mounted
guard of Light Horsemen followed.*

Isaac Isaacs was knighted when he was created K.C.M.G. (Knight Commander of the Order of St. Michael and St. George) followed later by the award of G.C.M.G. (Knight Grand Cross, Order of St. Michael and St. George). He carried out the duties of his office with tact and dignity, and upon his retirement after five years in office, King George VI honored him with the G.C.B. (Knight Grand Cross, Order of the Bath).

During his retirement he studied the Bible and wrote numerous articles and letters for the Jewish journals in Australia. It was in this closing period of his life (he was in his eighty-first year when he retired) that there rose dissension between Sir Isaac and the Jews of Australia.

In 1939 Britain issued a White Paper which so limited admission of Jews into Palestine that they would forever remain a minority there, even when a Palestinian state would in the future be created. Sir Isaac supported Britain's policy. To him, being a Jew meant being of the Jewish religious faith, and he was against setting up an autonomous Jewish state in Palestine with a Jewish majority.

He wrote against Zionism in letters to the *Hebrew Standard.* Two days before a public meeting to be held at Melbourne's Town Hall in 1943, to protest against the White Paper, a meeting at which non-Jews were scheduled to speak their support of the Jewish demand for opening the doors of Palestine to Jewish immigration, Sir Isaac published a letter in the public press warning against pressure on the British government on the issue of Palestine.

Emotions ran high. He was censured for the position he had taken. Professor Julius Stone (then Challis Professor of Jurisprudence and International Law at Sydney University and before that Assistant Professor of Law at Harvard, and later Academic Director of the Harry S Truman Center for the Advancement of

Peace in Jerusalem) addressed himself to the former Governor General in his book "Stand Up and Be Counted":

> *I render my tribute to your great legal contribution. I am conscious as well that you formerly discharged with great distinction the duties of the highest office in this land. . . . You cite "Mein Kampf" as accurately describing your conception of "political Zionism." You have shown persistent hostility to the Zionist Federation of Australia, a federation in which another great Australian Jew—Sir John Monash—whose loyalty to Australia will, I hope, never be questioned, held until his death the office of Honorary President. . . . In your letter of October 28, 1943, you denounced such a vision of Jewish nationhood as tending to weaken the "Australian patriotism" of your fellow Jews, as "ridiculous and even pestilential," as in tendency "treasonable" in Australian citizens and as "undemocratic."*

Despite Sir Isaac's opposition, the protest meeting was held, and on schedule.

When Sir Isaac died in 1948 at the age of ninety-two, he was given a state funeral, mourned by the nation, and the world paid tribute to "Perhaps the greatest Australian of our time, or any previous time," as one newspaper said.

In recent decades discord and divisiveness within Melbourne Jewry has been on another front—Orthodox vs. Liberal. Orthodox rabbis have refused at meetings of general civic interest to share a platform with a Liberal rabbi. At a recent dinner given by the Jewish community in honor of Australia's Prime Minister, no Orthodox rabbi attended because a Liberal rabbi had been asked to make the blessing over bread. Senior Liberal Rabbi Herman Saenger said, "If an Orthodox Jew wants to marry a Liberal Jew the marriage ceremony must be conducted in an Orthodox synagogue, or the children of such a family will not be acknowledged as Jews." One Orthodox rabbi wanted a wall erected to separate the Liberal section of the cemetery from the rest of the Jewish burial ground. However, from most recent reports, I understand the situation is improving.

A recent survey made by Liberal Rabbi John Levi (a fourth-generation Australian and a graduate of the Hebrew Union College in the United States) showed that intermarriage—now at a rate of 15 percent—occurs in both sectors of the community, the Orthodox as well as the Liberal branches.

It was refreshing to have met Rabbi Chaim Gutnick, leader of the Elwood Talmud Torah Congregation and a former Chief Jewish Chaplain of the Australian Armed Forces and an adherent of the Lubavitsher movement. When I expressed surprise at the fact that he was beardless (this was in 1965), Rabbi Gutnick explained that he did not want the wearing of a beard to stand between him and the young people whom he wanted to reach. Spiritual leader of one particular congregation, he felt he was "Rabbi to the whole community."

Rabbi Gutnick's approach to problems facing the twentieth-century Jew may be gleaned from the following excerpts of a conversation we had:

> *The faith practiced by Moses and by my grand-*
> *father is obligatory on me, but the way may*
> *change. . . . If a man has thrown off half of the*
> *Mitzvot let him uphold and maintain the rest. . . .*
> *Of the 613 Mitzvot, I specialize in one—my love*
> *for my Jewish people, for all of Jewry.*

◄§ FROM CONVICT TO SYNAGOGUE TREASURER IN TASMANIA §►

New Year's Day, 1966, found me in Hobart, chief city of the island of Tasmania, off the southeastern coast of the mainland of Australia. It was Sabbath day and I went to the synagogue, the oldest standing one in all of Australia. Three men and I formed the congregation that day—in a synagogue with room for a hundred and fifty.

Every detail of the building bespoke the love and care and devotion which had gone into its construction. Columns supporting the carved ceiling were trimmed with gilded palm and lotus decorations. The same designs were repeated on the ceiling from which hung five chandeliers containing eighty candles. Rugs covered the floor. The Ark, approached by circular steps and carved bronze railing, was screened off with a rich red velvet curtain. The Reading Desk was made of beautifully turned cedarwood. The seats, also of cedarwood, were cushioned in red velvet. Each seat number was placed within its own small bronze Magen David.

Inscribed on a wall tablet in letters of gold were these lines:

THE GROUND ON WHICH IS ERECTED
THIS EDIFICE
DEDICATED TO THE WORSHIP OF THE SUPREME
WAS PRESENTED TO THE HEBREW CONGREGATION OF
HOBART TOWN BY
JUDAH SOLOMON, ESQ.
WHO ALSO HANDSOMELY CONTRIBUTED
TOWARDS THE BUILDING

He had also been the first treasurer of the synagogue. But the incredible thing was that the man so memorialized, Judah Solomon, had been transported to Tasmania as a convict.

When England lost its American colonies as a result of the Revolutionary War, she sought a new place to which to send her surplus convicts, a custom that had been the norm in England for about two centuries. In addition to the New South Wales colony, another one was organized in Van Diemen's Land, so named by its discoverer, Dutch navigator Captain Abel Tasman, in 1642, in honor of the then Governor General of the Dutch East Indies. It was later renamed Tasmania in his own honor.

The fleets carrying the exiled ones sailed from England the long way around by way of the Cape of Good Hope, a route that took an average of 146 days. Ships were overcrowded, each prisoner having about eighteen inches of space for sleeping. Supplies were low, scurvy was rife and many died. In the second fleet, 267 died en route; in the third fleet 199 died during the voyage. Conditions on later trips were improved with a surgeon aboard, and a gratuity offered to doctor and ship master for each prisoner landed safely in the colony.

The convicts were not all criminals—some were political prisoners, others were debtors. Sentences were banishment for a term of either seven years, fourteen years or life.

Andrew Jamieson was convicted for life for stealing a cigar case, costing sixpence, and two promissory notes, each worth £5. One man drew a fourteen-year sentence for stealing a toothpick made of silver or ivory; another was exiled for stealing two prayer books valued at five shillings each.

Child convicts were to be counted among those banished from England's shores. A few boys, eight years of age, were deported, and twelve- to eighteen-year-olds were numerous. One twelve-year-old boy was sentenced to seven years for stealing knives. Sixteen-year-old George Wilkinson was indicted for stealing "one wooden till, value two shillings and five shillings in copper money." His sentence was seven years' banishment.

Half of the convicts were assigned as unpaid laborers or domestic servants to free settlers who had received grants of land in the area. The settlers were bound to feed, clothe and lodge these convict workers. In this manner the British government freed itself of financial obligations in the maintenance of many thousands.

Less dependable prisoners worked in road gangs and chain gangs. More incorrigible ones had to work in irons. The worst male offenders were sent to Port Arthur, about sixty miles southeast of Hobart, where a penal colony was built. A few miles away was narrow Eaglehawk Neck, guarded by savage dogs acting as a barricade, should anyone attempt a run for freedom from Port Arthur.

When a convict's sentence had been completed, he was given a grant of thirty acres of land on the island. Only if a man was given a "free" pardon, had he the right of return to England.

Jews were to be found among the banished convicts. The ship *Cambden,* reaching Australia in 1833, had one deportee "age 18—able to read and write—religion, Jew—single—trade, stable boy—height: 4 ft. 11½ inches—complexion dark, ruddy, nose large, tatooing on left arm." Ikey Solomon was also among those transported. This was the man said to have been the prototype for the character Fagin in Charles Dickens' *Oliver Twist.* Already well known to the police as a pickpocket at the age of fourteen, he later set up as a "fence" in Whitechapel. Papers in the State Archives of Hobart deal with Ikey Solomon.

Convict lists included such names as Isaac Cohen, Mordecai

Cohen, Moses Cohen and Nathan Cowan. There was an Abram Abrahams, Michael Isaacs, Abraham Jacob, Samuel Jacob, Hyman Jacobs, Samuel Solomon, Emanuel Solomon, Simon Solomon and even a Solomon Solomon.

But let us return to the Judah Solomon whose memorial tablet had so startled me in the Hobart synagogue. Judah and his brother Joseph, sons of Isaac Solomon of London, were indicted at the Kent Assizes for "capital offences." The records of the Kent Assizes do not give details of their "capital offences." In those days, committing a felony, in the nature of a debt owed on goods received in business, was held to be a "capital offence." Sentenced to life terms, Judah and Joseph Solomon were transported on the *Prince Regent* in 1819. Early the following year they were transferred to Van Diemen's Land on the *Castle Forbes.*

Apparently they were not assigned as convict laborers to any free settler and were not sent to Port Arthur. Instead, they were permitted to choose an occupation for which they felt suited. What that employment was is easy to surmise, for early the following year, the January 20, 1821 issue of the *Hobart Town Gazette* carried an advertisement by J & J Solomon, announcing the sale of drapery, jewelry and spirits at their home in Argyle Street. In the Hobart Library Archives it is recorded that Judah and Joseph Solomon were in business as "general dealers at the corner of Liverpool and Argyle Streets."

Within ten years of his arrival in Hobart as a convict, Judah Solomon was so well accepted by the community of Jews, that Sabbath services were held regularly at his home, which became known as Temple House. In the 1830s, both Judah and Joseph Solomon received conditional pardons—making them free men, but without permission to return to England.

Within twenty years of their landing, both brothers owned a number of business establishments, possessed homes, were ships' agents and were among the first shareholders in the Van Diemen's Bank. Judah had also become a money lender.

When, in 1842, the Jews of Hobart decided that they would build a synagogue, Judah Solomon offered a part of his garden in Argyle Street as a "gift in perpetuity." When there was a drive for funds for the synagogue, Judah Solomon's contribution topped all the others.

View from Mt. Wellington in Hobart, Tasmania.

The following year—in the seventh year of the reign of Queen Victoria—the foundation stone of the place of worship was laid. During the ceremonies, attended by "a great number of persons of every creed," the president of the congregation, Louis Nathan, said:

> *The Almighty has said "Where thou shalt record*
> *My Name, I will come unto thee and bless thee"*
> *and I hope the promise will be fulfilled to us, in*
> *this far distant land from the land of our ancestors.*
> *I must observe, referring to our small community*
> *here, that, Gentlemen, it reflects great honour and*
> *credit upon the whole of you, for the liberal man-*
> *ner in which you have responded to the call, and*
> *so generously subscribed to the erection of the edi-*
> *fice. I cannot refrain from commenting, individual-*
> *ly, on the very handsome manner in which Judah*
> *Solomon has assisted towards this laudable object;*
> *not only presenting the site, which is a portion of*
> *his garden, but the liberal way in which he has*
> *subscribed.*

Remains of penal colony at Port Arthur, Tasmania; incorrigible convicts from England banished here; colony closed in 1877.

Two years later, in 1845, the synagogue doors were opened.

Leafing through the recorded minutes of meetings of the first decade of the Hobart Hebrew Congregation, I visualized a small, courageous band of people struggling to maintain themselves, facing problems peculiar to the location, the numbers and the structure of the group in Van Diemen's Land.

For example, there was the question of the prayer Mashiv Haruah, referring to seasonal changes, to wind and rain. In the northern hemisphere these changes occur in the autumn of the year, so that the prayer is recited at that season. Hobart is "down under" in the southern hemisphere, and the seasons are the reverse of those in the northern hemisphere. Being traditional in their observance, the congregants found themselves in a quandary. Should they recite Mashiv Haruah simultaneously with their brethren in the northern hemisphere? Or should the prayer be read at a time appropriate to their own seasons of the year? In 1846, they put the question to Rabbi Nathan Adler, then Chief

Rabbi of the British Empire. He ruled that the Hobart congregation could be exempt from reciting Mashiv Haruah.

An uncommon problem facing this community was the question of its relationship with prisoners. The request of the Controller of Convicts at Port Arthur for prayer books for Jewish convicts was simple to fulfill. The congregation sent three Hebrew prayer books and one with an English translation for the men at that penal colony. For some years the local Jews had asked that any Jews in the Hobart prison be permitted to attend synagogue services and that such prisoners be permitted to refrain from work on the Sabbath. Finally, in 1847, the request was granted.

When convicts attended Sabbath service, the community also saw to it that they were invited to a Jewish home for a Sabbath meal. But soon another question posed itself. How were these convicts to be treated during the course of the religious service? Should they be counted towards a minyan? Should they receive an aliyah, be called up to the Reading of the Torah? Again the Chief Rabbi in London was called upon to solve their problem. His decision was that convicts could be counted toward a minyan, but they were not to have any honors given them during the service.

Conversion became a perplexing question. There was no qualified Beit Din to act when the need arose. Finally it was decided that the Synagogue Committee should take charge when anyone wished to become a proselyte to Judaism. Permission was granted to a member to be united with a non-Jewish woman "according to the custom of the Hebrew nation." When this problem was put before the Chief Rabbi for a directive, he urged that once having converted, proselytes be welcomed into the Jewish community.

Sabbath observance was strict. Complaint was made that Mrs. Widow Cohen kept her shop open on the Sabbath. The Synagogue Committee thereupon sent notice to every householder (and particularly to Mrs. Widow Cohen) that any one violating the ordinance "Remember the Sabbath day and keep it holy" by keeping his shop open on the Sabbath, would not be entitled to receive any of the benefits or privileges of membership.

Fines were instituted for breaches of discipline or laxity in synagogue behavior. Committee members who were late in coming to services were fined two shillings and sixpence. And no favoritism was shown. Judah Solomon, too, was assessed the same fine for coming late. It was recorded that Philip Phillips declined the honor when called to the Reading of the Torah. So he was fined twenty-one shillings.

The general composition of the Hobart community was unusual. When Colonel David Collins, the first Lieutenant Governor, landed with eighteen free men to organize a colony in Van Diemen's Land in 1804 there were no Jews among those original free settlers. The first Jews of Hobart were convicts—some of whom stayed on as freed men on the thirty acres which the government allotted to them at the expiration of their terms.

Ships continued to bring both convicts and free settlers. The land was waiting for the plough, and there was plenty of room for all. Prosperity in Tasmania attracted more immigrants, particularly at a time when England's recession was bringing many to a state of bankruptcy. Among the free settlers was Bernard Walford, who, although married in a church to a Christian woman, petitioned the authorities for a grant of land for a Jewish burial ground. His request was allowed. As fate would have it, Bernard Walford was the first person to be buried in Hobart's Jewish cemetery.

Among the early free Jewish immigrants was Samuel Moses, who came from England with his wife and children and servants. He went into the wine and spirit business, and also acted as the colony's mohel. Louis Nathan, president when the foundation stone of the synagogue was laid, had come with his wife and children in 1834, and ran a General Warehouse on Elizabeth Street. I. Friedman was a pawnbroker, other Jews became hotel keepers.

The community flourished and grew. By the year 1854 Hobart's Jewish population reached its peak of 435. Of these, 259 were free settlers and 176 were convicts.

When transportation of convicts from England ceased, this community's population declined. A total of 67,655 convicts had been banished to Tasmania by the year 1852. The Jews had prospered because of the commercial activity related to the needs of the penal colony. At about the same time that transportation stopped, gold was discovered on the Mainland, and men went off to try their luck in the gold fields. Then an epidemic of scarlet fever grew to such proportions that a public fast for the Jewish congregation was proclaimed.

When the penal colony at Port Arthur was closed in 1877, Jews began emigrating from Tasmania in search of a livelihood elsewhere. As the community diminished, still other families moved to the Mainland to raise their children among a larger Jewish circle in order to prevent intermarriage. And all the time the Hobart community continued to fall off in numbers. By 1933 only seventy Jews could be counted in all of Tasmania.

Throughout the years Hobart, like many small communities, had suffered from not having had continual spiritual guidance. Rabbis came and went—some staying only a year or two before moving on to larger communities. An early synagogue meeting resolved that "Mr. Henry Jones be appointed Reader at a salary of £12 per annum and as collector with 10 percent for any funds he may collect." As far back as 1853, Reverend Herman Hoelzel, appointed by Chief Rabbi Nathan Adler to the post of Presiding Rabbi of Jews of the Australian Colony, reached Tasmania after a voyage of ninety-two days. He was inducted into office with high hopes. But within three years Reverend Hoelzel left Hobart and was being installed as Minister of the Great Synagogue in Sydney.

Four other rabbis moved on, at various times, to Melbourne. Other cities on the Australian Mainland, such as Perth and Ballarat, attracted men who had come originally to serve in Hobart. New Zealand drew two rabbis from Hobart to its shores. And there were periods when Hobart was without any religious leader.

One such time was as recent as the close of World War II. Hobart advertised for a rabbi in publications around the world. There was just one response, that of Reverend Max Warse of Shanghai. He was accepted, but before long, he too had moved on to the larger field of Sydney.

Somehow, in spite of all vicissitudes, the small community

persevered. A happy occasion reported in the local newspaper *Mercury* in February 1905, was the wedding of Mr. Jno Levy to Miss Lena Glaser—the first wedding in forty years at the synagogue. The newspaper related the officiating rabbi from Melbourne and the groom were seated in the warden's box facing the Holy Ark. At the conclusion of the Minhah service, the rabbi led the groom to the canopy. The bride then entered and was placed at the right of the groom because, "the Psalmist says, 'Upon thy right hand did stand the Queen.'"

The high point in the life of the community during the twentieth century was also reported in the pages of the Hobart *Mercury*. This was the celebration held on August 9, 1963, marking the 120th anniversary of the laying of the foundation stone of the synagogue. President Clyde Epstein planned this great event. Rabbi Chaim Gutnick, former Chief Jewish Chaplain in the Armed Forces and Rabbi of the Elwood Talmud Torah Congregation in Melbourne, and Cantor Adler of the same synagogue, conducted the services. Leon Lasky, president of Victoria's Jewish Board of Deputies, was among a group of visitors from Melbourne. All of Hobart's Jews—men, women and children—were present to hear Rabbi Gutnick remark:

> *Here in this small township of Hobart, in this island of Tasmania, far away from Israel and European countries, brave courageous people laid the foundation for another synagogue 120 years ago and over the many years the small Jewish community has maintained it.*

Remembered in the memorial prayers that day were the first president of the synagogue, Louis Nathan, and its first treasurer, Judah Solomon.

Any mark of interest shown them by Australian Jewish Mainlanders helps keep alive within the Hobart community the feeling that they are not alone on this island. The Melbourne B'nai B'rith Harmony Lodge has adopted Hobart, and an occasional Sabbath visit by members of this lodge together with a Melbourne rabbi to lead in Sabbath services raises the spirit of the island group.

Today's Jewish community in Tasmania numbers less than the 136 persons recorded in the 1961 census. Of the Solomon family, none have remained Jewish, although one descendant, Magistrate Solomon, acknowledges his Jewish ancestry. Today's president of the community, Clyde Epstein, is the Australian-born son of Bialystoker Moses Epstein. Blue-eyed, silver-haired, nattily dressed, Clyde Epstein looks more like a man associated with the outdoors and racing events, than a synagogue president. But he is most sincere in his desire to keep the synagogue open. When there is a death he and two others act as a voluntary Hevrah Kaddisha to prepare the body for burial. Said Clyde (born Samuel) Epstein, "It's only a mitzvah."

Half of today's community reached Hobart as a result of the Hitler era in Europe. At first the "Australians" (native Jews) did not fully accept these newcomers, permitting only Australian-born Jews to hold executive positions within the community. But all that has changed.

Numbered among those of the latest wave of immigration is a man who was in a concentration camp, and a family that didn't leave Hungary until after the revolution there. Most were born in Germany and Austria, although some of Hobart's Jews are natives of the United Kingdom, Poland, the U.S.S.R. and Czechoslovakia.

Ferdinand Fixel was a managing director of a Viennese firm. Somehow he has managed to bring along a good Jewish library to Hobart, where he now works as a chemist.

Although the community is small, it is entitled to representation on the Executive Council of the Australian Jewish Board of Deputies. German-born Ludwig Hayes, accountant and director of a number of business firms, was Tasmania's representative on the Council at the time of my visit to Hobart in 1966.

The future of Tasmania's Jewry is indicated in the 1961 census figures, which showed there were ten Jewish boys between the ages of fifteen and twenty-four. In the same age group there was but one Jewish girl.

Where the families have sent their children to the Mainland for Jewish education, the young people have stayed and married there. Then the parents followed the children. Among the general population, too, there has been an exodus—so that in this island, the size of Austria, there is now only a total population of 380,000.

In spite of everything, the men are determined that the synagogue shall be open every Sabbath for services. To that end, each man is provided with a key to the synagogue. When I came at the scheduled hour of ten, there were three men present. Not enough for a minyan. But hope never dies in Hobart. We waited. Maybe tourists, in sufficient number, would drop in. Perhaps the unexpected would occur. In the meanwhile, the sedrah (weekly portion of the Scroll) was carefully gone over from a printed book, ready for use—just in case there would be a minyan and the Sefer Torah could be taken out of the Ark.

But no one else arrived, so we began. Mr. Newman led the service from the cedarwood Reading Desk facing the Ark. The other two men sat together on a red-velvet cushioned bench at one side. I was asked to sit in back of them, not up in the women's gallery (no other women being present). The two read aloud, strong and clear, the well-known verses: the "Shema," the "Yismachu" ("They that keep the Sabbath and call it a delight shall rejoice in Thy Kingdom"); and "In that day will the Lord be One, and His name One."

When I joined this congregation, numbering a total of three men, in the singing of Ayn Kelohenu and Adon Olam, I must admit I found myself singing through tears.

◄§ BALLARAT——GOLD RUSH TOWN §►

Gold! Gold! In Australia! News of the discovery of gold in the alluvial soil of Australia was flashed around the world in 1851, not long after California and her forty-niners. Soon the seekers after gold came pouring in to Australia. By the thousands they came—from England, from Russia, from Germany, from China, from America. No sooner was a ship tied to its wharf than the seekers of fortune thronged the roads, on their way to the fields where the precious metal was waiting to be picked up.

Chief magnet of the gold seekers was Ballarat, seventy-five miles northwest of Melbourne. What had been a pastoral area was quickly turned into a typical mining town with shanties, saloons and gambling. Shops of rough packing cases lined the narrow Main Street. Standing outside their shops, the owners called out their wares to entice the young bearded diggers in their high boots.

One evening in September 1853 Charlie Dyte, not quite five feet in height, moved through the crowds of diggers. From one booth to another he squeezed his way. He approached one shop where the owner was busy calling out, "Picks and shovels! Picks and shovels!" Charlie Dyte interrupted him with a whispered "Tomorrow night—six o'clock—at the Clarendon Hotel." Vendor Cohen nodded his head and continued with his "Picks and shovels! Picks and shovels!"

Little Charlie Dyte pressed through the throng. Outside another shop stood its owner urging "Shirts! Shirts! Dirt cheap—dirt cheap." To him, too, Dyte murmured "Tomorrow night—six o'clock—at the Clarendon Hotel." Then on to the bootmaker, to the watchmaker, the cigarmaker, to the lemonade seller, to the auctioneer and to others, Charlie Dyte pursued his course. To each he murmured the mystic formula "Tomorrow night—six o'clock—at the Clarendon Hotel."

The next evening at six o'clock at the Clarendon Hotel on Lydiard Street there assembled twenty men. Wrapped in prayer shawls over red shirts and high boots they had congregated for the "Kol Nidre" prayer ushering in the Day of Atonement.

For among the twenty thousand who were seeking their fortunes in Ballarat's gold fields were also Jews. Most of these were not actually diggers. They came, in the main, to provide for the needs of the miners. They were the storekeepers, the publicans, the hotel keepers—for Ballarat had forty-eight hotels to house the miners. The storekeepers would buy gold dust "on the side" from the miners and export it to England. The Wittkowsky brothers raffled gold nuggets, taking a share of the profits as the organizers of the raffles.

That Kol Nidre night in 1853 was the real start of the Ballarat Hebrew Congregation, and Henry Harris, owner of the Clarendon Hotel, became its first president.

As usual in a new developing town, the young men far outnumbered the women. So they wrote home to Poland or Galicia or England, or wherever they had come from, for their sweethearts to join them in the new land of golden opportunity.

They advised their sisters, too, to come out, for, they said, "There are plenty of rich young hosans waiting here for wives."

In 1851 there had been not a single Jew in Ballarat. By 1853 a minyan had been organized, and the following year kosher meat was being provided. In yet another year, a substantial wooden building was consecrated as Ballarat's first synagogue. The Town Council needed that particular site for Municipal Chambers, so the government made a grant of land on Barkley and Princes streets, adding £250 in cash for the synagogue to be built at the new location.

Dedication of this permanent structure of Congregation Shearit Yisrael was reported in the *Ballarat Times* of March 18, 1861:

> *It is now our pleasing duty to record the successful completion of an edifice in which our Hebrew bretheren can assemble and worship according to the faith of their forefathers. This result has been achieved chiefly by strenuous exertions of a few individuals who have at length succeeded in overcoming all the obstacles that lay in the path of their labour of love and religion . . . The building is sufficiently tasteful without being ostentatious, and the interior is remarkable for the simplicity, perfectly in keeping with the objects for which it is erected . . . The Evening Service and the chanting of the 150th Psalm terminated the ceremony which throughout was one of great impressiveness.*

But life was hazardous in the boom town. When a gold lead ran out, or there were rumors of richer fields elsewhere, the gold diggers would move on. The Jewish traders had to follow the diggers, using bullock teams to carry their goods on mere tracks which then served as roads. Occasionally a man would find himself stranded. Then the Jews of Ballarat "passed round the hat" among themselves to render necessary assistance. As early as 1857 the Ballarat Hebrew Philanthropic Society was organized in the age-old tradition of "each Jew being responsible one for the other."

This sense of responsibility for one another was displayed in

Monument marking centenary of discovery of gold in Ballarat, Australia.

the story of the man known as "Frenchie." Frenchie had no deep ties with the Jewish community, and spent his free time lounging around with companions. But when one of these called him a "Dirty Jew," Frenchie sent the man to the gutter with a few blows. The man died. Frenchie's trial was held on the Day of Atonement. During the afternoon service of the Holyday, two Jews left the synagogue, donned their top hats and went to court. Upon Frenchie's release, they led him to the shul, brought him up to the Reading Desk and there helped him recite the prayer repeated upon escape from danger. And—so goes the story— Frenchie became a good Jew.

Despite all this, the Jews of Ballarat were a contentious, quarrelsome lot. Congregational meetings were long and stormy. There were social differences between the Jews from England and those from Eastern Europe. Each wave of immigration from Russia had brought refugees without capital. Many started life in Ballarat hawking fruit on hand carts around town. The Annals of the Ballarat Hebrew Congregation relate that at one annual meeting, a man remarked, "I am an Englishman, while you're a mob of refugees" and that he "smiled condescendingly at the broken English and the gesturing hands of the others."

Different strains of immigrants had brought diverse forms of religious expression. There was the "froom crowd," as the ultra-Orthodox group was known, and the "linke," or Liberal left group. At first it was the "froom" faction that was in power and demanded that "No one should be elected to the Board of Management of the synagogue who did not keep his shop closed on the Sabbath and festivals and who did not keep a kosher home." Then came a time when the "linke" were predominant. When a later wave of immigration brought more Orthodox East Europeans, there was a schism and for a few years two rival synagogues existed in the small community.

To lead such a community was not an easy matter. The first minister was bachelor David Isaacs who came from England. As one congregant said, "Because Mr. Isaacs is an Englishman, some of the foreign Jews think he can do nothing right." His piety and his learning didn't measure up to the demands of the East Europeans. After a quarrel he resigned, suing the congregation for a sum which he said was owing to him. The matter was finally settled out of court.

David Isaacs was succeeded by the Reverend Samuel Herman, who came at the age of seventy from another Australian community. Soon he too left—for the people found him old and infirm, whereas Reverend Herman found Ballarat "too turbulent." After a short period Reverend Isaac Stone became minister. He was censured for having circumcised a child whose mother was non-Jewish, and within a year he resigned and went his way.

Stability and growth came only during the period when the Reverend Israel M. Goldreich served as rabbi. After a few years, he, too, had resigned. But this time things were different. The community gave him a testimonial and a purse of sovereigns. When he left the railroad station was crowded with well-wishers. Within a year, Reverend Goldreich returned to Ballarat, and this time he remained for thirty years until his death in 1905.

During the tenure of Reverend Goldreich Ballarat was made into the most orthodox center of Australian Jewry. The Hebrew

School, in its daily and Sunday classes, drew an attendance of fifty-eight boys and girls. Classes were held three times weekly for "young ladies desiring to learn Hebrew." Arrangements were made to supply kosher meat at low prices. Before long Ballarat felt strong enough to set up its own matzoh bakery instead of turning to Melbourne for the unleavened bread.

One year, the Ballarat *Star* reported in its columns, "Jewish juveniles to the number of fifty held a ball in the school room gaily decorated with flags. . . . The ball was held at the conclusion of Jewish religious festivities."

Another time the men spent the entire night of Hoshanah Rabbah poring over the Holy writings. At dawn the bell-toppered gentlemen formed a procession. Newman Frederick Spielvogel, scholar and writer, with prayer shawl over his shoulders, led the cavalcade carrying a new Sefer Torah. Behind him marched the men, two by two, down Sturt Street and on through Bridge Street and Victoria Street till they reached the synagogue. There they were met by a committee and the Reverend Goldreich, to whom they turned over the Scroll of the Law.

A few years later George Abrahams presented the synagogue with a stained-glass window for use over the Ark. Originally the window had graced an old Irish mansion dating from the time of Queen Elizabeth I. Its various colors, circles and sections are said to symbolize the three patriarchs, the twelve tribes, the bondage in Egypt and the tabernacle in the wilderness.

Alive and alert, the community continued in its tradition of responsibility for all Jews. In the 1870s the *Australian Israelite* reported, "Our brethren in Ballarat are to be congratulated on taking the initiative in this good work"—referring to the raising of funds for the relief of Jews in Persia. On another occasion the columns of the same weekly announced, "While Melbourne talks—Ballarat acts," in noting that a sum of money had been voted from the congregational funds to help alleviate the effects of famine from which the Jerusalem Jewish community was then suffering.

Unparalleled in synagogue history was what occurred in the 1890s. It was at that time that the Britannia Gold Mining Company found that a rich lode of quartz it was working ran below the synagogue. Britannia paid the congregation £400 for the right to continue the work with the understanding that the operations would not come within two hundred feet of the surface. What other synagogue could claim to be sitting on top of a lode of quartz?

But the glory of Ballarat was its human material—its sons and daughters. There was little Charlie Dyte who had made the rounds of the rough shops in 1853 with his whispered formula, "Tomorrow night—six o'clock—at the Clarendon Hotel." He's been called the father and founder of the Ballarat Hebrew Congregation. At one time or another he filled every honorary office of the group.

Charles Dyte was a descendant of the David Dyte who had saved the life of King George III at the Drury Lane Theatre in England. As the king was bowing from the royal box, a man named Hatfield fired a horse pistol point-blank at the king, only missing his aim when David Dyte struck up the arm of the would-be assassin.

Charles Dyte is remembered not only for his role within the Jewish community, but also for the part he played in the civic life of Ballarat as a whole. He was one of the five Jews who served as Mayor of the city, was a member of Parliament and laid the foundation stone of the Town Hall. Beloved and admired by all, he received a testimonial signed by the entire legal profession upon his appointment as Justice of the Peace. When he died in 1895, at the age of seventy-six, his remains were followed by Ballarat's Fire Brigade, of which he had been the founder and captain.

Rabbi Jacob Saphir, emissary from Jerusalem on a fund raising mission in the mid-nineteenth century, tells of finding Simon Hamburger sitting at his shop door reciting Psalms while waiting for customers.

Newman Frederick Spielvogel, a young rebel, ran away from home in Russia at the early age of ten, wandering through Europe, Asia and Africa. Lured by stories of the gold findings, he came to Ballarat in 1853, mining and keeping store. "Every night from seven to nine," his son Nathan recorded, "we sat with Father in the dining room and learned to translate the Bible from Hebrew into English."

At fourteen, Nathan Spielvogel became a teacher first in the school on Dana Street and later in the bush-country towns where, for a whole year, he tasted no meat "because it was tref." Following in the footsteps of his father, he had his own "wanderjahr (year of travel)," drawing out his savings to go on a world trip. Eventually he settled down in his home town of Ballarat, taught school and wrote of his experiences and of the history of the Jews there. In an address during World War II he welcomed the 108 Jewish American Marines who were stationed in Ballarat: "All our homes are open to you at any time. Our hearts are yours. Come and be made as much at home as you would be in your own father's house."

Another link between the gold rush days and the present was Dr. Fanny Reading. Her father escaped from Russia and ultimately wound up in Ballarat. With horse and wagon he peddled supplies in the smaller country places round about. Three years later the resourceful mother, with her young daughter Fanny, left the family home in Minsk and followed to Australia. As was common in those days, the Melbourne rabbi was asked to aid in reuniting the family. Word was sent to the father at Ballarat, "There's a woman and child waiting for you."

Born after her father's departure from Minsk, Dr. Reading told me she had worried as to what her reception would be when she met the handsome stranger. But she certainly had no need for fears. A warm, affectionate home was set up in which education for the children (three sons were born in Ballarat) was of primary importance. Fanny won a scholarship to the University of Melbourne, studied music, taught school for a year, then returned to the university to study medicine and got her degree in 1922. She joined one brother in medical practice in Sydney, but actually devoted most of her time to social welfare.

Recalling her own arrival as a child in a strange country with a strange language, she was determined to help new immigrants adjust to life in this country. To this end she was the moving force in organizing the National Council of Jewish Women of Australia in 1923.

Many honors came to this dedicated woman. She was awarded the King George V Jubilee Medal and the King George VI Coronation Medal in recognition of her social welfare work for all creeds and all causes. A settlement in Israel, Neve Zipporah, has been named in her honor by the National Council of Jewish Women of Australia. Most recently the decoration of M.B.E. (Member of the Order of the British Empire) was conferred on Dr. Reading by Queen Elizabeth.

Small wonder then that Rabbi Israel Brodie, who served in Melbourne and was close to Ballarat before becoming Chief Rabbi of the British Commonwealth said, "Wherever you see a spark of Judaism, the source was from Ballarat."

Then a change in fortune occurred. Returns from goldmining declined, economic opportunity generally deteriorated. People began moving to new places, seeking more favorable conditions. Wherever the diggers went, the Jews, whose hotels or trading catered to the miners, had to follow—from gold field to gold field. In 1870 there had been 400 Jews in Ballarat. Nathan Spielvogel recalled that in the year he became Bar Mitzvah (1887) there were twenty-seven other youths marking that event in their lives.

But from that time on, the number of Jews in Ballarat gradually decreased. At the turn of the century 266 Jews resided there. By 1921 only 91 Jews remained. Many had moved to the big center, to Melbourne. And the 1961 census counted only 51 Jews there—including men, women and children.

I went by train from Melbourne to visit what remained of the Jewish community in Ballarat. It was a two-car train—one car first class, the other for second-class passengers. We passed stations with such intriguing names as Moorabool, Cheringhap, Lal Lal, Yendon, Warrenheip. One place had a signpost but not even a station platform to assist the descending passenger. Within Ballarat itself the begonias were in bloom. Lovely gardens surrounded the homes which retained much of the old iron lace or grille work.

I found there, in 1966, only seven Jewish families. Adults, four university students and three younger children made up a total of twenty-two souls.

Mainstay of this small band is Marcus Stone, who lives across the road from the synagogue, in what once had been the Prince Albert Hotel, where gold diggers had been wont to hold their meetings. Of Marcus Stone it can be said that he is of Ballarat's

"Mayflower" stock, for his paternal grandparents came from Plymouth, England. His maternal grandparents came from Posen in Poland in the 1850s when Ballarat was a boom town. I photographed "Stone's," the house where both Marcus Stone and his mother had been born and where the family business was conducted. A large sign announced that "Stone's" was "Retiring from Business after 105 Years—Selling Out Sale."

Mr. Stone may have been selling out the business, but his interest in the community had not flagged. Carrying on the family tradition (for his grandfather and father had both acted as president of the congregation), Marcus Stone now headed the small flock. For almost twenty years, ever since Ballarat was left without a full-time minister, Marcus Stone has been training boys for their Bar Mitzvah ritual and has led religious services.

In 1961, in spite of the fact that the community then numbered only fifty-one, a centenary service of thanksgiving was held. At the consecration of the distinctive Shearit Yisrael Synagogue in 1861, it had been Charles Dyte who was president. In 1961 Marcus Stone said at the ceremony:

All Ballarat now needs is additional numbers to keep burning brightly the flame kindled by the early pioneers. We are determined to keep the spirit of our ancient faith alive in this city.

Polish-born Paul Simon and his wife, sister of Marcus Stone, live in a home graced by chandeliers of Venetian glass, inlaid French tables, Dresden china and carved Chinese chairs. Said Mr. Simon, Honorary Secretary of the group, "Ballarat needs professionals. It needs doctors, dentists, accountants. There are opportunities here for at least fifteen more Jewish families."

There is much in Ballarat of today that summons up remembrance of its gold rush days. Erected on the 100th anniversary of the gold strike is a replica of the "Welcome Nugget" weighing 2,217 ounces, largest single nugget of surface gold ever found.

The Eureka Monument is a unique reminder of a remarkable event that occurred in those days. By 1854 the alluvial gold finds were petering out and deep shafts had to be sunk into the leads. This meant months of hard work plus the cost for the land claim and license fees. From thirty shillings a month, license fees were raised to £3 monthly. The police, many of them formerly guards at the convict settlements, had regular "digger hunts," rounding up the men from their claims and ordering them to show their licenses. If they did not have the license on their person, they were chained until bailed out. At the time the diggers had no political rights, the franchise being held only by land owners.

Lieutenant Governor Sir Charles Hotham ordered license inspection twice weekly. As an incentive, it is said, the police received half the fines imposed on unlicensed diggers, or those who did not have their licenses with them at inspection time.

A miner named Scobie was murdered at Bentley's Hotel. His killer, the ex-convict hotel owner, was discharged by a corrupt magistrate. Aroused, the men burned down the hotel. More soldiers arrived. Then the miners made a bonfire of a thousand licenses saying, "Let the Joes [the soldiers] arrest us all."

The government sent police on another hunt for licenses. The miners defied the police, who fired over the heads of the men and took some prisoners. Ten thousand diggers assembled and took an oath to fight in defense of their rights and liberties. Then Lieutenant Governor Sir Charles Hotham sent a relief party to crush the rebellion of "foreign ruffians, scum of Europe." The diggings were declared under martial law.

On December 1 the men erected a crude stockade on Eureka hill, leaving an overnight guard of a hundred volunteers. During the night, soldiers and police, outnumbering the miners four to one, stormed the stockade and crushed the small band.

Two weeks later, during an opera performance, Digger Black, a leader of the men, climbed on the stage, trying to arouse the miners again. A hand from behind the curtain, the hand of Charles Dyte, pulled the miner back and smuggled him out the stage door showing him the sign on a tree trunk—"Reward of £400 for Black." Black vanished and Dyte, who had allied himself with the miners' cause, returned to the theatre.

The aroused people demanded that digger hunts be abolished. At the trial of the imprisoned diggers, their defense counsel (who acted without fee) asked why the Riot Act had not been read to the men. Quoting from English law, he said that until the Riot Act had been read, no soldier had any right to fire at the miners; therefore the miners were just defending themselves. The men were freed. The government resigned. No longer did the land-owners rule Victoria. The tremendous effect of the Eureka Affair on the growth of democracy in Australia is acknowledged to this day.

The Eureka Monument, a memorial to the men on both sides, is inscribed:

TO THE HONORED MEMORY OF THE HEROIC PIONEERS
WHO FOUGHT AND FELL ON THIS SACRED SPOT
IN THE CAUSE OF LIBERTY
AND THE SOLDIERS WHO FELL AT DUTY'S CALL

Among the list of fourteen defenders who fell here is the name of the Jewish lemonade seller, Edward Thonen. Prussian-born, it was said of him by a fellow participant in the "Affair": "His eyes spoke determination and independence of character. Thonen possessed the head belonging to that cast of men whose word is their bond."

Such was Ballarat—gold rush town, cradle of liberty and home of a once thriving, pulsating Jewish community.

◄§ HOLDING FAST IN GEELONG §►

If ever Jews have made a good real estate deal, it must have been the one in Geelong, for it was there that for a "yearly quit rent of one peppercorn for ever if demanded," the Jews received a crown grant of half an acre—at the corner of Yarrow and McKil-lop streets—to be used for erection of a synagogue. Another condition in this unusual real estate deal "reserved unto us [the Jews] our heirs and successors, all mines of gold, silver and of coal" that might be found on the tract.

Geelong, forty-five miles southwest of Melbourne, is today a manufacturing center with plants of the Ford Motor Co., International Harvester, Portland Cement, Alcoa Aluminum, Shell Oil, woolen mills, tanneries and other enterprises. Here also is the famous Australian Grammar School. Prince Charles of England was sent for part of his education to its next-to-nature house, Timbertop. And in Geelong today "not to be a football fan, indicates a somewhat perverse eccentricity," to quote a local public-relations pamphlet.

But back in 1851—in the year that the "peppercorn" deal was made—in the gold rush days, Geelong was known as The Pivot, for the majority of miners went through this port town in order to reach the gold fields of Victoria.

Jews, too, came through Geelong or stayed there. Some believe Abraham Levy, an auctioneer, was the first Jew to live in Geelong; others hold it was Benjamin Goldsmid Levien, a butcher from Melbourne, who in 1840 transferred to Geelong to open a tree nursery. Be that as it may, nine Jews were there by 1846. Some were in the drapery business, others were watchmakers or jewelers. One addition to the small Jewish colony (about whose arrival there is no question) was Morris Jacobs, who came from England in the year that the peppercorn deal was made. He also went into the drapery business.

Three years later the *Geelong Advertiser* of June 2, 1854, reported:

> *Last evening the ceremony of consecrating the Jewish synagogue in Yarra Street took place in the presence of a large assembly of people of that persuasion. The building being temporary until a stone building can be erected, a subscription was opened for that purpose and upwards of £200 was subscribed previous to the close of the ceremony.*

The congregation adopted the name Shearit Yisrael, the same as the one in Melbourne. Among the Rules and Regulations of the Geelong Shearit Yisrael were the following:

1. All persons who were members of the synagogue on the 5th February, 1854, (except such as are married to women not of Jewish faith or are living publicly with women in a state of concubinage), shall be considered privileged members.

2. Form of prayers shall be the same as read by the German Jews of England under the jurisdiction of the Chief Rabbi.

3. Committee men shall be fined one shilling sixpence when absent from the synagogue on Sabbaths and Holydays.

4. All bridegrooms and their unterfuehrers shall attend Divine Service in the synagogue on the Sabbath before and after their marriage, or pay a fine of ten shillings sixpence for each absence.

5. When paupers or other poor Jews shall depart this life their funeral expenses may be defrayed out of the funds of the congregation.

Twenty years later a visitor to Geelong wrote a Letter to the Editor in the February 6, 1874, edition of the *Australian Israelite:*

There are about a dozen Jewish families residing at the Pivot. The Geelongese have a neat little synagogue, where service is held on Holydays and festivals and also on Sabbath mornings but very irregularly. The synagogue is also opened every morning and evening when the Rev. Mr. Herman holds service by himself. . . . Night after night one may find him [Mr. Herman] sitting to a late hour, aye, even to an early hour in the morning, bending over the Talmud and Rabbinical writings. The old gentleman is engaged in writing a commentary on the Talmud. . . . On the Sabbath I saw several children enter the building. I was agreeably surprised to learn that they belonged to the Sabbath school. I found two ladies engaged in imparting religious knowledge and scriptural history to fifteen children. These two ladies, Mrs. Fink and Miss Levien, have now for the last eight years rendered their voluntary services to the Geelong Sabbath school. At a time when in Melbourne many Jewish children were unable to procure a little instruction in our faith, in Geelong a Sabbath school flourished.

But somehow the Geelong Jewish community never grew. When in 1886 the Reverend Mr. Brown was being considered for the post of minister, shohet and teacher at £2 a week, he was not engaged "due to insufficient funds." For most of the time since then, Geelong had no resident minister. Services were held only on the High Holydays. Intermittently the congregation had a teacher come from Ballarat or Melbourne.

And yet Israel Cohen reported that his appeal for funds for the Zionist cause in the 1920s brought contributions of £500 in this small community.

Notwithstanding their small number, the Jews of Geelong have played a significant role in the civic life of their home town. The Honorable Jonas F. Levien, son of pioneer Benjamin Goldsmid Levien, was a J.P. (Justice of the Peace) and a member of the Legislative Assembly of Victoria.

Julius Solomon, J.P. was councilman, alderman and when Acting Mayor welcomed the Duke and Duchess of Gloucester to Geelong in 1927. In true Geelongese spirit Julius Solomon was also an official of the cricket, football and racing clubs. At his funeral the Geelong City band preceded the hearse, which was followed by two hundred cars.

Sol Jacobs, son of Morris Jacobs, was Mayor on several occasions; fifth-generation Leonard Jacobs is a city councillor. London-born Benjamin Rosenberg became Mayor of the Borough of Geelong West.

His daughter, Frances Rosenberg, carries on the tradition. Deputy President of Geelong Region Red Cross, she is also the Honorary Secretary of the Geelong Hebrew Congregation and its representative on the Victoria Jewish Board of Deputies. In reality she is Geelong's "defender of the faith" and keeper of the keys of the synagogue, which she herself sweeps and cleans during the year, to maintain it in readiness for the annual services on the High Holydays.

Blue-eyed and with hair now turned iron grey, Frances Rosenberg starts making her rounds of the Jewish community weeks before Rosh Hashanah to remind everyone that his presence is needed for the minyan. The synagogue, still on the original site, has eighty seats, a reading desk of cedarwood and candelabra of

Sheffield silver. Tablets honor "King and Country." Preserved is the silver and gold "yad" (hand-shaped pointer for marking the place when reading from the Scroll of the Law) with a ruby in its index finger, presented to the congregation during the consecration year of the synagogue.

Although Geelong's population has doubled between the last decade of the nineteenth century and the 1960s (now numbering 105,000), its Jewish population has dwindled. From a count of 128 Jews in the 1861 census, the number declined to 84 in 1921. Although a few families from Germany and Poland were added in the Hitler period, by 1954 the number was further reduced to 61. At the time of my visit in the mid-1960s there were only 45 Jews in Geelong.

Of the "old" families there are still the Jacobs, the Pizers, the Crawcours and the Freedmans. In each of these families, some have "married out." Whereas formerly intermarriages meant a quiet civil ceremony, today it may mean a church wedding and the full gamut of social events. Of the descendants of Benjamin Goldsmid Levien none have remained Jewish.

Not since 1934 has there been a wedding celebration in the synagogue, and the last Bar Mitzvah observed there was in 1940. If a family does have an interest in the Jewish education of its children there is the correspondence course provided by the United Jewish Education Board of Melbourne. Teenagers find things difficult, for local youth groups are all church-affiliated. Generally speaking, the majority feel themselves Australians rather than Jews.

To my question, "What does Jewishness mean to you?" the answer of Geelong Jewry was, "Jewishness means attending synagogue services on Rosh Hashanah and Yom Kippur."

⊰ SHEPPARTON FARMERS ⊱

"Give your fruit plenty of water; pears like to live in moisture," advised 76-year-old Jack Rose, speaking to a dozen young people at the Hachshara—the Training Farm—at Toolomba, just outside of Shepparton, which is 113 miles north of Melbourne. More than a half century in age separated Mr. Rose from these eighteen- to twenty-year-olds to whom he was paying a neighborly visit.

Born in Poland, Jack Rose had studied at the yeshivot of Bialystok and Lomza to prepare himself for the rabbinate. Then he turned to business, but anti-Semitism made him leave Poland for Israel. Not meeting with financial success there, he proceeded to Australia.

Finding that strict orthodox observance of the Sabbath was difficult in Melbourne in that era, Jack Rose and nine other families decided to start life somewhere else where they could live freely and fully according to their orthodox religious precepts.

These ten Jewish families, seventy souls in all, settled in Shepparton, one of the districts that the Australian government was then opening up for agricultural settlement. Living in tents, they started dairy farming in 1912. Two years later, they lost all their cattle as a result of a drought. In time the government advanced each man £200 for the purchase of livestock. "In the meanwhile," Mr. Rose continued, "we had taken jobs as hired laborers in the fruit orchards to earn some shillings." Finding that more to their liking, the erstwhile dairy farmers became orchardists, selling their pears, apples and apricots to a canning company.

More families joined them as a greater number of Jews came to Australia following the 1917 Russian Revolution. During the Depression years of the late 1920s, the Victorian Jewish Immigrants Committee encouraged people to leave the hard-hit big city centers and try farming at Shepparton. A hostel was built for the newcomers and one family assigned to assist in their integration. With religious services, a shohet, a teacher and a functioning yeshiva, things looked bright for a viable, permanent community of Jewish fruit orchardists here.

"What happened to the dream?" I asked this lone remaining member of the original 1912 farm community. "Our children went on to higher schools of learning in Melbourne. They entered the professions, became doctors, lawyers, engineers, teachers. But they never returned to life as orchardists," responded Mr. Rose pensively.

So grey-haired Jack Rose adopted these young people and gave them of the wealth of his experience. Acquired in 1950, the eighty-acre farm was the property of the Jewish Agency and on it the young people were being prepared for aliyah to Israel.

The young people were a mixed group—half of them born in Australia, the rest coming from England, Russia, Holland or New Zealand. About 50 percent of them had come to Shepparton as a result of their affiliation with the Habonim youth movement, a few from other Zionist youth movements such as the Hashomer Hatzair or Betar. A few had had no previous Zionist connection or any specific Jewish association. Welding them into a unified social group, prepared to "go up" for its task in pioneering in Israel seemed to be the big problem here.

Of the half dozen Jewish families remaining in Shepparton in 1965, not all worked the land. A walk along Main Street brought me to Bloom's Fruit Store, operated by son-in-law Sam Leon, who brings in his "fancy fruit" from Melbourne.

A group apart, the Jews do not participate in the life of Shepparton, a community of 16,000 in what is still largely a fruit-growing and canning area, a place that goes in for all the sports favored in this part of the world: bowling, croquet, squash, water skiing, swimming, fishing, horse racing and trotting.

The few Jews may be in Shepparton physically, but their spiritual home is Melbourne. Some have homes there, to which they go for Sabbaths, for weekends or for holiday celebrations. And their children are sent to stay in the big city to get a Jewish education and to be in a Jewish environment. So they took the youths at the Toolomba farm to their hearts.

◄§ THE MONTEFIORES OF ADELAIDE §►

A synagogue whose income is greater than its expenditures? I can see you shrugging your shoulders in disbelief at such a statement. But this seeming anomaly does hold true—in Adelaide, South Australia, the city named for pious Queen Adelaide, wife of King William IV.

When in September 1848 the early Jewish pioneers met at the

Temple Tavern for the purpose "of forming members of the Jewish faith into a body," they decided as a matter of principle to start a subscription list for building a synagogue on a voluntary basis, and asked for no grants or assistance from the government (which was the accepted order of the day in Australia at that time).

A few months later they purchased land on Rundle Street for the sum of £280. And somewhat later, additional land on the same street was acquired on which stores were built. It is the rental monies from these shops, in what has become an important commercial area of the city, that bring the income of Beit Yisrael Synagogue above its expenditures. The synagogue entrance now is just off Rundle Street on a quiet roadway bearing the appropriate name "Synagogue Lane."

Adelaide and South Australia differ from other immigrant settlements in Australia in other ways. Never were any convicts transported here from England. Nor were the Jews who pioneered in Adelaide impecunious immigrants. The famous Montefiore family of England had very close ties with this city. Legendary Sir Moses Montefiore noted in his diary for May 7, 1835:

> *I called at 10 Downing Street on the Chancellor of the Exchequer. I thanked him for having at my request appointed Jacob Montefiore one of Her Majesty's Commissioners for the Colonization of South Australia.*

Jacob Montefiore, cousin of Sir Moses, and one of eleven commissioners appointed to the administration of the colony, never lived in Adelaide; but he visited there and was given a great civic welcome and dinner at the Shakespeare Tavern. His younger brother, Joseph Barrow Montefiore, did make his home in Adelaide's St. John's Street during the 1840s and 1850s. Prominent in the business community, he was a member of the Stock Exchange, the Chamber of Commerce and a trustee of the State Savings Bank of South Australia.

Another Montefiore, Eliezer Montefiore Levi, was a director of the Adelaide Mining Company back in pioneer days; Solomon

Mocatta, related to the family by marriage, was a shipbroker there. Much later, in 1876, another Montefiore—Moses H.—came and lived in Adelaide for the rest of his life.

Also related to the Montefiore family was Philip Levi, who was both a commercial trader within the city and raised sheep on a colossal scale. A man of energy and daring, he at one time owned 172,000 sheep and cattle. He, too, as other members of the Montefiore clan in Adelaide, was a director of the Adelaide Mining Company.

In addition to the Montefiore family and its branches, there was Emanuel Solomon, who came from Sydney on the ship *Lady Wellington* in the year following the founding of the colony. A man of many interests, Emanuel Solomon was a shipowner, a merchant, an auctioneer, a theatre promoter and had an interest in the Burra Burra Mine. Solomontown, north of Adelaide, is named for him and Dorsetta Terrace within the city takes its name from one of his brigs the *Dorset*. It was in his Temple Tavern that the organization meeting for the Adelaide Hebrew Congregation was held in 1848.

To encourage cultural life in the new city, Emanuel Solomon had the Old Victoria Theatre built, bringing over a dramatic company from Sydney, headed by Edinburgh-born John Lazar. It was actor John Lazar who led the Kol Nidre Service in a hired room in pre-synagogue days of 1848.

Adelaide attracted many big business firms headed by Jews. The Charles Jacobs firm became the largest Australian importers of sugar, tea and coffee; and the Alexander Kaufman Company sent its salesmen hundreds of miles into the back country to deliver its goods.

Two years preceding the foundation meeting at Temple Tavern, at a time when there were only forty-eight Jews in Adelaide, the Jews had petitioned the Lieutenant Governor and the Legislative Council:

That in any grant by your Honourable Council of monies for religious or educational purposes out of the public revenues, to which they so largely contribute, a fair proportion should be allotted to your

*petitioners for the purpose of building places of
worship and aiding the religious and moral training of the members of the Jewish faith within the
province.*

At the time government aid was being provided for Christian
religious and educational purposes. In the debate on a motion to
grant this petition, Captain Bagot (member of the Legislative
Council) said:

*The Jews, though few, are wealthy and probably
contribute thirty times as much to the revenue as
the average amount according to their number. The
Jews have as much right to their share as the
Christians have.*

But the Adelaide Jews did not pursue the matter any further,
not even accepting a treasury grant of £5 the following year, for
in reality they did not approve of state aid for religious purposes.
Instead, they undertook the plan calling for a "Subscription list
of one shilling per week to be paid by all persons professing the
Jewish religion in South Australia" for the purpose of erecting a
permanent place of worship.

Some light on the relations between Jews and Christians in
Adelaide is shed by the suggestion made by the *South Australian
Register* in its July 18, 1849, issue:

*As it is not intended to apply for any portion of a
government grant to complete the building [syna-
gogue] and as donations from private sources will
be thankfully accepted, we heartily recommend
those who can do so conscientiously to give their
mites toward the good work, the more especially as
many Hebrews had pecuniarily helped to rear
some of our Christian places of worship.*

When in September 1850 the Rundle Street synagogue was dedicated, the same publication reported the event:

*On either side wall are two conjoined tablets (one
in Hebrew and the other in English characters).
The tablets on the right contain a prayer for the
Queen—Prince Albert—Prince of Wales and the*

Royal Family. Those on the left contain the memorable words addressed to Moses when the Deity caused His glory to pass before him. Bronze chandeliers and other furniture are handsome, appropriate and strongly demonstrative of the liberal spirit which characterises the Jewish community in this province. . . . The consecration service commenced by certain members of the congregation arraying themselves in scarves of white silk with azure or purple borders, which simple preliminary being adjusted, four individuals (wardens) advanced from within to the entrance door, bearing a canopy supported on staves of turned and polished cedar. The voice of the Reader was heard without saying "Open unto us the gates of righteousness, we will enter them and praise the Lord." The entrance doors being opened he made his appearance bearing the sacred Scrolls of the Law, enveloped in a case elaborately adorned and took his position under the canopy.

The concern for charity had gone hand in hand with the consideration for the building of a synagogue. At the same meeting when they had decided to pay their own way, "Mr. Burnett Nathan brought forward a box containing the sum of £5/7/3 collected for the purpose of rendering assistance to all poor and unfortunate Jews in our colony." In 1852 the Adelaide Hebrew Philanthropic Society was formally established. Needs of Jews outside Adelaide were also remembered, the community responding to appeals for relief that came from Persia, from Damascus, from India and from Russia.

The community grew in numbers, so that within the short space of twenty years, a larger structure adjoining the original one was already being erected to serve the 435 Jews living in Adelaide in 1870. By that time the community's first ordained minister, the Reverend A. T. Boas had arrived from England on the sailing ship *Tamesa*. Amsterdam-born, suave and an authority on Shakespeare, Reverend Boas and Adelaide Jewry took to each other—he ministered there for almost half a century. The Consecration

Thrift shop, Australian style, in Adelaide, operated jointly by the Australian Council of Jewish Women and the Wizo.

Service of the newer, larger edifice was again chronicled by the *South Australian Register* of March 26, 1871:

> *The Minister's voice was heard outside the door exclaiming in Hebrew, "Open unto us the gates of righteousness, we will enter them and praise the Lord." The door being opened, the Minister and five past and present honorary officers of the congregation entered, each bearing a Scroll of the Law covered with handsome crimson mantles. The choir which consisted of twenty male and female voices chanted some verses commencing "How goodly are thy tents, O Jacob, thy tabernacles, O Israel."*

Within the same year Reverend Boas was already conducting a Sabbath school "assisted by twelve young ladies," and the *Australian Israelite* gave an account of a Bar Mitzvah in which "Festivities consisted of a grand juvenile ball given by the parents of the confirmant."

The imprint of the Jews is strong in the city. Six Jews were elected to the office of Mayor. First of these was John Lazar, he who had originally come to the city as an actor. Sir Lewis Cohen was Mayor for nine terms, with no one to oppose him in elections. Judah Moss Solomon, nephew of Emanuel Solomon, also was returned unopposed to a second term as Mayor. Mayor Solomon's son Vaiben Louis Solomon was a member of the Federal Parliament, a Government Whip, at another time the leader of the Opposition, and for a short period the Premier of the colony.

Emanuel Solomon had been a leader in all fields of cultural endeavor. In addition to bringing theatre to the city, he started the library and the art gallery, which later were directed by other Jews—Abraham Abrams and Henri Van Raalte, related to the Dutch painter Josef Israels.

The community grew and prospered, until the turn of the century when Adelaide numbered 728 Jews. But the first few decades of this century tell a different story. After the death of Reverend Boas there was a succession of ministers, and part of the time in the 1920s and the 1930s there was no rabbi at all. Added to this was the Depression of the late 1920s. The community shrank in numbers and by 1933 there were only twenty-five children enrolled in the religious school (down from 100). It was not only that the number of the community was down to 477, and continued to decline, but there developed an apathy, a lack of interest, as was constantly being commented on in the congregational records that I read.

Then came the Hitler period, and the largely "pukka" English stock of Adelaide welcomed refugees and DP's from Germany, Austria, Czechoslovakia and Poland. Particularly large was the group that began coming from Egypt. The story goes that a Mr. Liberman, leaving Egypt, could not get a visa to enter the United States due to quota restrictions there and decided on a temporary stay in Australia. Aboard ship he met an Adelaide family that was extremely warm and cordial, so Mr. Liberman came on to this city. The chain was strengthened so that by 1961 almost 22 percent of all Adelaide Jewry had been born in Egypt. Some Hungarian Jews and most recently a small number of South

Africans have found their way there. The declining tide has been stopped, for the 1961 census showed that 900 Jews lived in Adelaide.

Just a few years ago a mikveh was installed, with consideration for its need in cases of conversion. The question of conversion had come to the fore when recent immigrants arrived with wives who were not born Jewish, and there was need to accept them formally into the Jewish faith. Both Reverend Rafalowicz, Chief Minister of the Adelaide Hebrew Congregation and the second Minister, Polish-born Reverend Herman (who also acts as the shohet), were understanding and helpful in these cases.

I found Adelaide, early in 1966, a vigorous community seething with activities—youth groups, welfare and philanthropic committees, Zionist groups, Wizo, National Council of Jewish Women, B'nai B'rith, Hebrew classes, Jewish Board of Deputies—enough it would seem to enlist the energies of a group many times the size of this community.

Educational activities were vigorous under the leadership of Chief Minister Reverend Rafalowicz, a graduate of Jews' College in London. One hundred thirty children attended religious school on Sunday and two classes met in midweek. There were adult study courses and a Sabbath afternoon discussion group meeting at the home of Reverend Rafalowicz.

Notwithstanding all the buzzing Jewish activity, the question of "marrying out" and assimilation looms large in Adelaide. Forty-five percent of the Jewish men were married to non-Jewish women in South Australia in 1933. I met a woman with a very British name among a group of local Jewish leaders gathered at the home of Albert Hassan. I must have showed my surprise at finding a person with such an English name at this meeting, for she explained . . . "When I was a young girl, it was the custom for parents to send their daughters to live for a while in the larger Jewish centers of Australia, in the hope that they would thus find a Jewish marriage partner. But my parents were too poor to pay for my living away from home. What could I do? It meant either I remained a spinster (there were only a few Jewish young men at home) or that I "marry out." I married a Christian—but he has permitted our children to be brought up as Jews. . . . and I have remained a part of the Jewish community. . . ."

With the increase of Jewish population since that time, the rate of intermarriage has dropped, the 1961 census indicating that 23 percent of the Jewish men in South Australia were married to non-Jewish women. One of the main hopes of the existing Jewish youth organizations, I was told, was to encourage the youth to remain in Adelaide.

About ten years ago, a Liberal congregation was founded and has attracted a membership of seventy families, many of them professionals. The group has lay leadership with occasional visits from the Liberal rabbis of Melbourne. Said Dr. Ben Bellon, a leader of this congregation . . . "Assimilation had been rife here in Adelaide, particularly among the Jews of English background. Only twelve of our society had previously been members of the Orthodox congregation. The rest had been unattached, having no religious home anywhere. Now we have an average attendance of forty at our fortnightly Friday evening services and religious classes for sixty children led by volunteer teachers. . . ."

And amidst all the talk of assimilation I met a follower of the Lubavitsher movement, red-bearded artist Franz Kempf, who has studied in Europe with Oscar Kokoschka. Franz Kempf's work—serigraphs, etchings and lithography—clearly shows the inspiration derived from Hasidism and the Cabala.

When I said farewell to lovely Adelaide—with its wide-sweeping Sir Lewis Cohen Avenue and Montefiore Road—I really said farewell to Australia, for from there I proceeded to the Sydney airport to enplane for the nearly 4,000-mile flight to Manila.

• 5 •
OUTPOSTS IN AND
AROUND THE PACIFIC

ᴇᵍ PHILIPPINE ISLANDS ᵍᴇ

"I WAS DETERMINED TO CONVERT TO MY HUSBAND'S RELIGIOUS faith, the Jewish faith," said Filipino, Christian-born, black-haired and dark-eyed Helen Weinstein, president of the only Jewish women's group—the Auxiliary of Temple Emil and teacher in the religious school of this synagogue in tropical Manila. . . . "I came to this decision all on my own sometime after our civil marriage. I studied, was examined by Chaplain Kingsley and the two most learned and observant members of the Jewish community. After my official conversion, we were remarried in the synagogue 'according to the laws of Moses and Israel,'". . . continued petite, soft-spoken Helen, wife of American David Weinstein who had come as an engineer to Clark Air Base in the Philippines.

Helen Weinstein and I were among the luncheon guests at the home of Minna Gaberman, daughter of Hyman R. Levine (who was Life Honorary President of Manila's Jewish community). The home outdid some of Hollywood's finest specimens. The living room of adobe stone and monkeypot wood was open on one side to the garden, with no wall to separate one from the other. There were caged birds in the garden; orchids hung from the trees and poinsettias were in bloom.

Indoors was a table, seven feet in diameter, of monkeypot wood. Kuan Yins and other precious Chinese figures, and a superb Chinese screen brought their own flavor into the house. White-clad, white-gloved Filipino help provided deft service for the forty guests, including the wife of the Israeli Ambassador to the Philippines.

Life also seemed good in other Jewish homes in Manila. It was late January, but dinner could be served out-of-doors in this tropical island country only fifteen degrees north of the equator. Surrounded by spacious lawns, jade vine trees and the almost overpowering sweet-scented shrub, *dama de noche*, American energy and drive seemed truly a world away.

When not dining at a home, there were the facilities of the Polo Club or the Army and Navy Club. One did not really have to play polo or be in the military forces to belong, but membership in these clubs was *the* thing.

All this was a far cry from what had taken place in the Philippines during the Japanese occupation in World War II. Manila was heavily bombarded. The scars are still there, particularly in the old walled city of Intramuros. Within Intramuros, on the grounds of Fort Santiago with its large torture chamber, is a cross marking a mass burial site:

600 FILIPINOS—VICTIMS OF JAPANESE ATROCITIES— FEB. 1945: BODIES SUGGESTED STARVATION AND POSSIBLY SUFFOCATION . . . FOUND IN NEARBY DUNGEON HAVING INNER DOORS OF MASSIVE IRON BARS, AND OUTER DOORS OF IRON PLATE ON WOOD.

I could well understand the two Japanese tourists whom I met in the torture chamber saying, "It's embarrassing for us to be here."

From Luneta Park with its memorial to the martyred national hero José Rizal, executed there by the authorities in 1896 as a traitor to Spain, I took a jeepney—fringe-canopied, decorated jeep-turned-taxi—to reach Santo Tomas University. At the entrance to the main building of this university (older than Harvard), I read the plaque:

THROUGH THESE PORTALS PASSED UP TO 10,000 AMERI-
CANS AND OTHER NATIONALS OF THE FREE WORLD WHO
WERE INTERNED WITHIN THESE WALLS BY THE JAPANESE
MILITARY, SUFFERING GREAT PHYSICAL PRIVATION AND
NATIONAL HUMILIATION FROM JAN. 4, 1942, UNTIL LIBER-
ATED FEB. 3, 1945, BY THE AMERICAN FORCES UNDER
GENERAL DOUGLAS MACARTHUR.

Manila's Jewish cemetery bears witness to the losses sustained
by the community. On a monument of black Italian marble are
engraved seventy–nine names under the inscription:

IN MEMORY OF THE MEMBERS OF THE JEWISH COMMUNITY
OF THE PHILIPPINES WHO DIED AS VICTIMS OF WORLD
WAR CONSTITUTING PART OF THE MILLIONS WHO SACRI-
FICED THEIR LIVES FOR THE CAUSE OF FREEDOM OF ALL
MANKIND

VICTIMS OF BATTLE OF LIBERATION
[67 NAMES]
VICTIMS OF FORT SANTIAGO
[3 NAMES]
VICTIMS OF BATTLEFIELD AND IMPRISONMENT
[9 NAMES]

The Jewish presence in these islands is, historically speaking, a
recent one. It was in 1521 that Spanish explorer Ferdinand
Magellan discovered the islands for the Western world and
named them in honor of his sovereign—King Philip. For the next
few centuries word was heard only occasionally of any Jews
landing there. Among these were Spanish-born George Rodriguez
and Portuguese-native Domingo Rodriguez, with whom the Inquisition caught up in Manila. A small number of Marranos,
attracted no doubt by the fact that this was a Spanish-speaking
country, came to the Philippines. They, too, were accused by the
Inquisition and tried in Manila. A few German Jews came down
during the nineteenth century.

But not until the Philippines had been ceded to the United
States in 1898 did Jews from America and Europe begin arriving
in appreciable numbers. Refugees from the Russian pogroms also
found their way there; Iraqi Jews appeared on the scene, as did
some from Turkey, China and Egypt.

Jewish victim of incarceration by Japanese during World War II at Fort Santiago in old Manila; laid to rest in Jewish cemetery of Manila.

Hyman R. Levine, a Social Democrat in his youth, had gone from his home town Homel in Russia to America. Caught there by World War I in 1914, he later joined his brother-in-law Emil Bachrach, already established in business in Manila. At the close of World War I there were 150 Jewish families in the Philippines. The American Jews came as representatives of business concerns or as lawyers. Other Jews started as shopkeepers.

Economically they did well. But there was no organized community life. For the High Holydays services were held in a hired hall, with a Reader being brought in from Shanghai. For yahrzeit observance, somehow a minyan would be corralled. Not until 1922 was Temple Emil, named for philanthropic Emil Bachrach, erected on Taft Avenue.

During the 1930s a new chapter started for this small community. A Jewish Relief Committee of Manila, with Alexander Frieder as president, was organized to help bring over Central European Jews. A survey was made of the Philippines' need for men with professional skills, for university professors, doctors and lawyers.

The government permitted European Jews having the requisite skills to enter on a selective basis. In addition, temporary visas for two-year residence were granted to others. Some of the immigrants on these visas started life anew in the Pacific as peddlers. Manuel Quezon, first President of the Philippine Commonwealth, offered land on Mindanao Island for refugee settlement. More than a thousand Central European refugees found asylum in the Philippines.

Then came World War II. MacArthur and the American forces retreated. The Japanese swept in. Nationals of countries at war with Japan were interned. Jews with German passports were at first treated as allies and were not detained. During this period the German Jews were able to help others by providing needed medicines and food to those confined.

Those not interned had their business enterprises taken over. Homes were commandeered by the Japanese. People kept moving from place to place as the conquerors caught up with them.

For some time Temple Emil was left undisturbed. Then it too was seized and turned into an ammunition dump by the Japanese. In February of 1945, as the victorious U.S. 11th Airborne Division neared Manila, the retreating Japanese sacked and burned the city. The explosives in Temple Emil's community hall were set off. Only the walls of the synagogue were left standing—the rest was in ruins.

Gradually the community came back to life. Among the released internees was Morton Netzorg, who became president of the group and local representative for the American Joint Distribution Committee, which sent funds to supply the necessities of life. Homes had to be provided. People had to start in business all over again.

American Armed Forces Chaplains Colman Zwitman and Dudley Weinberg—and a committee of Jewish servicemen—helped sustain the local Jews. The Jewish Welfare Board dispatched supplies for a communal Seder, which included civilians as well as the military. Lectures were arranged at the USO–JWB Clubroom.

In November of the same year, on the anniversary of the 1938 Kristall Nacht destruction of synagogues in Germany, an open-air service was held amidst the ruins of Temple Emil. Those American G.I.s present pledged themselves to help rebuild this house of worship, as a memorial to their comrades who had died in the war to free the Philippines.

A joint Memorial Campaign and Hanukkah party was held. Fifteen hundred G.I.s were present and literally emptied their pockets. Relatives back home sent money. Within one month $20,000 was turned over to the local community. At a ceremony held in December, Lieutenant General William D. Styer, Commanding General of Armed Forces Western Pacific, who made the presentation on behalf of the servicemen said:

> Our forces came to the Philippines not as takers of freedom but as givers of freedom. Tonight's celebration is an expression of that true spirit of giving. American Jewish servicemen are giving a fund to be used in rebuilding the Manila synagogue as a memorial to their comrades who gave their lives in the Philippines. This synagogue, which was destroyed by the Japanese and which, it is believed, was the only synagogue under the American flag destroyed by the enemy in this war, shall be rebuilt.

And the synagogue was rebuilt—the local people raised a matching sum. Two and a half years after its destruction, Temple Emil was rededicated in August 1947. It was rebuilt to the same dimensions as the original, with the old walls being retained, on plans drawn by a local Jewish architect. Spacious and starkly simple, it seats two hundred. A small plaque honors ". . . all men and women of the Jewish faith of the Armed Forces of the United States and Allied Nations who laid down their lives in the defense and liberation of the Philippines—1941–1945—and [is] in tribute to the American Jewish personnel stationed in the Philippines who initiated the drive to assist the local community in the expenses of reconstruction." The following year Bachrach Hall Community Center was rebuilt.

In some ways the Jewish community in this island country— stretching a thousand miles from north to south between Taiwan and Borneo—is like the general population, a blend of Orient and

Occident. Of a predominantly Malay stock with a mixture of Indonesian, Chinese and Spanish, the Filipinos came under the Western influence of America. So, too, the Jewish community is a fusion of East and West in world Jewry. Half of Manila's Jews have come from Germany or Austria, Russia or Poland; 25 percent are from America; and the remaining are Sephardim from countries such as Syria, Iraq, Egypt, Morocco and Turkey.

Przemysl-born Dacha came to Manila via Hong Kong, where she had gone to visit an aunt. While on a stopover here, she met and married Hyman Meadows, who was born in Nagasaki, raised in Oregon and had spent some years in Palestine. Others came here from Shanghai and Harbin. One of three brothers from Syria is married to a German-born American woman who was at one time a student at the Teachers' Institute of the Jewish Theological Seminary, in New York.

Ezra Toeg is another good example of this fusion of Asia and Europe. Of Baghdadi parentage, he was brought to Shanghai, where the family lived near the Sephardi synagogue. Their Ashkenazi neighbor Rabbi Wallach also attended this synagogue. Young Ezra studied Talmud daily with Rabbi Wallach. To this day he speaks reverently of this Ashkenazi rabbi who had refused any payment for teaching the young Sephardi boy. And today in Manila the Ashkenazim say, "Ezra Toeg is our most learned man. He is a pillar of the community." Although the majority of the people are not strict observers of the Sabbath or of kashrut they hold in high regard the man who is their shohet and walks forty-five minutes each way from home to synagogue on the Sabbath.

The occupations pursued by the Jews of Manila, where nearly all the Philippine Jews live, differ proportionately from those which are classic in a European or American Jewish community. Here only 6 percent are professionals. Almost half of the Jews are connected with a manufacturing concern—either as owner, manager or in some other executive capacity. Embroidery is the most important industry with which these men are associated, the others generally being in the lumber, pharmaceutical or jewelry businesses. Owners or executives are three times as numerous as those who might be classed as employees. Large-scale export and import trading attracts 10 percent of the men. The general financial condition is good, and very few families are in need of relief.

Temple Emil serves all Jews, whether Sephardi or Ashkenazi. Services are held not only on the Sabbath but also in midweek. I witnessed one gala event at Temple Emil, at a Monday morning service. A large group of friends, including the Israeli Ambassador, had assembled to participate in the service when Dennis Greenfield, son of a family with German and American background, would for the first time put on his tefillin at a public service as part of his Bar Mitzvah ceremonies. It was a festive occasion with a breakfast in the community hall and photographers on hand.

Friday evening services, held in air-conditioned Bachrach Hall attached to the synagogue, had the flavor of an old-time East European shtiebel. There was a feeling of intimacy as the entire congregation chanted every verse of Kabbalat Shabbat songs. Nothing was omitted from the order of service as found in the United Synagogue of America prayer book.

Sabbath morning services were held in the synagogue proper, from whose windows swaying branches of palm trees were visible. Ezra Toeg read the portion of the week from one of the congregation's seven beautifully attired Scrolls of the Law. Some of the men called to the Reading of the Torah wore the Philippine formal tagla, an embroidered, long-sleeved, open-throated shirt made of banana or pineapple fiber.

Religious leader of the community was Israeli Amnon Wallenstein who had begun his university studies in Tel Aviv in the field of law. Coming from a traditionally observant home, he accepted the post in Manila although not an ordained rabbi. In Israel he had been affiliated with the orthodox youth movement Bnai Akiva and he introduced the chants or niggunim of this movement into the Philippines.

Sabbath morning was a busy time for spreading Torah in Manila. Following the kiddush at the close of services, the youth took over Temple Emil. Wherever I went there were classes—up and down stairs in Bachrach Hall, in a small passageway, in a sitting room, in the synagogue proper. Seven classes in all, led by Amnon Wallenstein and his wife, by native-born Helen Weinstein, by the wife of the Israeli Ambassador and by three other women of the community. The Hebrew language, Jewish history and holiday customs were being taught. The general feeling as expressed by more than one mother waiting after the service for her son or daughter was, "The school is more important than the shul." In the middle of the week a bus collected the children from the wide reaches of Manila for classes led by the Wallensteins at the community center.

Philippine Jewry feels close to developments in Israel. In December 1947 there was public worship hailing the U.N. decision favoring partition of Palestine. And in May 1948 the proclamation of the State of Israel was marked by a service during which the shofar was blown. Later that year, hundreds of trees were planted by Manila Jews in Upper Galilee's Freedom Forest in the name of the Republic of the Philippines, which had voted in favor of partition. Each year on Tu B'Shevat the children present the Israeli Ambassador with a gift of money for the planting of trees in Israel. (Preceding the days of ambassadors, Ernest Simke, a local leader, had for years been Honorary Consul for Israel.)

President of the community at the time of my visit was German-born Jack Haberer, son of Oskar Haberer who won the Grand Prix at the International Art Exhibition in Seattle in 1909 and the Golden Medal at the Exposition Universelle et Internationale de Bruxelles in 1910. (His mother, artist and art writer Ilse Kirschstein Haberer, was related to Max Lieberman and Walter Rathenau.)

The Jewish community is only a minute segment of this land of 36 million people. During the Hitler period, when Manila was a place of refuge for Central European Jews, the number rose to 1,800. But many of the refugees looked upon the Philippines only as a way station, and left at the close of the war for Australia or America. In 1966 I found only 250 Jews remaining there.

The intermarriage rate was 16 percent at that time. However, one third of the non-Jewish members of these mixed marriages have become converts to Judaism. Turkish-born Susanna Gadol dealt with the problem of intermarriage within her family in her own way. She sent her three children to a Catholic school where boys and girls were taught in separate classes. When they grew up, she encouraged her children to go to America where the opportunities for meeting other young Jews would be greater. "If you marry out of your faith, I'm not your mother anymore," she told her children. Mrs. Gadol seemed a happy mother, although thousands of miles away from her children—all of whom had married Jewish partners in America.

American influence is strong in the Republic of the Philippines. Its Constitution and Bill of Rights, its compulsory education system—all are based on the American way. When a street sign at one corner of Manila showed Harvard Street meeting Princeton Street, or when the billboards cried out "Put a tiger in your tank" and "Happy Motoring," I knew the American business influence was strong.

At the same time anti-American feeling was brewing. Talk of "American Imperialism" is intensifying. Particularly resented is the Parity Law—in effect until 1974—which gives the American businessman equal rights with the Filipino, who says such competition is too strong for the native businessman.

What will happen in 1974? Will American Jews (25 percent of Manila Jewry) be able to continue in business when parity is withdrawn? And, if not, will there be a continuing Jewish community in this area?

⊸ SINGAPORE ≈⊷

Jews had the monopoly of the opium trade! True—in Singapore, about 130 years ago, when opium traffic was a perfectly legal pursuit.

Only twenty years earlier, Singapore had been a sleepy little fishing village on a swampy island full of jungle growth three-quarters of a mile off the coast of the Malay Peninsula. But its location at the crossroads of Southeast Asia and the Pacific Ocean intrigued the imagination of England's Sir Stamford Raffles. He saw vast possibilities for trade in just such a location.

A man of tact, of great courtesy, with a speaking knowledge of the Malay tongue, he came ashore one day in 1819 and talked with the representative of Sultan Hussein Mohammed Shah, the

Sultan of Johore and owner of the island of Singapore. When he left that evening, Sir Stamford had in his pocket an agreement giving the East India Company of England the right to establish a trading post at the mouth of the Singapore River. Five years later England was given sovereignty over the entire island, a little over 200 square miles in area.

That trading post at the mouth of the Singapore River has grown to be the fifth busiest port of the world. It is a tax-free port: "the trade thereof open to all ships and vessels of every nation in the world free of duties." To it come ships laden with goods from all over the world. So many ships come that there is no room for them at the docks. Many have to wait their turn and anchor out in the harbor, as I saw when riding around the port. Among them were moored the Chinese lighters, each with two eyes and two sharp teeth painted on them "to keep the evil spirits away." Singapore is now one grand bazaar, with goods from East and West.

As an island, Singapore had but one avenue for expansion—to reclaim land from the sea. Jungle growth from the interior was hacked down and brought to the waterfront. Today's popular and lovely Esplanade—with its walks and restaurants and carts selling orange juice made of Jaffa oranges—is built on just such reclaimed land.

Bits of Victorian England are still to be seen in the architecture of several of the public buildings, like the Supreme Court. A fine example of another era is famous Hotel Raffles. With an air of fine disdain for such new-fangled notions as streamlined modern construction and air conditioning in a location only seventy-five miles from the equator, Hotel Raffles continues on in its serene way, with ceiling fans whirring away. I had reserved a room in this hotel beloved of Somerset Maugham. My "room" at the Raffles included a 27 × 15 foot bedroom, an anteroom, a 9 × 9 foot bathroom and a 15 × 11 foot sitting room overlooking the charming Palm Court with its frangipani flowers, fanlike traveler palms and impeccable outdoor dining service in this land of eternal summer.

Today Singapore's population is a mixture of European, Asian and Eurasian. Heading for some Jewish point of interest I realized I was the only Western-clad woman passenger on the bus. One Indian woman wore a flowing white sari and nose ring, another one was in Punjabi wide pantaloons worn with a knee-length dress; a Chinese girl was in trousers and long blouse with high collar; Malay women, fine-featured and delicate, were wearing long narrow sarongs with overblouses. Bearded Sikhs in turbans sat next to men in Western suits. My own American dress did not draw any particular attention in many-faceted Singapore in which 75 percent are Chinese, 14 percent Malays, 8 percent Hindus and the remainder Europeans.

The British authorities had permitted each community to retain and observe its own religion and customs. The coming of independence did not interfere with this diverse calendar and way of life. The Chinese take two weeks to celebrate the coming of their New Year. Driving through the Chinese area on "Chap Goh Meh," the fifteenth and closing night of the New Year celebration, was a dangerous undertaking. A dense pall of smoke filled the streets. And no wonder—for the belief is that the more firecrackers one explodes, the more good luck one will have in the New Year.

As so much of life goes on out of doors in Singapore, one evening's walk brought me into the midst of a Chinese wake. Mourners were dressed in sackcloth, big wreaths were placed on sidewalk easels, as were the long streamers bearing condolences. At tables, also set out on the sidewalk, friends were eating food to the accompaniment of music.

On Thaipusam Day, the Hindu festival of penitence, I was in the midst of a throng assembled at Mariamman Temple. Here had assembled Indian adherents who had vowed they would do public penance if they were restored to health, or their children would be spared, or for some such other good reason. Steel skewers were driven into their chests and backs. Across their shoulders was placed the *kavadi* (an open, decorated boxlike container made of bamboo, in which gifts to the god had been placed). Accompanied by family and friends to lend encouragement, they started out in procession. Bearing their burden they went through the streets to Chettiar Temple on Tank Road. I saw one devotee, nearing the end of his penitential walk, fall to the ground in agony. He was helped to his feet so that he might, in truth, complete and make good his vow.

Among these Chinese and Hindus, the Malay Mohammedans, Sikhs and Christians—each with his own traditional customs— live the Singapore Jews, numbering 500 souls. Jews have been here since the days of Stamford Raffles. Hearing of his plan for the new trading post, Jews of Baghdad came and were "in" on things right from the start. It was they, too, who started that fabulous trading center near the waterfront known as Change Alley. Nearby they built their homes, going back to Baghdad to find wives. By 1849 they were a large enough group to have need for a synagogue building. Soon thereafter a cemetery plot was leased in a location well away from the center of town. Now that small plot (burials since 1928 taking place in a new area) is in the midst of fashionable shopping-center Orchard Street—and is worth millions.

Today the Jewish section of old Singapore is completely Chinese. All that remains of Jewry's early days is a street sign "Synagogue Street," indicating where the house of assembly had once been. I walked about the old neighborhood. Brick buildings covered with plaster discolored by the rains housed the crowded population. Vegetable stalls, attractively arranged, filled the streets. Among the buyers were the "samsui" members of the guild of Chinese laboring women, distinctively garbed in blue with a red head covering. More numerous than the food buyers were the people eating at simple tables in the out-of-door restaurants. The food, I was told, was good and very inexpensive.

By 1878 the old synagogue, seating between thirty and forty, had been outgrown and a larger structure was built on Waterloo Street in a new part of town. Maghain Aboth, as the synagogue is named, remains on the same site to this day.

Name plates on the pews of Maghain Aboth gave evidence of the Iraqi origin of many of the families. For here I saw such family names as Sassoon, Meyer, Joshua, Ezekiel, Joseph, Benjamin, Isaac and Menasseh, it being customary for the oldest son to take his father's first name for his own surname or family name. Other name plates (among them Grimberg, Ellison, Sissauer, Jacobson) indicated the coming of the other lines of Singapore

Jewry—the Russian Jews who came via Harbin, at the turn of the century, and later on the German Jews.

Maghain Aboth serves both Sephardim and Ashkenazim. Rabbi Jacob Shababo, born in Safad of a Romanian mother related to Leon Blum (first Socialist and first Jew to become premier of France) lived in Palestine until World War I, when he moved on to Lisbon and later to Egypt. "I was in Egypt when the second World War broke out," Rabbi Shababo said as we chatted before the start of the Sabbath service. "I began burning my Zionist books. The smoke attracted attention and I was put into prison. Finding the halif or knife I used for slaughtering animals, for I was the shohet, the Egyptians claimed the knife was intended to kill them. Had it not been for the intervention of a Jewess married to a high official, things would surely have gone much worse for me. As it was, I was released after forty-three days." For over two decades Rabbi Shababo has been rabbi, shohet and mohel in Singapore.

In his seventies, he is active in the interfaith movement, and served three terms as President of the Inter-Religious Organization—embracing in its membership Hindus, Buddhists, Mohammedans, Sikhs, Catholics and a Mecca-born officer of an Arab country consulate.

Rabbi Shababo lived at some distance from the Waterloo Street synagogue, so he traveled to synagogue in a trishaw whose driver was paid before the start of the Sabbath.

There is no ghetto area, but names such as Menasseh Street, Nathan Street, Elias Road and Nissim Road indicate where Jews had had their business or where once the Jews had lived close to one another. Solomon Street is named for one among the early Iraqi settlers who had continued to wear Arab robes of the type customarily worn in his native Baghdad.

Along Wilkie Road, where once many Jews had lived, I visited on Sabbath afternoon one of the Jewish families still remaining there. Wilkie Road is a street of two-story buildings with shops and "back of the store" living quarters on the ground floor, and a shuttered upper floor also for dwelling purposes. Rooms are high, simple and almost bare. The children of this family attended a missionary school and did not get any Jewish instruction. The mother goes to synagogue only on Rosh Hashanah and Yom Kippur, as do all the other women.

Most famous of Singapore's Jewry was Sir Menasseh Meyer, knighted for his public service in raising the cultural level of the city. He came from Baghdad, a poor lad, at the age of fifteen. Eventually he became an importer and exporter, an opium trader and a real estate dealer, and was said to have owned half of Singapore's real estate property. He, too, had been among those returning to Baghdad to find a wife. Deeply religious and observant, Sir Menasseh had his own poultry yard, cattle shed and a private shohet.

After a dispute with a fellow member of Maghain Aboth Synagogue, Sir Menasseh had his own private synagogue, Chesed El, built on the grounds of his palatial home on Oxley Rise. Chesed El—an imposing, lofty cream-colored structure on a hill—has two rows of eight columns each, a marble floor, 125 teakwood seats and a Persian rug on the bimah. A network of wires extends from wall to wall, from which are suspended glass bowls with coconut oil and wicks to serve as yahrzeit lamps.

"Minyan men" were employed to attend services regularly at Chesed El. Israel Cohen, who visited Singapore in 1920–21, reported that the minyan men had gone on strike and that their demands for increases in salary and for rickshaw allowances were satisfied. Today, the synagogue is still served by a paid minyan. But instead of rickshaws a bus collects the minyan daily— morning and afternoon—and returns them to their homes.

Mrs. Nissim, daughter of Sir Menasseh Meyer, is a legend in Singapore. She continues in the path started by her father. Observant and generous, her home is open to all on Sabbath eve, and she sends food from her home to the hotel to provide for visitors wishing to comply with kashrut. Loved and respected by all, everyone quiets down naturally in her presence. "Mrs. Nissim is our goddess," was the way several people spoke of her.

Provisions from the Menasseh Meyer Fund, since his death in 1933, have enabled promising Jewish youth to study abroad, have supplied food for the poor and have furnished religious education at the Talmud Torah in Singapore and at a yeshiva in Jerusalem.

Another fund, the Amber Trust Fund, was set up by the Elias family to provide for higher education of Jewish youth. The Flora and Abdullah Schoker Fund also supplies aid for Jewish purposes.

The Jewish Welfare Board, constituted in 1949 by the organized community, gets its funds from real estate income and donations. It administers a home for the aged, assists widows, provides medical aid for the needy and scholarships. A former president of the Welfare Board remarked, "The curse of our small community is the existence of all these funds. People have come to expect a handout."

Across the road from the Chesed El Synagogue on Oxley Rise is the Communal Hall. Built only nine years before my visit in 1966, the center was already becoming an empty shell. Here was the Talmud Torah providing two hours' free daily religious instruction for the children who get their general education in mission schools, where the New Testament and catechism are required subjects. Each time I visited the Talmud Torah, I found only two boys there. And these two seemingly were drawn by the free hot lunches provided, for both came from needy families. As for the curriculum—that was limited to the repetition of prayers.

On Sunday mornings a volunteer member of the community led a group of twelve children in the study of the Torah portion of the week. All were reading the selection from Soncino Bibles. The leader came to his work with commendable devotion. But some of the children were too young to cope with the reading itself, let alone to show an understanding of the material.

On the upper floor of the center was a spacious youth headquarters, donated by the Reuben Menasseh Meyer Fund, established by the son of Sir Menasseh Meyer. The parquet floor, a stage and screen all recalled former activities, concerts and amateur theatricals that took place there just a few years ago. Today the place stands empty.

Only twenty years ago the youth, organized as Habonim, with emphasis on Zionism and Jewish culture, was 300-strong. Some members wanting activities of a more social nature broke away and formed the Menorah Club. Today neither the Habonim nor the Menorah Club is in existence. Frank Benjamin, a leading force of the defunct Menorah Club and editor of its bulletin *Kadimah* said, "The trouble was that my generation did not train the younger ones to step in and succeed us."

"Occasionally a few of us hold a function in the premises of the former Menorah Club," a present-day teenager told me. I learned that a function meant a dance.

Even the observance of the Bar Mitzvah ceremony, which in many places is the highlight in the life of Jewish youth, here in Singapore is not very important. Fifteen-year-old Raymond told me he had not yet observed his Bar Mitzvah. It is not a question of lack of funds, I was told. The parents choose any year, any week they desire. The boy then learns the Torah portion of that particular week and the ceremony is held whenever they wish.

To arouse the women's interest in cultural matters, a Women's Group was holding an all-day session once every two weeks. The day started with tea and sandwiches in mid-morning, followed by a speaker. Then came a lavish lunch after which the women settled down to an afternoon of card playing, interrupted only by tea in the afternoon.

World War II had its impact upon the Jewish community as a whole. A British Naval Base still being added to as late as 1938, Singapore was believed impregnable, surrounded as it was on three sides by water. But the Japanese attacked from the rear, coming down through the mainland to Johore in December 1941—Pearl Harbor month. By February 1942 unassailable Singapore had fallen. For a short time the Jews, then numbering two thousand, had carte blanche and services continued. Then they were required to wear arm bands and medallions with the word "Jew" on them. Two months later, the men were interned and had to till the fields. A year and a half later, the women and children were interned. But there were no atrocities committed against the Jews, as was the case with the local Chinese; for here, too, the conquerors pursued the old tradition of animosity between the Japanese and the Chinese.

One leading Jewish personality, David Marshall, was a problem to the Japanese. Born in 1908 to a Baghdad-Persian family, he was by upbringing a mixture of East and West. At school he was the Jew. In England where he studied law, he was treated as an

Asian. To the Japanese in World War II, in which he served as a volunteer in the British army, light-skinned David Marshall was not an Asian and so was sent to a labor camp in Japan's northernmost island Hokkaido. Hating colonialism, David Marshall became his country's "Father of Independence" and Chief Minister in Singapore's first real election in 1955—a post he held for fourteen months. In 1968 he represented his country at the U.N. David Marshall has also served the Jewish community as president of the Jewish Welfare Board and by intervening with Chou En Lai he made it possible for the Jews to leave Shanghai.

In recent years Singapore has called upon Israel and Israelis to help find a solution for some of its vexing problems. One of these problems was the automobile traffic which was choking Raffles Place, the local Times Square. Itzhak Ben-Asher, chief engineer for roads in Haifa, on loan from the Israeli Government, helped unravel the situation. Already there is an underground car-park at Raffles Place, above which is a breathing space where fountains spout and people promenade. Underground pedestrian crossings were also built under Mr. Ben-Asher's direction.

Singapore was also recently beset with the problem of juvenile delinquency. Called in to help solve this condition was Aryeh Levy of Israel. His background included membership in a kibbutz, service in the British army at sixteen and a three-year stint in the Palmah. A graduate of Teachers' Training College with a university degree in sociology and political economy, Aryeh Levy had also had much experience in working with youth before he was commissioned to Singapore.

At the Residential Training Center for professional youth workers, which he had instituted outside of the city, Aryeh Levy showed me charts which vividly reflected the situation. Singapore had a population of 420,000 between the ages of twelve and twenty-one. Only one out of four of this age group attended school. The labor market could take in only 60,000. "For all the rest there is frustration," said Aryeh Levy. "Frustration leads to anxiety and then aggression. Repeated aggression leads to delinquency. The 255,000 are exposed to vice elements and to the tongs or secret societies."

Now there are Youth Labor Services giving vocational guidance, a Youth Labor Exchange, a Works Brigade where Chinese,

Malays and Indians learn to live together and to work together, a youth movement to counteract the influence of the secret societies; Community Centers and training of professional youth workers.

Jewish youth has its own specific problems. In the labor market they have to compete with the Chinese. I found them in a mood to leave Singapore and go searching for a "better life" elsewhere. Their land of golden dreams was Australia. Already there was in Perth, on the west coast of Australia, a colony of former Singaporeans. Nearer to home, the two Jewish families I found in Kuala Lumpur, capital of Malaysia, were also Singaporeans.

Jewish life in this outpost of the Pacific is fast disappearing.

◄§ EXOTIC MALAYSIA §►

Do you want to escape to the sun? Then get away to Malaysia, land where the white frangipani and the purple-flowered jacaranda, the hibiscus and the orchid bloom, land of such exotic trees as the flamboyant (royal poinciana), the pepper, the palm and the rubber. Just north of the equator, Malaysia juts out at the southeast corner of Asia, between Thailand to the north and Singapore to the south. A peninsula, it is almost entirely surrounded by the waters of the South China Sea and those of the Straits of Malacca.

With a mean temperature of 81°, it can be hot in Malaysia, but don't let that bother you. You need not even think of carrying drip-dry clothes. For every morning before leaving my very comfortable Merlin Hotel in the capital city of Kuala Lumpur, I was asked for my laundry—including dresses—and courteously reminded, "There's no charge." How wonderful to return after a day's exploring to find everything washed and neatly ironed, and indeed "no charge!"

But watch your step as you walk along the sidewalks with the roofed-over verandas attached to the exterior of the buildings, for every so often you come to steps bridging open drains which carry off flood waters. Don't miss the cobbler plying his trade at a street corner or the "satay" meat being grilled on bamboo sticks over charcoal in the open. And don't be surprised seeing automobiles that carry no numbers on their plates. These belong to important people; they are distinguished not by numbers, but by carrying the legend "Chief Justice" or "Minister" or whatever office the owner holds.

The Moorish architecture of government buildings and the railroad station is a reminder of the many streams of traders and conquerors who had their day in Malaysia on the main sea route between the Persian Gulf, India, and China. There were the Arabs trading in aloewood, camphor, sandalwood, ivory, tin, ebony, rattan and bamboo. Then came the Portuguese and the Dutch, avid for the spices that Europe sought.

The old port city of Malacca still retains Dutch street names and architecture. In Kuala Lumpur, the Selangor Club is built in the British Tudor style, recalling that the British East India Company came here in the eighteenth century.

"What does being a Jew mean to you here in Kuala Lumpur?" I asked Harry Elias as we sipped cold drinks on the veranda of the prestigious Selangor Club of which he was a member. Singapore-born, educated in England and now practicing law in Malaysia, Mr. Elias is head of one of the two Jewish families living in Kuala Lumpur.

"Being a Jew means observing the mitzvot," came the sure, prompt reply of warm-hearted, quick-witted Harry Elias. "When I was a boy in Singapore, I did not mix with my schoolmates, for they were pork eaters. When I touched the Torah in the synagogue or was called up for an aliyah a holiness descended upon me. When kaddish has to be recited, you do it—no matter what the inconvenience—morning and evening for one year."

Talk of mitzvot, Torah, aliyah and kaddish seemed incongruous in this Far Eastern country the size of England, with its population of 7½ million a melange of races—50 percent easygoing Malays, 37 percent energetic Chinese and 11 percent Indians—each group with its own customs and religion.

The Malays are Moslem and their newly constructed National Mosque on its thirteen-acre plot gives the effect of lace in stone, surrounded by lawns and many pools. The National Museum proudly displays the large mythical bird on which thirteen-year-old Moslem princes rode to their circumcision ceremonies. Buddhist temples serve the Chinese. High on a limestone outcropping is the shrine of the Batu Caves. With sharp metal skewers thrust into their chests and backs, devotees climb the 272 steps leading to the shrine, fulfilling their vows on the Hindu Thaipusam, the day of penance.

At the modern Weld Supermarket, actually a shopping center, I met with Meyer Elias, of the only other Jewish family living in Kuala Lumpur (the two families are not related). Meyer Elias also comes from a Singapore family of Iraqi descent. He transferred to Kuala Lumpur for economic reasons, opening a store in this shopping center close to the Merlin Hotel. A successful businessman, he now owns four specialty shops selling apparel, shoes, jewelry and other merchandise.

We sat for some hours in the small restaurant on the second story of the shopping center, where Mr. Elias could be easily reached if needed. In Chinese and Malay surroundings we talked of Jewish matters. Every morning Meyer Elias puts on his tefillin and recites the Shema. Meat is provided by a Moslem butcher "to assure us that no pork will be used and that the shehita will be observed." On the Sabbath Eve there are prayers at home and a festive meal. On Saturday the family eats at a restaurant to avoid cooking at home.

I was taken aback when Meyer Elias added, "We do not light candles for the Sabbath lights," until he went on to explain, "the candles may be made of pork oil. Instead we dip a wick into peanut oil."

A special custom is observed by this family on the opening day of a new shop. On such an occasion, a prayer book, bread, water, a penknife, sweets and a mirror are left overnight on the premises after appropriate blessings have been recited. Why the mirror, I wondered. Responded Mr. Elias, "To avoid the evil eye. Upon seeing his reflection in the mirror, anyone with evil intent will surely be frightened away."

Years ago, Saul Meyer opened a general store in Seremban, forty miles south of Kuala Lumpur. With a family that numbered seven sons—and some assistants—he had a ready-made minyan. Morning services were conducted daily and the business was closed on the Sabbath when Mr. Meyer read the complete weekly portion of the Torah to the family. Kosher meat was brought in by bus from Singapore. Today the Meyers are scattered, only two sons remaining in Seremban to carry on the family business in the original one-story building.

At Gombak, eleven miles out of Kuala Lumpur, I came upon members of yet another group of the native population. These are the aborigines, of whom there are 100,000, many living in the mountain jungle areas. An English doctor opened a medical center here and helicopters are used to bring them out of the jungle to the 300-bed hospital at Gombak. Their families are encouraged to come along and arrangements are made for them to do their own cooking, if they so desire.

Among one of these aboriginal tribes, the relatively fair-skinned Semai Senoi, custom holds that if a man dies young, his brother marries the childless widow. But he is not forced to do so against his will, a practice reminiscent of the Jewish yibbum and halitzah.

One continues on through lush rubber estates and tin-dredging operations, past peaceful lovely villages with thatched huts built on stilts; the olive-skinned, black-haired, small-boned women in long sarongs and short muslin jackets; the men in knee-length sarongs over their trousers, and wearing small round velvet caps. It seems a never-never-land with its hibiscus and frangipani flowers, with its cloves and nutmegs as well as the flame and jacaranda trees.

Two hundred and fifty miles north of Kuala Lumpur is the island of Penang, just off the western coast. Sir Francis Light came here in 1786 with a group in tailcoats, knee breeches and swords, and raised the English flag "in the name of His Britannic Majesty and for the use of the East India Company"—the Sultan of Kedah having ceded it to the English. Officially the city of Penang is called Georgetown, in honor of the British monarch George III.

On the outskirts of the city is the Snake Temple, where eggs are offered as food for the many vipers kept there. The imposing Ayer Itam Temple—with its large marble Buddha—draws many devout worshippers.

One of Penang's many charms is that it is a free port offering ivories, woodcarvings, jade and curios from many countries at low prices in the many shops run by Chinese, who make up a large segment of the population.

In 1966 in this veritable tropical paradise, lived half a dozen Jewish families, all of Baghdad background and all related. After the death in 1964 of its hazzan and shohet Hayoo Jacob, kosher meat was imported for a while from Singapore (then part of the Federation of Malaysia), almost 500 miles away. But government regulations requiring certificates of meat inspection and import permits put an end to this practice. In the years since, these Jews have not tasted meat—subsisting on fish, cheese, eggs and vegetables.

Riding in a trishaw with an overhead canopy and propelled by a cyclist, I reached 28 Nagore Road, just off the New World (a Chinese amusement park), where the Jews had been wont to assemble for services. Actually it was not a synagogue building, but a small room in the home of the late Hayoo Jacob.

Around the walls were simple plaster seats for use on High Holydays. On Sabbaths and the year round, the men sat on rugs spread on the floor. Fifteen glass containers filled with coconut oil were used as yahrzeit lamps. The Ark held eight Sifrei Torah, all but one in unadorned cylinders, having been stripped of their silver ornaments by the local Chinese during World War II. The one Scroll retaining its velvet and silver trimmings had been hidden by the hazzan during the war. In one corner of the room stood the special chair used for Brit Milah ceremonies.

Head of one of Penang's Jewish households was Baruch Ephraim. Obliged to work on the Sabbath (he was in the civil service), he nevertheless tried to make the day different from the rest of the week. At home he touched no money, nor would he do any writing on the Sabbath.

In his youth there had been fifteen Jewish families in Penang, numbering seventy people. In those days, Mr. Ephraim recalled, fathers prepared their sons for Bar Mitzvah and all Jewish festivals were observed. Part of the Purim celebration was to make a Haman figure of straw, dressed in old clothes. The holiday would close with "Haman" being thrown into a fire and firecrackers exploded.

Among customs followed was that of keeping the havdalah

spices overnight under one's pillow to ensure that the coming week would be a good week. When a bride received her ketubah she would seal it. Never would it be opened, for to do so might bring divorce or death.

But whom can one marry now in a Jewish community as tiny as Penang's? There is no Jew available as a marriage partner for the Ephraim daughter, and to this family, marriage outside the faith is not to be taken into consideration. She would not think of leaving home to try her luck in a larger group. Said her father, "What is fated for her, will be." Another solution was found by Mordecai David Mordecai, manager of the well-known Eastern and Oriental Hotel. His young son resembled the child's Chinese mother—a convert to Judaism.

From the Ephraim house I walked past Chinese homes, with their tiny sidewalk shrines, on my way to the Jewish cemetery on Yahoodi Road, with its special section reserved for the burial of kohannim.

Since my visit to lovely Penang in 1966, the Jewish group has grown even smaller, for death has taken its toll. No more is there public worship on Nagore Road, for Penang lacks a minyan, and its Sifrei Torah are waiting to be sent where they can be used.

So keen is Baruch Ephraim's desire to maintain a link with Judaism, that he asked to be supplied with a Jewish calendar to enable him to mark the special days of the year in common with Jews in the rest of the world.

Fascinating Penang may be a tropical paradise for the traveler, but it is not a Garden of Eden for its few remaining Jews.

◄§ THE STAR OF DAVID IN THE LAND OF THE RISING SUN §►

FLASH——————

There are now about 8,000 Jews in Japan organized into a group called the Union of Jewish Japanese. The group is led by two university professors—an atomic scientist and a prominent naval engineer, both of whom took part in the 1941 attack on Pearl Harbor. Union members speak only

> *Hebrew among themselves, circumcise their chil-*
> *dren and attend services in their own synagogues.*
> *They also bombard the Israeli Legation in Tokyo*
> *with requests for immigration visas [to Israel].*

This March 2, 1958, *New York Times* dispatch (dated Jerusalem—Feb. 26) set off a glow of excitement among Jews around the
world. The romantic thought that thousands of kimono-clad
people had converted to Judaism in the land of cherry blossoms,
in the land of picture-postcard beauty of Fujiyama and of red-
lacquered torii gates at Shinto shrines, remains imbedded in the
hearts of many, despite the fact that only one month after the
above news item another report, from Tokyo this time, appeared
in *The New York Times* of April 8, 1958:

> *A scholarly interest in Judaism by Prince Mikasa,*
> *youngest brother of Emperor Hirohito, has resulted*
> *in rumors that many Japanese were being con-*
> *verted to Judaism. The reports were denied here by*
> *Asher Naim, chancellor of the Israel Legation. . . .*
> *Denying that thousands of Japanese were con-*
> *verted, Mr. Naim said, "I know of only one man*
> *who expressed an interest in being converted.*
> *There are no organizations of Japanese Jews. The*
> *reason is simple, because there are no Japanese*
> *Jews.*

One of the few cases of authenticated conversion to Judaism is
that of Setsu Zau Kotsuji, member of an upper-class family that
had been Shinto priests for 1,200 years in Kyoto, ancient capital
of Japan, a city with hundreds of Shinto shrines and almost 900
Buddhist temples. As a boy it was his duty to kindle the Shinto
altar fire daily. Religious doubts began creeping in, and at the age
of thirteen he began reading a Japanese translation of the Bible he
had picked up at a secondhand bookshop. "My life was forever
changed," he says in his book *From Tokyo to Jerusalem*. Study
with Christian missionaries brought baptism to that faith. Later
he became a church minister, and when twenty-eight years old,
he came to America for further study at the Theological Seminary
in Auburn, New York and the Pacific School of Religion in
Berkeley, California. While in California he met Jews and began

attending synagogue services in San Francisco. "I left America [1931] as a Jew more than a Christian," said Kotsuji back in his homeland. "I began to find myself thinking and feeling more like a Jew, as if there were a Jew living inside me. I felt closer than ever to the persecuted people of Israel. I knew that some day I would become a Jew."

That day came closer to actuality when on August 8, 1959 he enplaned at Hanedo Airport in Tokyo and flew directly to Lydda in Israel. A month later he appeared before the Beit Din in Jerusalem. Formally received into the Jewish faith and circumcised at the Shaare Zedek Hospital (he was sixty years old at the time) he received the name of Abraham ben Abraham. After a year's lecture tour in Israel and America, Abraham Kotsuji returned to Japan, making his home thirty miles from Tokyo at Kamakura.

Another confirmed case of conversion is that of Hiroshi Okamoto, a high-school teacher. After the traumatic experience of the Japanese surrender in World War II and the shedding of the cult of belief in the divinity of the emperor, there began in Japan a search for a new faith, new ethical values. Hiroshi Okamoto came in 1958 to the United States to study the Jewish religion at the Hebrew Union College in Cincinnati. Three years later he and his wife, the former Kyoko Sato, were converted by a specially convened Orthodox Rabbinical Court. In June of 1964 he was ordained a rabbi, receiving honors in rabbinics upon his graduation. He returned to Japan and for two years directed a Jewish seminar in Tokyo. Graduate study at Oxford University in England followed. Today this rabbi is back in the United States as an assistant professor in the Department of Religion at the University of Miami.

Conversion or no conversion, there has been in Japan a strain of belief that there is some affinity, some kinship, some relationship between Israel and Japan. Particularly so is the conviction that the Ainu, the aboriginal inhabitants of Hokkaido, northernmost island of this 1,300-mile-long island country, are descendants of the Lost Ten Tribes; for unlike the rest of the Japanese, the Ainu are Caucasoid or European in appearance, the men are bearded and their hair is wavy.

Dr. Jenichiro Oyabe, with degrees from Yale, is one of those who holds that the Japanese stem from the Lost Ten Tribes. He claims that some of the Shinto practices have their basis in the Old Testament—that the torii, the two-column gateway forming an approach to Shinto shrines, originated in the two ornamental pillars Jachin and Boaz that stood before the vestibule serving as the entrance of Solomon's Temple; that the "haidan" (place of worship) and the "okuden" (holy of holies) of the Shinto shrines are founded on the Hekhal and the Holy of Holies of the Temple in Jerusalem; and that the sacred music performed by musicians who are placed at the side of the altar of Shinto shrines is based on II Chronicles 5:11-12 "And it came to pass when the priests were come out of the holy place . . . [they] stood at the east end of the altar."

The Japanese Imperial Regalia (a mirror, a sword and a jewel), so sacred that they are never removed from their sanctum within the Imperial Palace, asserts Dr. Oyabe, were brought to Japan by Jippon, eldest son of Gad, for whom the country is named.

Dr. Allen H. Godbey, in *The Lost Tribes A Myth*, also claims a connection between Jews and Japan:

> *In the province of Yamato are two ancient villages,*
> *Goshen and Menashe. The legend is that in the*
> *third century a strange people appeared. A temple*
> *known as the "Tent of David" still stands where*
> *they first settled. A folk legend says that the*
> *founder of the sect, when a child, was found in a*
> *little chest floating on the water. The people today*
> *call themselves Chada "The Beloved," [this is*
> *traditionally the meaning of the name David]. . . .*
> *In the city of Usamasa, on a site belonging to one*
> *of the oldest of the Chada families, is a well some*
> *1,500 years old. Upon the stone curbing the word*
> *"Israel" is engraved. A village near Usamasa is*
> *Kando-a-mozi, "River-crossing + Journey cakes"*
> *which suggests the Red Sea and the Passover.*

Historically speaking the arrival of Jews in Japan from other parts of the world is said to date from the fifteenth century, when some came with the Portuguese explorers, and in the sixteenth century, when others came with the Dutch traders. After 1853 when Commodore Matthew Perry sailed his frigate into Uraga harbor, thus opening Japan to the commerce of the world, Jewish traders from Iraq, India, Syria and Europe settled in the port cities of Nagasaki, Yokohama and Kobe. Among the first was Elias David Sassoon who opened branches of his father's mercantile firm, the D. Sassoon & Co. of Bombay. By the mid-1880s there was an organized Jewish community in Nagasaki which lasted until the Russo-Japanese War of 1904–05.

The name of Jacob H. Schiff, New York financier and philanthropist, is linked with this conflict between Russia and Japan. It was he who induced Kuhn, Loeb & Co., of which he was an influential member, to underwrite over 50 percent of three war loans for Japan to the amount of £52,000,000. Baron Takahashi, Vice-Governor of the Bank of Japan and Financial Commissioner of the Japanese Government, who had been sent to London and New York to negotiate loans for his government, said:

> *Mr. Schiff's move to throw in his lot with Japan was taken before her first decisive victory at the battle of the Yalu . . . How Mr. Schiff became interested in Japan I did not know fully at the time. . . . Mr. Schiff's deal was a very bold venture especially if the fact is taken into consideration that foreign investment was not yet a beaten track of American high finance and surely he did not make the venture for the sake of mere profit. . . . He had a grudge against Russia on account of his race. He was justly indignant at the unfair treatment of the Jewish people by the Russian Government. . . . The financial support of our foreign friends and the foreign investors largely contributed to our success in the war and the consummation of peace.*

Visiting Japan in 1906, Mr. Schiff was received in private audience and for lunch by Emperor Meiji and invested with the Order of the Rising Sun, in addition to the Order of the Sacred Treasure which he already held. Mr. Schiff's name is revered in Japan, and Japan's representatives to America "visit him," that is, make pilgrimages to his grave.

All that remains now in Nagasaki to recall a Jewish life there are the tombstones with Hebrew inscriptions in a small walled section of the cemetery overlooking the epicenter of the atom bomb that blasted this city.

During World War I Yokohama, only eighteen miles from Tokyo, was the hub of organized Jewish life in Japan. After the 1917 Revolution more than 20,000 Jewish refugees sought escape from Russia. European ports being closed, they turned eastward, wandering across the Urals and across Siberia. It was then that Japan became a way station on their route to reunion with families in places of safety around the world.

The Benevolent Society of the local Yokohama Jewish community was inundated with requests for assistance. Then the HIAS sent its representative, Samuel Mason, to centralize aid to the refugees. In visits to Vladivostok and Harbin, where he also set up relief and Central Information Bureaus, Mr. Mason told of finding these former middle-class Jews sleeping in railroad stations, in sheds and in courtyards. From Vladivostok they proceeded by steamer across the Sea of Japan, and from Manchuria they went by rail to Korea and then by steamer to Japan. One group of four families roamed for three years from Russia across Siberia until they succeeded in reaching Yokohama. The great majority of the refugees joined families in the United States.

In February 1918 Yokohama's Hotel Royal, old and dilapidated despite its regal name, became the HIAS hostel for refugees. All requirements for traditional religious observance—shohet, prayer books, Sifrei Torah, shofar, megillot, tefillin—were provided; classes and lectures in English were started.

Following the devastating earthquake of 1923 which leveled the city, people scattered and the Yokohama Jewish community declined.

Good relations between the Jews and the Japanese continued. Japan was one of the first countries to support the Balfour Declaration, issued in 1917, which "viewed with favor the establishment in Palestine of a national home for the Jewish people." By nature the Japanese are a tolerant people, many practicing both the Shinto and the Buddhist faiths simultaneously. But anti-Semitism was brought in from the outside. The White

Russians who had found a haven in Manchuria claimed that the Bolshevik seizure of power was "Jewish conspiracy and plot."

When the Hitler period came, again the escape route led Jewish refugees across Siberia for shelter in Japan and in Japanese-occupied territory in Manchuria and China. Their military alliance with Germany, Japanese authorities and newspapers pointed out, did not imply acceptance of the Nazi theory of race superiority or race hatred. In Kobe the Jews removed a Hebrew signboard from in front of their synagogue because of the presence of German agents in the city. But Japanese police officers told the Jews there was no need for fear, "This wasn't Germany," and the signboard was replaced.

Eventually, however, the work of Nazi agents in the country did bear results. Shanghai stateless refugees (those coming from Germany or any Nazi-occupied territory in Europe) were interned in the Hongkew area of that city and surrounded by barbed wire. Within Japan itself some German-Jewish professionals, among them a symphony conductor, an engineer and a professor of chemistry, were dismissed from their posts.

Much has changed since those days for the thousand Jews now living in this island country, somewhat larger than the state of Montana (but with a population equaling half that of the entire United States).

I had come to study at the University of Tokyo in the summer of 1961 and was living at nearby traditional Shinsen Inn in a warren of narrow alleys that served as streets, unnamed as were most of the streets in this city with a population of ten million. And traditional it was—shoes worn out of doors were removed upon entering the inn and exchanged for sandals, these in turn thrown off before going into my own room—a six-mat room, with bed mat and covers stored along one side, a low table and cushions, a lovely scroll on one wall and windows of paper. The house-supplied yukata, or kimono—for indoor wear—was welcome, but I soon gave up any attempt to sit back on my heels in Japanese manner while dining at the low table.

Walking back from classes in the middle of the day, I could see the hot lunch being brought from the noodle shops by vendors, guiding their bicycles in and out of traffic with one hand while the other held aloft a tray with a number of small bowls containing hot noodles or rice. At other times of the day I learned to enjoy seaweed, abalone and the raw-egg sauce that accompanied the sukiyaki.

On the first Friday that summer I ventured out to attend Sabbath services at the Jewish Community Center at 102 Hanezawa-cho, Shibuya-ko. I use the word "venture" advisedly, for although the Japanese are among the most literate people in the world, don't expect Tokyo taxi drivers to understand or read English. And the Shinsen Inn staff, bowing and giggling, was not too helpful when it came to communicating in English. I had therefore taken the precaution to supply myself with two cards at the USO office on famed Ginza Street—one giving the location of the Center and another indicating the University, all in Japanese characters. Showing the appropriate card to the driver, we set off, careening in and out of traffic at furious speed. No wonder taxis here are named Kamikaze, or suicide cabs.

The Jewish Community Center in Shibuya, in a residential area of wide streets and large homes, is surrounded by a garden and wall carrying signs in Hebrew, English and Japanese indicating the nature of the building. Built as a private mansion, part Japanese and part European in architecture, it was purchased in 1953 by the Jewish community.

The synagogue room, seating 120, with wood-paneled walls, white silk curtains before the Ark, on the bimah and at the windows, was not well filled. The order of service was Orthodox, the prayer books from the Hebrew Publishing Company of New York, and the chants familiar. It was a period when the city was "between rabbis" and knowledgeable Mr. Milewsky, originally from Wilno in Poland, was the lay leader.

At the conclusion of the service I went on to the outdoor dining room overlooking a swimming pool. Well-dressed people, many more than at the service, were enjoying food from the Center's kosher dairy kitchen, kosher meat and delicatessen being imported from the United States. Some groups were playing cards. For the Center actually functions as a Jewish country club within the city where Jews go to meet and be with other Jews, to spend their leisure hours together, to see movies and hear concerts.

Yiddish and Russian, English and Hebrew were the languages I heard, for most of Tokyo's Jews are those who came after the war from Shanghai and Manchuria. Some refugees who tried living elsewhere returned to Japan. To these have been added Americans there on business or those who married Japanese women and decided to remain after completing their tour of military duty. Israeli diplomats and those with business connections are also to be found in Japan.

Back in the house with its card rooms and place for billiards, I turned the pages of the Visitors' Book and came across the name of Jacob Craven, whom I had first met when he was a member of a Zionist youth organization in America, and who now lives at Kibbutz Ein Hashofet in Israel.

Later on in the summer I could find my way to the Center by subway, which in Tokyo is clean and attractive with plush seats—and a good vantage point for seeing the mingling of the old and the new in the country. A perfect example is a man I saw on one such trip: a kimono-clad man squatting back on his heels on the subway seat, his sandals on the floor, a Western hat on his head.

One Sabbath there was a special service addressed by a Lubavitsher Hasid on his way to Australia. The Jews of Tokyo being well off (most in import-export business or trading in pearls), he thought it worthwhile to stop for a few days of fund raising. He made no appeals at the service, only announcing he would call on the men individually at the conclusion of the Sabbath. Kiddush following the service featured lox and gefillte fish.

For Sabbath luncheon that day I was invited to the nearby Milewsky home (the Milewskys now making their permanent home in Tokyo), a house furnished in Western style but with Japanese touches, including a doll in a glass case, flowers arranged according to local custom and a live-in maid receiving $25 a month. But the lunch we enjoyed that day—the Lubavitsher Hasid, his wife and I—was one all of us could enjoy, for the meal included that world-wide favorite Sabbath dish of "cholent."

While spending a summer in hot and humid Tokyo (similar to New York climate), I escaped one weekend to cool Karuizawa, 3,000 feet high in the mountains, only ninety miles from Tokyo. It seemed a little bit of Cape Cod and Provincetown set in a mountain area, with its many tiny shops featuring the locally made art and craft work. The summer colony of foreign diplomats were walking about in Western summer attire. Near the tennis court, pointed out as the place where Crown Prince Akihito first met his commoner wife, now Princess Michiko, I visited with Dina Waht at the boardinghouse she operated in this summer resort town.

Originally from Odessa, Dina Waht came from Shanghai to see the famed Japanese cherry trees in blossom, a visit which turned into a residence of over forty years. As we talked, a Japanese youngster about five years old ran into the room and Mrs. Waht addressed him in Russian and Yiddish terms of endearment. I must have had a quizzical expression on my face, for Dina Waht explained that he was the child of a former maid who had worked for her for eighteen years. Realizing that her end was near, the ill Japanese woman worried about the future of this young child who would be left alone in the world. Mrs. Waht assured her that she would raise the child, and the tone of the warm relationship between the two spoke eloquently of how the former Russian Jewess was observing her pledge.

During the summer I went to Kobe to visit with the Jewish community there. On Osaka Bay, with a natural backdrop of mountains, Kobe is the second-largest port in the country, with ocean liners stopping there on trans-Pacific routes. It was the Jews from Iraq who first settled here to trade, to import and export. Later the Russian Jewish merchants established themselves. Soon two synagogues were erected, one Sephardi and the other Ashkenazi. Refugees were assisted during World War I and the Nazi periods. Included among these was the group from the Mir Yeshiva who had escaped by way of Wilno and Kovno, crossing the continent of Asia by the Trans-Siberian Railroad, reaching Kobe as an intact group of three hundred students, faculty and family members. From Kobe the Mir group went on to settle in Shanghai.

To reach the synagogue I climbed the hillside up from the port to Kitano-cho, an area of attractive homes built of concrete. Initially a warehouse contributed by the Sassoon family, the bare building served the largely Sephardi community. We waited for a full minyan to be present. The president of the group himself was not present—he had gone to Israel to find a wife (I have since learned he was successful). Communal leader Mr. Moshe came in, followed by his seven children—but that did not help, for none of them had reached Bar Mitzvah age. Three more arrivals—brothers who were to recite kaddish—came in. Still the required ten men were not present. Not until one man went out into the immediate neighborhood, inhabited chiefly by Jews, was the search for the "Tenth Man" crowned with success, and the service started.

Two years before my visit Kobe had suffered from a severe typhoon and the Jews were unable to secure a lulav and etrog for use in the celebration of the Sukkot festival. They appealed to Rabbi Matthew H. Simon, then chaplain attached to Commander Naval Forces Japan, but he had only one lulav and one etrog which had been sent to him by the Jewish Welfare Board Commission on Chaplaincy for use of the Jewish sailors at the Yokosuka U.S. Navy Base—and Yokosuka was 250 miles from Kobe. What followed is told by Chaplain Simon:

> The next morning, after being blessed by the naval
> congregation, the "fruit of the goodly trees" and
> the "branches of palm trees" were passed to Lieu-
> tenant Lawrence Steiger [who had volunteered]
> who was waiting at the controls of his F2F
> "Tracker." Two hours later the religious symbols
> which had originated in the soil of Israel, been
> shipped to New York and then expressed to Japan,
> were placed in the hands of Kobe worshippers
> seeking to "rejoice before the Lord."

The current picture of the Kobe Jews is a far brighter one. Now a community of forty families—half Sephardi and Ashkenazi, and half Israelis associated with the Israel Zim Lines—they joyously dedicated on March 10, 1970, a new synagogue, the first structure to be built specifically for synagogue purposes. Driving force and now president of Kobe—The Jewish Community of Kansai—is Albert Hamway, whose interests may be gleaned from the fact that the meat used at the Hamway table is kosher meat imported from the United States.

In this country with its tales of conversions, of legends and folk tales of affinity with the Jewish people, there is a Japanese scholar who is making a serious attempt to bring a real knowledge of Jews and Judaism to the Japanese. This is Masayuki Kobayashi, professor of history at Waseda University in Tokyo. He has written on Jewish history and has translated, among other works, Norman Bentwich's *Israel* into Japanese.

The Star of David and the Land of the Rising Sun seem to link up in the following story told by Rabbi Victor M. Solomon, chaplain of the U.S. Air Force in Japan. Chaplain Solomon had gone in December 1968 to lead a Hanukkah candle-lighting ceremony for the Jewish airmen stationed at Wakkanai in the northwestern tip of Japan's northernmost island of Hokkaido. Within view across the narrow sea passage was the Soviet island of Sakhalin. Chaplain Solomon reported:

> *As we were kindling the Jewish lamp of freedom within sight of that country in which our people are not free to practice the faith of their ancestors, the Jewish Welfare Board banner triumphantly waved in the breeze on a windy point high above the sea. . . . A deep impression was made on the Japanese citizens who were present because, as I later learned, the Star of David on the Jewish Welfare Board banner is also the official seal of the city of Wakkanai.*

✑ HONG KONG
ISLE OF FRAGRANT WATERS ✑

Lunch on Wednesday at the Jewish Recreation Club—70 Robinson Road—is something uncommon. For this 70 Robinson Road is in Victoria City, better known as Hong Kong on the island of the same name, in the South China Sea off the Mainland of China.

From my hotel in Kowloon at the tip of the Mainland peninsula, I crossed the mile-wide channel to the island of Hong Kong by Star Ferry, a spectacular introduction to the sights and sounds of busy Hong Kong harbor—high-sterned junks with their unusual billowing sails, laundry flapping in the breeze from the smaller sampans propelled by sculls, cargo freighters flying the Communist China flag, an American luxury liner anchored in the roadstead, walla-wallas (small water taxis) dashing about, and the Star Ferries disgorging people who were 99 percent Chinese.

A taxi took me from the waterfront esplanade with its commercial houses and banks and made a twisting climb, for Hong Kong mounts to its peak over 1,950 feet high. Along the way was 70 Robinson Road, a quiet enclave with synagogue and Jewish Recreation Club and lawns. Every Wednesday a luncheon is held—no speeches, no appeals for funds, no business—only a display of togetherness with other Jews.

Soon after the island was ceded to the British in the wake of the Opium War in 1841, astute David Sassoon sent his son Elias David Sassoon to open a branch of the Bombay family firm here. Enough Jewish employees and their families were sent along from Bombay so that Jewish life would take root, and all needs and requirements for ritual observance were supplied. The monopoly of the opium trade, a legal business, was the start of the Sassoon success story in this part of the world.

In 1867 Elias David Sassoon organized his own company, E.D. Sassoon & Co., branching out in Shanghai and Hong Kong into banking, finance, real estate and land investments. Associated with E.D. Sassoon & Co. at one time was Shanghai-born Denzil Marcus Ezra, son of a family that became prominent in the charity and the literary life of that city.

Well remembered also is the name of Sir Matthew Nathan, Governor of Hong Kong in 1904. London-born, he was the most distinguished cadet of his term at the Royal Military Academy, and later created Companion of the Order of St. Michael and St. George. He was the first Jew to be appointed to governorship in the distant colonies of Sierra Leone and the Gold Coast. His administration in Hong Kong is remembered for his ability, wisdom and zealousness.

And then there were the Brothers Kadoorie, Ellis and Eliezer (the latter known as Elly), who came from Baghdad. Starting at the bottom with the Sassoons, they went out on their own and in time became multi-millionaires. Sir Ellis, knighted in 1917 for his services to Great Britain in the East, contributed to both

Jewish and non-Jewish institutions, and left a fund for the building of agricultural schools in Palestine—one for Jews and another for Arabs. Sir Elly, knighted in 1926, founded the firm of Sir Elly Kadoorie & Sons. A philanthropist, he is known for his assistance to hospitals and schools in the Far and Near East. (At Bombay I was to visit the Elly Kadoorie School for the brown-skinned Bene Israel children of the Jewish community there.)

His sons, Lawrence and Horace, are now partners in the firm of Sir Elly Kadoorie & Sons and play a large role in the life of Hong Kong today. Each one's list of directorships covers a full page in the Who's Who of Hong Kong. Cross the harbor in a Star Ferry, ride the Peak Tramways cable car to Castle Peak for a view, stay at famed Peninsula or Repulse Bay hotels, buy a rug at the Hong Kong Carpet Manufacturing Company (after all, Nelson Rocke-feller was a customer), go down to the wharfs, stop in a bank, or turn on an electric light, and you are in touch with some of the business interests controlled by Sir Elly Kadoorie & Sons. Law-rence Kadoorie was Chairman of the Board of the China Light and Power Co., which recently combined with Esso Standard Eastern to form the Peninsula Electric Power Co.; and Horace Kadoorie is more specifically concerned with "trams, ferries, wharfs, rubber plantations."

But beyond all this, the names of Lawrence and Horace Kadoo-rie are associated with refugees, and in Hong Kong refugees mean the Chinese "illegal immigrants" streaming in from Mainland China. These refugees come pouring in to Hong Kong, pursued and fired on by border guards, swimming rivers, stopping to rest on the island of Macao and covering the remaining forty miles by junk, hidden in secret compartments.

A charming, intelligent woman I had met in Taiwan, while en route to Hong Kong, had seemed very depressed. I learned she was worried about her mother, who was at the time trying the underground escape route from the Mainland via Macao. Arriv-ing in Hong Kong I made contact with friends of the family and was able to meet the newcomer. It was the day after her arrival, and though she showed signs of the strain of her ordeal of walking, swimming, climbing and the junk trip, one could not but be charmed by the gentleness and good breeding of this

Hong Kong—High-rise housing built for refugees streaming into the British colony from Mainland China.

woman in her sixties. She was taken into her friends' home and was absorbed into the multiplying population of Hong Kong.

But not all have such friends here, as attested to by the squatters' huts that dot the hillsides of Hong Kong. And the population, which at war's end was a half million, has expanded to nearly four million. The government has resettled more than a million in apartment houses, eight, nine or ten stories high, with schools atop the roofs.

The Kadoorie brothers had another approach to solving the mass refugee problem. Recalling from their own earlier life in Shanghai what good farmers the Chinese were, their plan was to set up the refugees in villages of the 350-square-mile area of the New Territories, stretching twenty-two miles from Kowloon to the Chinese border, which were leased from China by the British Colony in 1899 for a term of ninety-nine years. The Kadoories devised an agricultural project with a quick turnover which would speedily transform refugees into self-supporting people. The refugee farmers were given flowers and vegetables, fowl, pigs and pigsties and interest-free loans for feed. Through the Kadoorie Agricultural Assistance Association and the Kadoorie Agricultural Aid Loan Fund Association hundreds of thousands of refugees have been made independent farmers in hundreds of

Hong Kong—Ohel Leah Synagogue; built by the family as a memorial to Leah Elias Sassoon.

villages. Into this project have gone not only Kadoorie millions, but the hearts of the two men. Horace Kadoorie devotes part of each day working at the family experimental farm and being close to the farmers.

In 1962 the Kadoories received the distinguished Magsaysay Award, named for the late Ramon Magsaysay, President of the Philippine Islands, "In recognition of meritorious contributions to the public good in Asia." Before that, in 1960, Allen M. Strook, then Chairman of the Board of the Jewish Theological Seminary of America, in New York, had gone to Hong Kong to personally present the Kadoories with the Solomon Schechter Award of the World Council of Synagogues (Conservative Movement) in testimony of the fact that:

Strong in their faith in God and loyal to the teachings of His prophets, the Kadoorie brothers have throughout their distinguished careers loved righteousness and championed human freedom and opportunity.

Rising from strength to strength, their commitments to the welfare of mankind have sanctified the name of God and have been a source of blessings to the world and an inspiration to free men everywhere.

Remnants of the early Sephardi families in Hong Kong remain, all with large financial interests—Ellis Joseph Hayim, C.B.E., born in Baghdad and educated in Bombay; Charles David Silas, director at one time of E.D. Sassoon & Co.; Denzil Marcus Ezra, who in addition to his connection with the E.D. Sassoon & Co., was co-owner of the China Press.

To these Sephardi families have been added Russian Jews whom war had swept across Asia into Shanghai before they found a resting spot in Hong Kong. More recently a new element has been coming, one not interested in sinking its roots here. These are people who see the Colony as a place where one can make money fast, and then return home, wherever that is. For Hong Kong's success story is based on its being a free port, where taxes are low and there are no controls, where there is no lack of cheap labor working round the clock in small sweatshops making the garments, the sweaters, the textiles, the plastics or whatever else the world will buy. China was encouraging exports of many things prized by the Western world, for in this way she could get foreign currency. You learned not to ask too much about a man's business. Most of the Jews in Hong Kong now are Ashkenazim from various countries.

It was with this community that I observed Rosh Hashanah 5722, corresponding to the year 1961. For a while it looked as if I wouldn't be able to get to the synagogue, for a September typhoon had blown in the previous day and all ferry crossings had been canceled. But the winds subsided and I reached 70 Robinson Road and its synagogue, a large structure with two pagoda-like turrets, named the Ohel Leah Synagogue.

Built as a memorial in 1901 to Leah Elias Sassoon by the

family, it has a marble floor with a simple Ark and the bimah in the center. Iraqi Haham Eleazar had just retired after thirty years' service and his place was being taken by Rabbi Joseph Adler, a native Britisher who had spent twenty-five years in Australia. His blistering sermon that Rosh Hashanah eve took the congregation to task for not contributing in larger measure to charitable causes and for their irregular attendance at Sabbath service.

Morning services were scheduled for eight o'clock. I was there—but the required ten men were not. At last a minyan was completed, but the congregation numbered far fewer than the previous evening. Many men were already back at business.

My feeling that Jewish life in Hong Kong is a temporary affair was confirmed in the conversation of the women sitting in the gallery during the hour-long repetition of the Eighteenfold Benediction by the Reader, and the rest of the lengthy service. Families came to Hong Kong, stayed for a while and left. There was a coming and a going, the children being sent abroad for their education. The only real expression of Jewish interest was in the annual appeal for the United Israel Fund, and the women's activities benefiting the Youth Aliyah program.

This coming and going extended itself also to the leadership, for the year following my visit in Hong Kong, Rabbi Adler had moved on to a new flock in Tokyo. Retired American Reform Rabbi Ferdinand Isserman, vacationing in Hong Kong, was induced to take over the leadership of Ohel Leah Synagogue. He carried on for a short period of eight months in 1963.

The question now is—is there a future for the rootless community in this Isle of Fragrant Waters?

❧ AMID BUDDHIST TEMPLES IN BANGKOK ❦

Bangkok, city of four hundred temples rising heavenward in a Chinese-influenced architecture; Bangkok, city of saffron-garbed and shaven-headed monks, casts a spell over the visitor. Far from the rush of the marketplace and the stir of the city, large areas are set aside for these monks who live in quiet seclusion, devoting their days to religious study in veritable Thai "yeshivot."

In a country where 90 percent of the population is Buddhist, every man—no matter what his social status—must spend some period of his life as a monk. During this time he may do no outside work for livelihood, nor may he ask for alms. But he may receive donations.

So every morning these distinctively dressed monks go out into the city carrying their begging bowls. And the Thais, feeling that they are storing up merit in heaven for themselves by the giving of alms, stand ready on the sidewalks with large pots of boiled rice waiting for the monks to come by so that they may be privileged to fill the begging bowls.

Despite its charm, Bangkok homes are very plain, of unpainted wood. Why bother painting the wood? I was told. The heat will soon make it peel anyway. But its people are enchanting. Small-boned and delicate of form, they are very friendly.

I stood one day in front of a Thai sidewalk food stand. A batter of papaya paste was dropped in small pancake size on a griddle over a charcoal fire. When baked, the pancake was filled with coconut or shrimp and folded over in half, ready to be popped into one's mouth. I watched as a young woman paid one tical (five cents) for a serving, consisting of three of these delicacies. Immediately she offered part of her serving to me, a stranger in town.

Amidst Bangkok's population of two million live a handful of Jewish families, some Sephardi and some Ashkenazi. These permanent residents are far outnumbered by Jewish transients, serving a tour of duty with either the United States or Israeli embassies or agencies of these governments, or as technical experts. But whoever they are, or wherever they come from, the Jews in Bangkok pray together as a unit.

On my first visit to Bangkok, in 1961, I spent Yom Kippur there. Services were held then at the home of Aleppo-born Isaac Djemal. In the large home were decorative pieces such as Chinese ivories, Indonesian and Russian woodcarvings, Japanese coral and Siamese figures. Mrs. Djemal's own paintings graced the walls. The Sephardi ritual was followed in the service, except for the Kol Nidre, which was chanted in a quavering voice by Odessa-born Henry Gerson, who settled here half a century ago.

After Neilah (the closing prayer of Yom Kippur) all of us—residents, transients and tourists—broke fast together on the terrace of the Djemal home, overlooking a garden with hibiscus, bougainvillea, mango and coconut-palm trees. On the menu that evening was banana shtrudel (apples do not grow in that tropical climate).

In preceding years, services had been held at the home of ophthalmologist Dr. Fritz Jacobsohn. Leaving Germany, Dr. and Mrs. Jacobsohn had wandered through Ethiopia, Israel, India and Burma before settling in Bangkok. Their first home was commandeered by the Japanese in World War II. Their second home was an old Thai wooden structure rented from the King of Thailand, which they had filled with Chinese rugs and porcelains, sculpture and brass. But the Jacobsohns are no longer in Bangkok. Again they have moved on, this time to America.

Lately there has been yet another change in the locale of the services. This time, hopefully, it will be a permanent one. Mrs. Alisabeth Zerner, only Bangkok-born adult of the group, donated a building for use as a Jewish Community Center, and services are now being held there.

The Jewish Association of Thailand, including all Jews—Sephardi, European Ashkenazi, American and Israeli—plans monthly cultural and social activities, classes for the children in Hebrew language and history, and a library. Event of the year is the festive Communal Seder in which the American servicemen, residents and Israelis participate. Supplies of matzoh, wine and gefillte fish are flown in from Okinawa for the servicemen, and the rest of the meal is provided by the local people.

Presidency of the Jewish Association shuttles back and forth between Sephardi Isaac Djemal and Ashkenazi Henry Gerson, who also headed the local Rotary. When Mr. Gerson became a citizen of Thailand, he was directed to assume a Thai name, the standard procedure for all naturalized citizens. In his case, however, the government settled for a change only in his first name, so now it's Thai citizen Haim Gerson!

Honorary Secretary of the Association in 1966 was American Freda Lyman who had also succumbed to the lure of Bangkok. Transferring from Washington, she and her husband took over a

Saffron-robed and head-shaven monk in Buddhist temple precinct in Bangkok, one of the city's 400 Buddhist temples.

large law office on Suringwonse Road. Another permanent resident is former New Yorker Robert Golden, also a lawyer and author of a Thai-English dictionary.

In Bangkok, as in other small Jewish communities scattered around Asia, it was the Sephardim who were most punctilious in the observance of traditional Jewish rituals. Elie Chouweke had come from Beirut to work with his brother-in-law Isaac Djemal in the export and import trade. A problem faced Elie Chouweke and his wife when their son Jacob was born. There was no mohel in Bangkok to perform the rite of circumcision. Mr. Chouweke contacted Bombay, Calcutta and Hong Kong with no success. The Chouwekes would not hear of a physician carrying out the prescribed rite. They decided to take their son to Beirut for the circumcision. When the infant was ten days old, he was finger-printed and photographed for the necessary passport documents. An official asked, "Why not perform the ritual here? There are Moslems who can officiate." But the Chouwekes would hear of nothing but a mohel. When the baby was twenty-five days old, the parents took the infant on a direct flight from Bangkok on the South China coast across the continent to Beirut on the Mediterranean coast of Asia. There, in true traditional fashion, the Brit Milah and the Pidyon Haben were celebrated. After that, the family flew back to Bangkok.

And it was Selim Eubbani, a Sephardi, who imported kosher meat from the United States, almost half-way around the world. It was he, too, who prepared the boys for their Bar Mitzvah ritual. Should the boy be of an Ashkenazi family, Selim Eubbani considerately used records with an Ashkenazi chant for the purpose. Small wonder that Mr. Eubbani was known as the Honorary Rabbi of Bangkok.

Native-born Alisabeth Zerner personified a union of Orient and Occident. Using Yiddish expressions, Mrs. Zerner told me the story of her family, a tale which sounded like a Jewish United Nations epic in itself. Her mother, a Russian Jewess who was living in France, and her father who was a Romanian Jew, met in Colombo on the island of Ceylon. Her father was on a business trip at the time (gems were his line of business). Her mother had gone there on a visit. They were married in Singapore and came back to her father's base in Bangkok. Here the daughter was born and educated in a convent school.

Later a young Dutch Jew, born in Java, who was also "in gems" called on Alisabeth's father when passing through Bangkok. And so the young people met and were married. In spite of a lifetime in Bangkok and a convent upbringing, Alisabeth Zerner, now a widow, still enjoys borscht, kreplach and gefillte fish.

With a Jewish Center and classes for the youth, and with the active encouragement of an Israeli Ambassador who looked upon the "keeping alive of Jewishness" as one of his main purposes in Bangkok, I found renewed hope for the continuance of Jewish life amid Buddhist temples in this exotic corner of the world.

ৰঙ্গ TEMPLE BELLS OF BURMA ৪ঃ

If you've heard the east a-callin', why you won't
'eed nothin' else
No! you won't 'eed nothin' else

But them spicy smells
And the sunshine and the palm trees and the tinkly
temple bells
On the road to Mandalay

For the temple bells are callin' and it's there that I
would be
By the old Moulmein pagoda, looking lazy at the
sea

On the road to Mandalay
Where the old Flotilla lay
. . .
Oh, the road to Mandalay
Where the flyin' fishes play
An' the dawn comes up like thunder
outer China 'crost the Bay!

Thus sang England's Rudyard Kipling of Burma, tucked away in southeast Asia—with China to the north, Thailand to the east and the Bay of Bengal on the west. The "tinkly temple bells" are heard not only in Mandalay, but throughout this country where one stores up one's merit in heaven by building a pagoda. In Rangoon, 300 miles south of Mandalay, the temple bells of Shwe Dagon Pagoda, Burma's largest shrine, can be heard.

From an eminence 168 feet above street level, one goes barefoot up hundreds of steps flanked on either side by stalls selling votive candles, incense sticks and flowers to a marble-paved platform. Here, encircled by miniature pagodas, Shwe Dagon rises from a base 1,335 feet in circumference and tapers in the form of a cone to its summit 368 feet higher up.

Covered with gold leaf from base to summit, Shwe Dagon's spire is topped by a diamond lotus bud ten inches in diameter and crowned with an umbrella of gold on whose rings hang gold and silver jeweled bells which tinkle with every passing breeze.

Jewels are so much a part of dress in this country that when a servant girl enters employment in a home she is presented with a gold chain or wrist bangle. Burma, land of star sapphires and emeralds, is also known for its rubies. Mogok, north of Mandalay in a high valley surrounded by jungle-covered hills, has been the home of the ruby since time immemorial. Set in an area troubled by armed robbers and bandits, most of Mogok's ten thousand inhabitants are engaged in the mining, cutting, polishing or selling of rubies, said by the Burmese to be made from the "fire and blood of the earth itself," and regarded by them as the very pinnacle in the hierarchy of jewels.

Among Mogok's fifteen hundred traders in rubies has been the Jew Julius, with whom French writer Joseph Kessel lived for some time. Born of a Russian Jewish Orthodox family, and wanted by the police for his activity in a secret revolutionary socialist group, sixteen-year-old Julius escaped to Istanbul, where he became errand boy to a pearl and diamond broker.

Restless, he moved on to Lebanon, to Palestine (where he worked as a halutz on the land) and to Bombay when that city was the big pearl market. After World War I he traveled for a jewelry firm to Ceylon, Calcutta, Indonesia, Bangkok, Shanghai, Hong Kong, finally making his base in Mogok. In the simple Burmese hut which was his home, the living room was equipped with apparatus necessary for weighing and evaluating the precious ruby.

One advantage Julius held over the hundreds of other traders of precious gems in Mogok was the fact that he could make notations on the tiny packets holding the valuable stones in a language unknown to the others—that language being Hebrew.

Returning southward to Rangoon from Mogok on the once-a-week flight, one comes down for a halt at Mandalay, home of ancient Burmese kings, where today only a cemetery recalls the memory of a once-thriving community of Jewish pioneers. Further south in this country, almost equal in size to the state of Texas, one comes to the area where two million Karens live—the second most important tribal minority group within the country.

Considered by some to belong to the Lost Ten Tribes of Israel, their origin is obscure. The Karens are believed to have come to Burma with a Thai-Chinese wave of immigration in the sixth or seventh century. They have lighter skin than the Burmese; they are clannish, marry within their own tribe, and they have a great love of learning. Their religion is a mixture of animism (worshiping the spirits within nature), Buddhism, and most recently a layer of Christianity.

The Karens believe in the Eternal God Y'wa (some scholars believing Y'wa to be the Jewish Yaweh or Jehovah) who gave them *The Book,* later lost through their own unbelief, and which according to their tradition, will be restored to them by white men coming across the sea—hence their easy acceptance of the faith brought by the American Baptist missionaries. In their oral tradition are found stories of the creation, of the fall of man through eating forbidden fruit, stories of a flood and of the division of people at Babel. Their poetry employs the device of pairs of parallel lines with each thought being repeated—a technique characteristic of Biblical poetry.

The real center of modern Burmese Jewry is in the capital city of Rangoon, with its Buddhist Holy of Holies the Shwe Dagon Pagoda; Rangoon with its British colonial-type buildings now streaked with black as a result of rain and humidity; Rangoon, where both men and women wear the longyi, an ankle-length skirt folded over in front or to the side, topped by a short jacket for the men or by a white transparent muslin blouse sporting diamond buttons (on special occasions) for the women.

Center of all cultural and religious life within the community is the Musmeah Yeshuah Synagogue, maintained by the income from a number of shops and buildings in which synagogue funds have been invested.

Among the early Jews in Rangoon were the Indian merchant, Solomon Gabirol, who was in charge of the army commissariat for one of the Burmese kings, and Galician Shlomo Reichman, who came here with the British army in 1852 and stayed on after the war. The core of Rangoon's Jewish community was the group that came from Baghdad in the 1870s for trading purposes. As in other places, the Baghdadis soon became tri-lingual, speaking Arabic among themselves, Burmese to the natives and English to the Europeans in their shops.

Following the British annexation of Burma as a province of India in 1885, Bene Israel from India proper began coming to this province. The Bene Israel had made their home in India for many centuries. Brown-skinned and speaking the Indian Marathi tongue, they were fine-featured, dark-eyed and dark-haired. The lighter-skinned Baghdadis were condescending toward these darker-skinned co-religionists.

Rangoon Jewry was marked by disagreements, bickering, dissensions and by a whole series of suits between rival factions of synagogue trustees in the 1920s. Of a larger dimension, however, was one particular case of litigation—Civil Regular Suit No. 85 of 1934 in the High Court at Rangoon. Plaintiffs in this case were J. M. Ezekiel and another member of the Bene Israel; defendants were C. S. Joseph and other trustees of the Musmeah Yeshuah Synagogue.

What led to this exceptional suit was that in the 1926 election of synagogue trustees the Bene Israel were excluded from the list of those eligible to run for office. Again in 1929, the Bene Israel were barred. Before the next election, scheduled for 1934, the Bene Israel asked to be included in the list. This time the trustees not only refused the request, but in addition struck off all Bene Israel names from the list of voters. The suit followed.

In his judgment delivered April 9th, 1935, Justice Mr. Leach said:

> . . . The plaintiffs are suing for a declaration that they and the Bene Israel generally are eligible for election to the Board of Trustees of the synagogue and are entitled to vote at such elections. . . . The plaintiffs claim that the Bene Israel are members of the Jewish faith and community. . . . The defendants deny the validity of this claim and say that the Bene Israel are not of the Jewish faith or community . . . because they do not observe the Mosaic law with regard to divorce, yibbum and halitzah. (The marriage of a man to the widow of his deceased brother who has died childless is known as yibbum. The procedure which follows the refusal of the surviving brother to marry his sister-in-law is known as halitzah and when it is carried out it has the effect of setting the widow free to marry again according to her own choice.)

Justice Leach continued:

> *The plaintiffs maintain that the Bene Israel are*
> *orthodox in all respects. It is admitted by the de-*
> *fendants that the modern Jew refuses to marry his*
> *brother's widow and openly disobeys the Mosaic*
> *law in this respect . . . and the halitzah ceremony*
> *has been modified . . . and consequently it cannot*
> *be said that failure on the part of the Bene Israel*
> *to observe this law would make them unorthodox.*
> *There is no doubt that the Bene Israel in Burma*
> *have for many years been looked down upon by*
> *other Jews in the Province. The attitude of the*
> *General body of Jews in Rangoon to the Bene Is-*
> *rael may be gathered from the fact that the latter*
> *have not been allowed to take any prominent part*
> *in services in the Musmeah Yeshuah Synagogue.*

This last is a reference to yet another matter in which the Bene Israel were not treated as equals—the matter of synagogue honors. The Bene Israel were not called up for aliyot to the regular seven portions of the weekly reading from the Torah. In 1913 synagogue rules had reiterated "the old custom" of not calling the Bene Israel to the Torah except for "extra readings not regarded as an essential part of the service."

During the course of the trial it became clear that the trustees were ready to allow full rights to the Bene Israel if the latter would give "an undertaking in writing" that they would follow Jewish law in regard to divorce, yibbum and halitzah. This the Bene Israel refused to do on the ground that it was a reflection on their faith and observance.

Justice Leach said further:

> *The evidence convinces me that there is no differ-*
> *ence in the observance of these laws so far as the*
> *Bene Israel in the Province are concerned. . . . The*
> *two plaintiffs are supported by Mr. A. J. Cohen*
> *and Mr. J. E. Joshua, both of whom are uncon-*
> *nected with the Bene Israel. On the other hand*
> *there is no evidence worthy of the name in con-*
> *tradiction. Moreover, defendant 1, who is one of*

*the most prominent Jews in Burma, made it quite
clear that it is merely a matter of belief that the
Bene Israel do not observe the laws referred to.*

Finally Justice Leach ruled:

*There will be a declaration that the plaintiffs and
other Jews called Bene Israel are eligible for appointment as trustees of the Musmeah Yeshuah
Synagogue and are entitled to vote at elections of
trustees. . . . Defendants are not entitled to exclude
from the lists [of those eligible for election to the
office of trustee, and of those entitled to vote at
election of trustees] a Jew merely because he is a
Bene Israel. I consider that the costs of this case
should come out of the [Synagogue] Trust Fund.
Order accordingly.*

At the time of this suit the Jewish community had grown to
1,300 souls, and by 1940 it was at its zenith with 1,500 people.
Then came the Japanese invasion. Burma became a World War II
battleground, its cities bombed and battered. Most of the Jews
fled to India, where they were assisted by the Indian Jews. At
war's end only a few hundred returned to Burma to pick up life
once again.

After a period of upheaval an independent state of Burma was
proclaimed on January 4, 1948—the day and the very hour of the
day being set as most favorable by the country's astrologers. The
new state's foreign policy was announced to be neutralism, a term
interpreted as aloofness toward the West and the signing of a
treaty of friendship with Communist China.

In 1962 gentle U Nu, Premier of the new state, was ousted and
imprisoned in a *coup d'état* staged by General Ne Win, Defense
Minister and Commander of the Armed Forces. Ne Win introduced an authoritarian one-party political system and the
much-vaunted Burmese Way to Socialism. Under the concepts of
this way of life all business which before independence had been
in foreign hands—British, Indian, Chinese or Jewish—was nationalized.

Burma Unilever Company became the People's Soap Factory No. 1, stores became People's Stores, banks became People's Banks. Retail stores, down to the small neighborhood shops, were expropriated and nationalized; many of the owners never received any compensation and some individual owners were deported.

A spirit of xenophobia, a fear of and antagonism toward anything foreign, swept the country. Tourists had to show tickets for onward passage—and even at that were limited, until 1969, to a twenty-four-hour stay in the country.

In such an atmosphere life became difficult for the Jews who were merchants and traders. By 1960 there were only eighty-seven Jews in all of Burma.

It was at the season of Sukkot in 1961, before Ne Win came to power, that I visited with the remnant of Burma's Jewry in Rangoon. From the almost-deserted Hotel Strand—a vestigial remain of British colonialism, with its lazily whirring ceiling fans and British-style food—I walked to the Musmeah Yeshuah Synagogue. Within the large impressive building, marble-floored and with memorial lamps suspended from the carved ceiling, assembled a total of nineteen worshippers, including Israeli diplomatic representatives and children. No local women being present, it was suggested that I sit at the side of the main sanctuary rather than alone in the large, empty women's gallery.

At the conclusion of the service I joined the men in the simple undecorated sukkah which had been raised between the synagogue front and the sidewalk, for the kiddush and the blessing and breaking of bread.

This fragment was the remainder of a community that had once played a respected role in the general civic life; for Jews had held office as magistrates, municipal councillors, commissioners and even sheriff of Rangoon. Yehuda Ezekiel Street honors the memory of a Jew who was Mayor of the city.

Though far removed geographically from the main centers of Jewry, the Burmese community had maintained links with Jewish life elsewhere. The *Jewish Chronicle* of September 21, 1888, reported:

> *The new Jewish congregation at Mandalay has*
> *given evidence of its existence in a manner com-*
> *mon in the East. Learning that there was in Cal-*
> *cutta a messenger from Aleppo who was collecting*
> *funds in aid of the Talmud Torah schools in his*
> *town, the Mandalay congregation sent a contribu-*
> *tion for this object.*

And Rangoon was on the route for Zionist fund raising around the world. In telling of his mission in Rangoon for that purpose in 1925, Israel Cohen described local leader Meyer Meyer's magnificent home with its complement of thirty-six Burmese servants.

To mark the Declaration of the State of Israel a meeting was held at the synagogue on May 22, 1948, presided over by yet another Meyer—Nissim Meyer.

Since then Israelis have come to Burma as experts and advisers in the fields of agriculture, building and medicine. U Nu visited Israel; Ben Gurion spent some time in Burma; and the late Israeli President Ben Zvi made a state visit to Burma. During the course of this visit Mrs. Ben Zvi was photographed together with a Karen singer. Other pictures show U Nu in company with David Hacohen, first Israeli Ambassador to Burma, both in the national costume of the country.

Gone are the days of dissension and factions within the Rangoon Jewish community. Now Jews cling together, with the Meyer and Davis families at the head of whatever remains of Jewish life among the pagodas, the saffron-robed monks and the tinkling temple bells of Burma.

· 6 ·
INDIA

✑ CALCUTTA'S SIMHAT TORAH BEAUTY QUEEN ও৵

THE DRIVE FROM DUM DUM AIRPORT TO INDIA'S SPRAWLING
metropolis of Calcutta was an introduction to the sights and
smells of India. It was evening, but there was no escaping the
heat. Rows of tiny shops, dimly lit by kerosene lamps, lined the
way. Sidewalks and streets teemed with people, the men in once
white *dhotis,* most of them barefoot. Cows stepped with a slow,
seemingly supercilious air, as if they knew they were sacred and
that automobile traffic would have to adjust to their gait.

Morning brought into view people making their ablutions and
brushing their teeth at sidewalk spigots. There simply was not
sufficient housing to accommodate the vast multitudes who were
swarming into the city seeking a better lot than had been theirs in
their home villages or the Hindu refugees pouring in from Moslem East Pakistan.

A walk through this city of six million on the Hoogly River,
near the Bay of Bengal, calls to mind that until 1911 Calcutta was
the capital of British India. At one end of the two-mile-long
Maidan (Park) is Government House, where the Viceroy of India

had once lived; there is the white marble Victoria Memorial and Fort William, originally built to protect the trading post set up here by the British East India Company at the close of the seventeenth century. The names of Robert Clive and Warren Hastings are bound up with the history of Calcutta. Chowring-hee, an avenue facing the Maidan, once a row of stately Victorian mansions, is now the focus of hotels, fine shops and restaurants.

Stepping out of my hotel, the Great Eastern—which the guide-books list as a luxury hotel—I walked, that first evening, directly into the midst of a mass of people already settled down for the night on the pavement stones fronting the hotel. Intermingled with the people were cows which had also chosen the environs of the Great Eastern Hotel for their night's rest. I beat a hasty retreat indoors.

Another night, however, I did go out—for kiddush in the sukkah of a Jewish family. Kiddush, in true Oriental Sephardi fashion, turned out to be dinner. The home was an apartment chosen because its open terrace lent itself to the making of a sukkah. Braided palm leaves were used for walls and roof of the sukkah. Multicolored balls, lights and flowers were strung along one side, half open to the street. A hanging lamp with seven glass containers for oil held the customary holiday lights.

In one corner was a lectern on which an open Bible had been placed. According to tradition, a very special "worthy guest" is welcomed to the family feast. On the first night it is the patriarch Abraham who is the worthy guest, the second night Isaac, the third night Jacob; then in turn Moses, Aaron, Joseph and David. Each night the Bible is opened to a selection bearing on the life of the "worthy guest" of that evening.

The silk hallah cloth was embroidered with the words "L'Shonim Rabbot," wishing one many years. To the wine in the kiddush cup some water was added, my host told me, "So that the words of the 23rd Psalm 'my cup runneth over' might be ful-filled." On the menu that evening in Calcutta was roast chicken. As the old skilled shohet had died and the new one was not sufficiently trained for the ritual slaughter of mutton (the govern-ment forbids the importation of beef) the observant Jews of Calcutta were limited to the use of chicken. Custard apples and a drink made of cut beets and lime juice closed the meal.

After the recitation of Grace After Meals, the children kissed the hands of mother and father. Then the father, placing his hand on the child's head, blessed and kissed each one.

My host in that sukkah was a sixth-generation member of a family that had come from Baghdad. Most of the Jews in Calcutta trace their ancestry to Baghdad or Syria. The very first Jew to settle in Calcutta was Aleppo-born Shalom ben Aharon Obadiah Cohen who came by way of Baghdad in the first decade of the nineteenth century. A jeweler by profession, he went into partnership with Saleh Semah in the import and export business, trading with Bombay and Baghdad in silks and indigo.

An inveterate traveler, Shalom Cohen moved on to the Punjab, in northern India, where he became court jeweler first to the maharajah and later to the King of Oudh. It was the latter who showed his high regard for this Jew by inviting Shalom Cohen to ride together with him on the monarch's own elephant.

Shalom Cohen's son-in-law was Moses Duek Cohen, of a family that had settled in Aleppo after exile from Spain (the name Duek referring back to the title of Duc held while in Spain). Moses Duek Cohen became the religious leader of the young Calcutta community, serving as honorary minister and mohel.

Ezekiel Musleah, whose grandfather Rabbi Salah ben Yosef Mazliah had been the Nasi or head of the Yeshiva in Baghdad, came to Calcutta as an indigo expert for the British East India Company. Ezekiel Judah, like most of the early prominent settlers of the community, came to trade in indigo, silk and Dacca cloth. Soon they were speaking Bengali with the natives, English with the British government officials and among themselves continued the Arabic with which they had grown up.

Two Baghdadi families that played a preeminent role in the life of the Jewish community were the Ezras and the Sassoons. David Joseph Ezra, first of his family to make his permanent home in Calcutta, also started as an exporter of indigo and silk to Baghdad and Aleppo. Then he branched out into the export of opium to Hong Kong and was the agent for merchants and ships from Muscat and Zanzibar. Later he began investing in real estate and became the city's largest property owner.

The Sassoons, with headquarters in Bombay, established a branch in Calcutta, and following family tradition a member of the Sassoon family assumed control of this branch. The Ezras and Sassoons intermarried. Most frequently it was a daughter of the house of Sassoon who was united in marriage with a son of the Ezra family, so that it is the name Ezra that remains conspicuous in Calcutta for outstanding devotion in all fields of social welfare.

Hailing as it did from Baghdad and Syria, the Jewish community was traditionally orthodox in its way of life:

> *On Monday the 25th of Elul 5585 since the creation of the world by our calculation here in the city of Calcutta situated on the river Ganges which flows into the ocean, which corresponds to the English date of 29th of August 1825. We the undersigned, have taken upon ourselves, our future generations and all those connected with us, a procedure for all times, to appoint an officer and manager of the affairs of the Synagogue existing in the city of Calcutta.*

Thus began the constitution of the first synagogue in Calcutta—Neve Shalom.

Twenty-five years later the Beth El Synagogue, founded by David Joseph Ezra and Ezekiel Judah, rose on Pollock Street, then in the heart of Calcutta Jewry. Matzoh was baked in this synagogue compound; ritual wine was manufactured in the godowns (warehouses) attached to the synagogue and a ritual bath was constructed on the grounds.

Sometime later a Prayer Hall was started on Blackburn's Lane at the home of Haham Shelomo Abid Twena. A distinguished scholar, he was brought from the Yeshiva at Baghdad to act as shohet and dayan. In a dispute with synagogue authorities over the two-hour-long sermons he was wont to deliver in Arabic, he started services in his own home which soon attracted a loyal following of young and old. Before the Sabbath afternoon prayers he would expound the Talmud for two hours.

To earn a living he sold religious articles, taught Hebrew to the children and was a shohet. Of Haham Shelomo it was said:

> *His poverty-stricken home was situated in the poorest section of the city. His impoverished demeanour stood in bold relief against his spiritual*

*opulence and gigantic mental capacities. For sel-
dom has anyone been so impecunious and seldom
at the same time so affluent in the Torah.*

Largest and most imposing synagogue in the city is the Maghen
David, a red-brick structure with a 142-foot-high steeple, in
whose base is a clock imported from London. Its lofty columns
topped by floral designs, the arches above these columns and the
stained-glass windows make a most impressive interior. Built by
Elias David Joseph Ezra as a memorial to his father David Joseph
Ezra, it was erected on land adjoining the old Neve Shalom
Synagogue, on which there had been a number of shops. To make
up for the loss of rental income from these shops, Mr. Ezra set up
a trust fund for the benefit of the Neve Shalom Synagogue.

With great ceremony the new Maghen David Synagogue was
dedicated in 1884. The Torahs were carried from the old synagogue and up to the entrance of the new one where the leader
called out, "Open to me the gates of righteousness, I will enter
into them, I will give thanks unto the Lord" (Psalm 118:19). From
within came the chant, "This is the gate of the Lord, the righteous
shall enter into it" (Psalm 118:20) and the doors of the new place
of worship were formally opened.

Ten years later a set of rules was adopted. Rule No. 10 referred
to seats (pews were not sold, instead they were claimed by usage):

> *If any seat holder of this synagogue shall leave
> this city or shall attend other synagogues for one
> month—he loses the right over his seat.*

And Rule No. 13, on discipline, said:

> *No one shall audibly felicitate congregants in any
> way such as the Arabic-speaking Jews who con-
> gratulate brides etc. with a shrill outcry. No one
> shall throw sweets and flowers in the Synagogue at
> any time. . . . Confetti of any sort of paper, or of
> sweets shall not be brought to the Synagogue. Dur-
> ing the feasts of Purim the use of fireworks in the
> Synagogue and the producing of any sound from
> any kind of instrument even in the compound of
> the Synagogue are forbidden. . . .*

Despite Rule No. 13, however, I found that the custom of "audible felicitations" was still in vogue in the 1960s.

Minister of the Maghen David for well over half a century was the Reverend Elias Moses Duek Cohen—affectionately known as E.M.D.—and the grandson of the Moses Duek Cohen who had been honorary minister of the community. Modest, progressive and zealous in his work, E.M.D. was the guiding spirit not only in the synagogue, but in the life of the entire Jewish community and in the life of Calcutta as a whole.

At that time Jewish children were educated in Christian schools. When it became evident that these schools were undermining the faith of the children and one Jewish girl was ready to convert to Christianity, Reverend Cohen issued a call for the erection of a Jewish school that would provide general education combined with study of Hebrew language and religion. In 1881 the Jewish Girls' and Infants' School was opened. At first a primary school to which boys were also admitted, it developed into one of the best secondary schools in Bengal, boys attending only in the early grades. Throughout his life, Reverend Cohen remained the "life and soul" of this institution, now known as the Jewish Girls' School.

For eleven years Reverend Cohen published *Paerah,* a popular weekly Jewish gazette that became known the world over.

Court cases between Jews and non-Jews were referred to him for arbitration and his decisions were always accepted. The first Jew to be elected municipal councillor, he held that post for over twenty years. When British royalty visited Calcutta, Reverend Cohen was in the welcoming party, greeting the Prince of Wales, now the Duke of Windsor, and King George V.

Reverend Cohen died on a Friday night, January 14, 1927. The obsequies were reported by D. S. Sassoon in the *Jewish Chronicle* issued February 11th of that year:

> The funeral was timed for Saturday evening . . .
> and started at nine o'clock. The whole community
> followed the bier which was carried all the way
> from the house to the cemetery. Six torches were
> carried on either side of the bier along the route . . . .
> He was removed to his last resting place in the

cemetery at Sura (a suburb of Calcutta). We returned about 2:00 o'clock in the morning from this
most impressive funeral.

It was to the Maghen David Synagogue that I went that Simhat
Torah Eve of 1961, accompanied by its minister of a more recent
era—Rabbi Ezekiel Musleah, sixth-generation descendant of that
Ezekiel Musleah who had come from Baghdad to Calcutta as an
indigo expert for the British East India Company. Twentieth-
century Ezekiel Musleah also had traveled—from Calcutta to
New York, where he received his rabbinical training and ordination at the Jewish Theological Seminary of America.

A thrilling sight met my eyes as I entered the synagogue that
evening. Ranged across the wide pulpit were the Scrolls of the
Law, about fifty in number, each one encased in silver—
altogether a glittering, gleaming display.

The mantles in which the scrolls were usually enveloped had
been removed and were hung in tiers on the columns or suspended from the women's gallery. Their silks and satins and
velvets, multicolored and richly embroidered or textured, made a
breathtaking scene that made me think of jousting fields when
knighthood was in vogue. But the only armor these twentieth-
century "knights" had were their embroidered velvet yarmulkes
and the scrolls they carried in glad procession, an honor won by
auction held in the Arabic tongue.

For this special occasion women were permitted on the main
floor of the synagogue. All were in holiday finery, most in saris,
making a colorful sight as they moved about gracefully. One of
the women, her dark brown skin set off by a blue silk sari over a
gold lamé blouse, made a particularly enchanting picture.

"Make a wish and kiss the Torah. Then your wish will come
true," the women advised me. There was a constant surge of
women and children to the pulpit all through the course of the
seven circuits. Starting at one end of the pulpit, they advanced
from scroll to scroll—kissing each in turn—proceeding rhythmi-
cally until they reached the far end of the pulpit. I was mesmer-
ized into feeling that I was watching the movement of a Greek
chorus emphasizing the action of a dramatic play.

But I was quickly brought back to reality by the sight of the

*Author embracing Queen of Beauty chosen at Sim-
hat Torah Ball in Calcutta, just after crowning
Sheila Joshua the Queen of the 1961 ball.*

rickshaws, lined up and waiting for patrons as I left the Maghen
David Synagogue at the conclusion of the service.

Holiday festivities closed with the choice of a Queen of Beauty
at the annual Simhat Torah Ball held at the Judean Club. Two
portraits ornamented the clubrooms—one of Theodor Herzl, the
other of Lady Rachel Ezra. Of the house of Sassoon by birth, she
had married Sir David Ezra and gave of herself and of her wealth
to every community need, both Jewish and non-Jewish. People
still spoke of her as "our fairy godmother."

"Every Queen of Beauty has been married in the year following
her selection," said Ezra Nissim, president of the Judean Club, as
he asked me to join the judges for this important event limited to
unmarried young women. Our choice, a unanimous one, was
lovely seventeen-year-old hairdresser Sheila Joshua. Shining-
eyed, winsome, tall Sheila had to bend her head so that I could
crown her Queen of Beauty.

But over the joyous occasion hung an air of poignancy, of
melancholy. The line-up of participants for the procession from

which a Queen of Beauty is chosen was becoming smaller and smaller with each passing year, an indication of what was happening in Calcutta. In 1945 there had been 4,000 Jews there. In the early 1960s only a thousand remained. "A hundred leave each year," said Rabbi Musleah. "They look for a better life in England, in Israel, in America or in Australia." Since then Rabbi Musleah himself has left Calcutta for the United States.

Of those who remain, the majority are destitute, 60 percent of them depending upon a dole they receive from Trust Funds set up by the Ezra family. "People living in the Bengali heat are lethargic and they're lazy," say other Indians. I am no judge. But in November 1948, the *Shema* (publication of Calcutta Jewry) reported that when an attempt had been made to open a center for teaching handicrafts to needy Jews, only one applicant reported to the center, the rest "preferring the dole."

As far as Jewish education is concerned, "It isn't fashionable any more to send your children to the Jewish Girls' School," said Rahma Luddy, devoted headmistress of the school for over thirty years. Succeeded by a Hindu as principal of this institution, Rahma Luddy carries on as a volunteer bringing Jewish awareness to a small group of children.

Go to Calcutta during Sukkot season, but go soon, while there still is a Jewish community there.

⊷§ JEWTOWN, COCHIN ℞⊷

In the land of the pepper tree, in the land of ginger and cardamon, where waving coconut palms fringe the shore and Chinese fishing nets bring in the wealth of the seas, lies Cochin—"Queen of the Arabian Sea"—a Venice of the East near land's end at India's southwestern tip, in the state of Kerala.

Here one is lulled by the beauty of the quiet lagoons, the canals, the calm waters of this safe, landlocked harbor. Small valloms (tiny cargo boats) ply back and forth transporting their wares to the ocean steamers moored in the deep waters of the harbor second in importance to Bombay on India's western coast.

What had drawn me to captivating Cochin was its Jewtown and its community of Black Jews and White Jews soon to mark the

400th anniversary of the founding of the historic Paradesi Synagogue. From the Malabar Hotel on Willington Island I went by public ferry to Mattancherry, the area where Jewtown and the Paradesi Synagogue are located. As I handed my ticket to the brown-skinned, khaki-uniformed, barefoot ticket collector, he smiled and inquired if I was going to see Jewtown's synagogue. When I asked his name, his proud response was, "Saul—like the name of the first Jewish king."

I arrived in Mattancherry in 1961 and turned down a rickshaw driver in favor of walking through Jewtown. Small shops lined both sides of narrow Jewtown Road. There was the Sorabji Company's Ahura House—a shipping, clearing and forwarding house. Morris & Sons, whose address also is Jewtown, Cochin, were ship chandlers and commission agents. Store-name plates bore the legend "Jewtown" even where Hindus had taken over from previous Jewish owners.

For here the term "Jewtown" carries no overtones of anti-Semitism, no stigma. It is merely a statement of a fact of life. When Jews in the sixteenth century fled Cranganore, fifteen miles to the north, they came to Cochin and asked for asylum. The Rajah responded with a gift of land adjacent to his palace. There Jewtown was built, and there most of Cochin's remaining Jews still live. According to the original understanding, still faithfully adhered to, they pay no taxes on their property.

A "Mudaliar"—Jewish chieftain—with a silver knob topping his wand of office, had jurisdiction in civil and criminal cases and authority to impose fines. The Rajah reserved only the right to try capital offenses. Now the Rajahs are gone and the duties of the Mudaliar, theoretically a member of Cochin's Hallegua family, are no longer practiced.

As I walked along Jewtown Road's shop district there was an air of busyness, of activity, of people coming and going. This was the section where the Black Jews once lived. They were the petty traders, selling eggs, bananas, vegetables. Others were fishermen, oil pressers, carpenters. Here stands the Kadavumbhagam Synagogue, now shuttered, for its former congregants have migrated to Israel. Further north was the community of the Emancipated group, the bookbinders and the clerks.

As I continued north through Jewtown, shops gave way to residences and a greater calm prevailed. Here was the section of Jewtown where the White Jews lived. They were the more affluent ones—the merchants, professionals, government officials. Homes were two-storied with sloping tiled roofs, cream-colored walls and small, barred and shuttered windows. The architecture was a reminder that the Portuguese and the Dutch had once ruled here.

It was a warm November day and doors were open, people sitting on the doorsteps, calling one another or running across the road to visit. There was an intimate feeling. Small wonder, for everyone seemed to be a cousin of one another. Before long I, too, was invited indoors to visit with the Cohens, the Halleguas, the Sassoons.

Wide stairways led from the ground-floor kitchen and servants' quarters to the sparsely furnished living quarters above. Mosquito netting canopied the beds. Chairs were of Dutch-Portuguese design. Large wooden chests had brass handles and trimmings. Window seats, comfortable and wide, overlooked the street.

One of the houses bore the brass name plate "Dr. Blossom Esther Hallegua." Dr. Blossom, as she is fondly called, is a graduate of Madras University and is a gynecologist at the government hospital in nearby Ernakulam. Asked how she was able to combine a professional career with the demands of a family, she replied, "In Cochin we are nearly all one family. Someone is always around to look after the children when I am at the hospital."

The last structure at the north end of Jewtown Road is the Paradesi Synagogue. Only a fence and gate separate it and the rest of Jewtown from the former Rajah's palace grounds, with the Hindu temple a mere thirty yards away. Betel nuts were drying on the compound ground. The synagogue clock tower, a landmark, has dials fronting in different directions. Facing the Rajah's palace the numerals are inscribed in English letters; the side facing the harbor has numerals in the native Malayalam writing; and the front facing Jewtown has Hebrew numerals. Granite steps lead to an antechamber, where an iron safe is affixed to the outer wall of the synagogue for alms contributions.

Forty feet long, the Paradesi Synagogue has two rows of crystal chandeliers and hanging silver lamps. Brass pillars support an upper gallery to which the Scroll of Law, with its golden crown (gift of a Rajah) is brought from the carved Ark for ceremonial reading on Sabbath mornings. Behind this upper gallery and separated from it by lattice work, is the women's balcony. Paradesi worshippers face west toward the holy city of Jerusalem.

A striking feature of the synagogue is the floor made of Chinese tiles in a willow pattern. Many legends have grown about these tiles. One story is that the Rajah imported a large quantity of Chinese tiles to pave his audience hall. Told by Jews that bullocks' blood had been used in the making of the tiles the Rajah became distressed at the indignity done to the sacred Hindu animal and asked the Jews to remove the tiles from his sight. They did—and used them in the synagogue. Another story has it that they were ordered especially for the synagogue. At any rate, the commerce of Cochin was almost entirely in the hands of the Jews at that time, with ships going to Malacca, Singapore and as far as China—and the tiles are Chinese.

Accompanying me on that first visit to the Paradesi Synagogue was the community's leader, Dr. Shabbetai Samuel Koder, of the Indian branch of the well-known Kadoorie family. A graduate of Madras University, having wide commercial interests, Dr. Koder is also a scholar and historian. He was a member of the Cochin Legislative Council for over twenty years and president of every Jewish organization.

From the Holy Ark Dr. Koder brought the community's most prized possession—the "Copper Tablets," historic proof of the existence of a free Jewish principality on India's southwestern coast. Scholars disagree as to the date and the accuracy of the translation from the original Malabar language. But Cochin tradition holds that it was in the fourth century that this charter was given to the Jew Joseph Rabban by the then king and worded:

> *Hail and Prosperity! The following gifts were graciously made by him who had assumed the title of King of Kings, His Majesty Sri Parkaran Iravi Vanmar . . . We have granted to Joseph Rabban the*

*village of Anjuvannam together with seventy-two
proprietary rights, tolls on boats and carts, the revenue and the title of Anjuvannam, the lamp of the
day, a cloth spread in front to walk on, a palan-
quin, a parasole, a vaduga (Telegu) drum, a trum-
pet, a gateway, garland, decoration with festoons,
and so forth. We have granted him the land tax
and weight tax; moreover we have sanctioned with
these Copper Plates that he need not pay the dues
which the inhabitants of the other cities pay the
Royal palace, and that he may enjoy the benefits
which they enjoy. To Joseph Rabban, Prince of the
Anjuvannam and to his descendants, sons and
daughters and his nephews, and to the sons-in-law
who married his daughters in natural succession,
so long as the world and the moon exist, Anjuvannam shall be his hereditary possession. Hail.*

Signed by the king and witnessed by five chiefs, the commander
of the forces and the prime minister, these Copper Tablets became the charter of freedom of the first Jewish principality in the
Diaspora.

But "so long as the world and the moon exist" did not last
forever. Trouble shattered this Eden of Anjuvannam near Cranganore. Dissension broke out between the ruling Jewish prince
and his brother. Intervention of outsiders was sought. By that
time Portuguese traders had come, seeking control of India's
spice trade. With the traders came the Cross and the Inquisition.
Jews were hunted in various places along the western coast. In
Cranganore, homes, property and synagogues were destroyed.
The land was laid waste. The Jews fled Cranganore in 1565 and
came south to Cochin, where the Hindu Rajah took the refugees
under his protection. Jewtown was built, and there Jewtown
remains to this day.

But Jewish history in this area goes further back than the
Anjuvannam Eden. Origins of Jewish settlement on the western
coast of India are lost in antiquity. Some believe it goes back to
the days following the Assyrian and Babylonian captivities of the
First Temple era. Many are said to have found their way to India

when freed. From Persia a wave of immigration is believed to have come down the western coast of India, particularly in the fifth century to Cranganore.

Some say that many thousands came to southwestern India from the island of Majorca, to which their ancestors had been taken captive when the Second Temple was destroyed by Titus.

The apostle St. Thomas, who introduced Christianity to India, arrived in Cranganore in 52 C.E. According to tradition, he was received by a Jewish flute girl and lived in the Jewish quarter. At a marriage feast he sang a Hebrew song in praise of the bride. But it is also said that he baptized forty Jews.

In the following century a Roman merchant ship recorded having found a Jewish colony at Cranganore. And the Talmud mentions a Rabbi Judah, a Hindu convert to Judaism.

Down through the thousand years of the existence of the Anjuvannam Jewish principality, reports of the Jews on the Malabar coast of India drifted back to Europe from travelers, from missionaries, from explorers.

Judah Ha-levi and Abraham Ibn Ezra both visited Shingli (Cranganore). Moses Maimonides, in his "Epistle to the Yemenites," says there are "Jews still further in India." Benjamin of Tudela, also in the twelfth century, wrote in his *Itinerary* of his visit to India:

> The pepper tree grows in this country. Cinnamon, ginger and many other kinds of spices also grow in this country. . . . All the cities and countries inhabited by these people contain only about a hundred Jews who are of black color as well as the other inhabitants. The Jews are good men, observers of the law and possess the Pentateuch, the Prophets and some little knowledge of the Talmud and its decisions.

Abu Ullah Mohammad Ibn Batuta, the greatest Mohammedan traveler of the Middle Ages, described the Malabar Jews in his *Travels in Asia and Africa* in the fourteenth century: "It [Cranganore] is inhabited by Jews who have one of their number as governor." Franciscan missionary Friar Odoric de Porde reported:

*In that land growe the pepper in the Forest that
men clepen [call] Combar, in a forest wel an 18
days journey in length. In the forest ben 2 good
cytees—Flandrina and Zinglantz . . . and Jews in
gret plentee.*

Marco Polo carried news of the presence of Jews in South India
in the thirteenth century. Portuguese explorer Vasco da Gama,
who lies buried in Cochin's St. Francis Church, chronicled that
the first person he met in Calicut on India's western coast was a
Jew. In India Admiral Vasco da Gama met the former European
Jew Gaspar, who was baptized, assumed Admiral da Gama's
name and joined the latter's retinue. When the first Portuguese
Viceroy of India sailed for his post, Gaspar accompanied him as
interpreter. Also on this voyage was a Dr. Pinheiro, bringing a
trunkful of Sifrei Torah rescued from the destroyed synagogues
of Portugal, for possible sale to the Jews of Cochin. It was the
wife of Gaspar, who had remained a loyal Jewess in Cochin, who
arranged for the buying of thirteen scrolls in that year of 1505.

Dutch Commander Jan Huyghen Van Linschoten, who traveled to the East Indies in 1584, reported, "The Jews have built
very fair stone houses and are rich merchants and of the King of
Cochin nearest Counsellors."

The sixteenth and the seventeenth centuries witnessed a see-
saw struggle between the Portuguese and the Dutch for supremacy along India's western coast. The Portuguese swept down
from Cranganore to Cochin, plundering and destroying homes
and damaging the Paradesi Synagogue. When the Dutch appeared the Jews looked upon them as liberators and gave them
"victuals and all other assistance." But again the Portuguese
triumphed and again the Jews suffered at their hands. The Dutch
launched another attack in 1663—this time a successful one—
ushering in a rule that lasted well over a century. During Dutch
sovereignty, the Jews of Cochin were safe in Jewtown and the
Paradesi Synagogue was rebuilt.

The Dutch rule in Cochin forged a close bond between the
Jews of Holland and their brethren in India. Dutch Rabbi Manas-
seh Ben Israel, appealing for the readmission of the Jews to
England said in his "Humble Addresse to His Highnesse the

Lord Protector of the Commonwealth of England, Scotland and
Ireland [Cromwell]":

> *How Profitable the nation of the Jewes are—It*
> *would be a matter of too large extension if I*
> *should make a relation of all the places under*
> *whose Princes the Jewes live . . . . These in India in*
> *Cochin have four synagogues. One part of these*
> *Jewes being there of a white color and three of a*
> *tawny; these being most favoured by the King.*

Moses Pereyra de Paiva, member of a commission sent by
Dutch Jewry to visit the Indian Jews published *News of the Jews
of Cochin* in 1687 in which he reported:

> *. . . loving welcome which we experienced. [There*
> *were] many tears and joyful demonstrations and*
> *repeating with them the verse of the Psalmist "This*
> *is the day which the Lord hath wrought." The joy*
> *of the people was so great that if the king Messiah*
> *were to enter their homes it could not be greater. In*
> *the synagogue they sang liturgical hymns in*
> *thanksgiving because God had shown [them] their*
> *brethren from remote lands and so beloved to*
> *them.*

In crossing to Angicamal (near Cochin) a boat came out to greet
him with music. Even those who were in mourning appeared in
festive clothing. He reported finding Jews there from Aleppo,
Damascus, Shiraz, Germany, Jerusalem and Castella, in addition
to the original Cranganore group.

Eighty years later, Rabbi Thubia Boaz inquired by questionnaire as to the state of the Cochin community. The reply came
from the local leader Ezekiel Rahabi, whose grandfather had
come from Aleppo in Syria. A learned man and a devout Jew,
Ezekiel Rahabi conducted business correspondence with other
Jews in Hebrew. It was he who had presented the clock tower to
the synagogue. Ships anchored at his warehouses directly on the
waterfront. "Chief Merchant" of the Dutch East India Company,
Rahabi was highly esteemed for his diplomacy in dealing with
the native kings who controlled the pepper land, and served as
the unofficial envoy of the Dutch government.

Ezekiel Rahabi's reply to Rabbi Boaz's questionnaire stated that the Cochin community followed Sephardi religious rites to which some Ashkenazi forms had been added, and that authority for all judgments in ritual matters was the Shulhan Arukh code and the decisions of Rabbi Moses Isserles. At the time, 1768, there were 40 White Jewish families attached to the Paradesi Synagogue and 150 Black Jewish families with three other synagogues.

At the request of the Cochin community, prayer books, Scrolls of the Law and the Babylonian Talmud were sent from Amsterdam. So great was the joy of the people upon receipt of this material, that the fifteenth of Ab—the day on which the ship carrying these ritual objects landed—has remained ever since a day of glad celebration in the calendar of the Cochin Jews.

Their own book of *Prayers and Hymns for Special Occasions* is inscribed: . . . "Printed in the Year 1757, by the publishing house of Joseph, Jacob and Abraham Salomons, Props. in Amsterdam; According to the customs of the people of Shingly [Cranganore] and the Holy Congregation at Cochin." Included is the order of service for Circumcision of Slaves, and for weddings—not only for the marriage ceremony itself, but for all the many rites which made Cochin's wedding celebrations so colorful.

Marriages were formerly arranged by the parents. Custom still demands that the father of the young man formally approach the father of the young lady. When approved, the groom's family presents the bride-to-be with a small ivory casket of family jewelry and the betrothal is announced.

Wedding preparations begin almost at once. The groom's wedding outfit is made at home. As the tailor opens his shears to make the first cut into the cloth, sweets are thrown over the table. On the Thursday before the wedding, a nuptial-bed ceremony is held. Married women raise and lower the canopied cot.

The bride performs several rites. Attired in simple white muslin and accompanied by a few women companions, she proceeds to the mikveh. It is now a quiet, modest ceremony, but in earlier days she would have been escorted there with the sound of timbrels and dancing.

Then comes the bride's pre-nuptial formal visit to the synagogue. As she steps out of her home, her mother throws a handful of coins into the road symbolizing the hope that prosperity will always follow the bride. Accompanied by a band and women companions, she moves down Jewtown Road. Along the way she stops at each house to humbly "kiss the knee" of elders, both men and women, who await her coming in their doorways. (In token form, that is to say, she touches their knees with her hand, then raises her hand to her lips.)

At the synagogue she is met by the rabbi, who greets her with such phrases as "O beautiful as the moon." The sacred Scroll of the Law is opened to the Ten Commandments. With hands over her eyes, the bride kisses the Scroll seven times. She is hailed: "Arise, shine, for thy light has come," a verse from Isaiah, and other Biblical verses referring to Sarah and Rebekah. The totality of blessings in all the Holy Writings is invoked for her:

> *May they be realized for you and your offspring;*
> *may you merit long life with sons and daughters*
> *engaged in works of the Law; may you have length*
> *of days, honor, gratification of spirit, piety, tran-*
> *quility; may the Lord give you a good reward in*
> *this world and a good portion in the world to*
> *come.*

On Monday evening a dinner is given at the bride's home. Dressing at a relative's home, she is attired in a white, gold-embroidered costume, the skirt draped to the side in local fashion, with jewels in her hair and around her neck. Drums sound and the groom and a party of his friends call for her. Clapping their hands and facing her all the time, the men walk backward as they escort her to the function at her home.

And now Tuesday, the day of good augury, the day of the actual wedding service has arrived. At three in the morning the women are already assembled in the bride's home. Seated on benches arranged against two sides of the ground-floor corridor, they sing old love songs in the Malayalam tongue to the bride, who faces them.

Preceded by a drum and brass band, the women next move

down the length of streamer-decorated Jewtown Road, making public announcement of the marriage. "Won't anyone complain of the noise at such an early hour of the day?" I asked. "Of course not," I was told, "the street is ours; we can do what we want." By five in the morning, they are back at the bride's dwelling, where breakfast has been laid out.

The groom, too, has his ceremonies to carry out on this day of days. He and his friends must have their hair cut. Now it is his turn to deferentially "kiss the knee" of the elders along Jewtown Road. A luncheon and a songfest held in his honor are "for men only." The men greet him with the following from the Book of Esther:

> *And Mordecai went out from the presence of the*
> *King in royal apparel of blue and white and with a*
> *great crown of gold and with a garment of fine*
> *linen and purple and the city of Shushan rejoiced*
> *and was glad.*

And from the Book of Genesis with excerpts addressed to Abraham and to Jacob:

> *I will make of thee a great nation and I will bless*
> *thee and make thy name great; and thou shalt be a*
> *blessing; and I will bless them that bless thee and*
> *curse him that curseth thee and in thee shall all*
> *families of the earth be blessed. God give thee of*
> *the dew of heaven and of the fat places of the*
> *earth and plenty of corn and wine.*
>
> *The Lord Almighty make thee fruitful and mul-*
> *tiply thee; and I will make of thee a company of*
> *peoples.*

From Psalm 91 the following is repeated:

> *There shall no evil befall thee, neither shall any*
> *plague come nigh thy dwelling*
> *For He shall give his angels charge over thee;*
> *to keep thee in all thy ways.*

A rather florid version of Grace After Meals closes the luncheon.

Finally the hour for the marriage ceremony arrives. Dressed in white, with prayer shawl and a white skull cap embroidered in gold, and the customary Indian garland of flowers, the groom starts out. Attended by friends, and heralded by a band, he makes his way to the synagogue to await his bride. Meanwhile she is being helped into a white gown by friends singing Malayalam songs. Escorted by her brother, and a band, she arrives at the synagogue, and is seated with a high round canopy covering her face and head.

The marriage vows begin:

GROOM: *By your leave*
RESPONSE: *By God's leave*
GROOM: *With the permission of our rabbis*
RESPONSE: *By God's leave*
GROOM: *Praise to the Lord for He is good*
RESPONSE: *For His mercy endureth forever*

The groom chants the blessings over the wine, and to the bride he says:

You are betrothed and sanctified unto me. By means of this cup and this ring, by this silver you enter my jurisdiction, in the presence of witnesses, according to the Law of Moses and Israel.

The wine is sipped and the ring placed on the bride's finger.

With a "By your leave" to which the assembly responds "By God's leave," the rabbi reads the ketubah. The groom hands one end of his prayer shawl to the rabbi and the following colloquy is repeated three times:

RABBI: *By the command of the Holy and Sanctified, by the Mighty One who revealed the Law at Sinai. Her support, her clothing and her conjugal rights he shall not diminish*
GROOM: *Her support, her clothing and her conjugal rights I will not diminish*
RABBI: *Dost thou undertake this?*
GROOM: *I undertake this*
RABBI: *An affirmation before Heaven and earth?*

GROOM: *An affirmation before Heaven and*
           earth
ASSEMBLY: *Blessed be He Who sanctified Israel*

The marriage contract is signed by the groom and two witnesses. The rabbi rolls it up and hands it to the groom who transfers it to the bride with the words, "Here is thy ketubah. By virtue of all that is written therein you enter into my jurisdiction, in the presence of these witnesses, according to the Law of Moses and Israel."

As the bride is now unveiled, all break into, "O beautiful as the moon!" Then follows the Sevenfold Benediction, a liturgical poem beginning "Praise ye the Lord" and "This is the day which the Lord hath wrought."

The bride is honored with excerpts from the Bible about women, such as this from Proverbs:

> *Who can find a Woman of Valor, for her price is far*
>   *above rubies;*
> *The heart of her husband doth safely trust in her; . . .*
> *She will do him good and not evil all the days of her*
>   *life*

And from the Book of Ruth:

> *The Lord make the woman that is come unto thy*
> *house like Rachel and like Leah which two did*
> *build the house of Israel.*

And again from Proverbs, "Rejoice with the bride of your youth."

With a final invocation for "Life and Peace," the couple leave for the wedding feast, led by torchbearers and music. During the evening the groom dances with the men, the bride with the women. Feasts and the repetition of the Sevenfold Benediction continue for a week.

At the Sabbath services following the marriage, the groom is honored with an aliyah, being called up to the Reading of the Torah with the words, "Arise, groom, arise to read the Torah in reverence." At the conclusion of the service, he receives manifold blessings including these lines:

> *May Priests bless you and Levites minister to you*
> *May Kings rejoice at your table*
> *Depart, O groom, for your home.*

Following the festive Sabbath meal at his home, in which many people have shared, the company sings for a long time, a favorite diversion in Cochin. One of the selections sung is the "Ehod Mi Yodeah" ("Who Knows One")—which we in the West are accustomed to include at the Passover Seder ritual.

After the Minhah Service, many join the couple once more to share in the Seudah Shelishit (the third Sabbath meal). One of the hymns sung at this time includes these lines:

> O good and beneficent God
> Make us rejoice in Thy Torah
> And in the joy of groom and bride

Wedding gifts are presented at the final feast held on the seventh day after the marriage. It is a particularly gay evening. Again the groom greets his bride with "O beautiful as the moon" and the men dance before the groom. Heard this evening is the Song of Songs, a Song of Wine, and a melody with the chorus of "A good omen, a good omen." The week's celebrations come to a close with the Sevenfold Benediction and these wishes:

> You shall have length of days
> And years of life
> May peace be added to you.

Just as weddings were celebrated with great ceremony and splendor, (and with some rites unique to this community), so were festivals celebrated throughout the year. During the thirty-day period of Slihot a town crier would go up and down Jewtown Road at three o'clock in the morning calling out the names of individual men and announcing "Time for Slihot—Time for Slihot." Young boys, wishing to be counted among the adults, paid the town crier so that he would call out their names, too, in the early morning hours when it was "Time for Slihot."

As God was supposed to be seated on the seat of mercy during this time of year any male child born during Slihot time was named "Rahamim." .

Preceding Yom Kippur, some of the men observed the rite of Malkot, or Penitential Scourging, submitting to thirty-nine lashes administered by a synagogue functionary. Six-foot-tall candles, six in number and six inches in circumference, burned in the synagogue all through this day.

Sukkot booths were constructed of coconut-palm leaves. Accepted in Cochin was that interpretation of the lulav and its components which compared them to human beings—the palm branch said to resemble the spinal cord, the citron similar in shape to that of the heart, and the leaves of the myrtle and willow branches corresponding to the shape of the eye.

Repeatedly I was told I had missed one of the year's greatest events in Cochin life by not being there for the celebration of Simhat Torah. On that day the Paradesi Synagogue's walls are draped in cloth of gold and yellow satin, the sweet scent of jasmine is everywhere and the people are dressed in gaily colored robes of crimson, amber, orange, green or yellow. Women are permitted on the floor of the synagogue proper so that they may kiss the Scrolls of the Law.

For the festival of Purim the 1757 prayer book contains the following song:

> *Blessed be the Lord*   *God of Israel*
> *Blessed be Mordecai*   *Cursed be Haman*
> *Blessed be Esther*   *Cursed be Zeresh*
>   *[Haman's wife]*
> *Blessed is all Israel*   *Cursed are the wicked*

A more modern version puts it this way:

> *Blessed be Mordecai*   *Cursed be Haman*
> *Blessed be King George*   *Cursed be Hitler*
> *Blessed be Israel*   *Cursed be the Nazis*

Two mallets were struck together twice each time a "cursed" name was mentioned in the song.

Another favorite Purim custom was to have two wooden figures, elaborately clothed, swatting each other until one was in fragments. The broken form represented Haman, the victorious one—Mordecai.

Passover preparations started long before this holiday season. During the preceding harvest, some of the grain was stored in tins for safekeeping until time for the baking of the unleavened bread. Baking of matzoh had once been a cooperative venture, each family bringing its flour to one house—usually the Koder home—and there all the matzoh were baked.

Dramatic elements were introduced into the Seder. A child

dressed as a wanderer with knapsack on back and staff in hand trudged round the table until asked:

FATHER: *Where are you coming from?*
CHILD: *From Egypt*
FATHER: *Where are you going?*
CHILD: *To Jerusalem*

Then the "wayfarer" would be invited to join the family.

The "Four Questions" were asked by the father and only he read out the ten plagues, pouring out the wine as he did so into a wooden bowl which was immediately emptied. Part of the "afikomen" was preserved for the entire year. When traveling by sea, this piece of the afikomen was carried along, for it was believed to be efficacious in calming stormy waters.

During the Shavuot service, the Chief Elder ascended to the synagogue upper gallery, usually reserved for the Reading of the Torah, and there solemnly declaimed the Ten Commandments as the entire congregation stood. The 613 religious commandments were recited during the Musaf (Additional service), that morning, the Book of Ruth being read in the afternoon.

Tisha B'Ab was observed with great solemnity. The synagogue was darkened, all decorations removed, the congregation wore mourning clothes and went barefoot as Lamentations were read on the day commemorating the destruction of the Temple in Jerusalem. Women wore no jewels.

Sabbath had its special foods. Cold cakes of rice and ground coconut, baked with onions and eggs, were eaten in the morning. Hot hamin, a Cochin-style "cholent," was served at mid-day. Here's the recipe: To make the hamin, you start with a fat duck or chicken, add rice, onion and ground coconut, all flavored with turmeric and some raw eggs in their shells, and bake it in the oven overnight from Friday to Saturday lunchtime. Good eating!

And how Cochin Jewry enjoyed singing! Their Standard Book of Songs has many of the compositions used at weddings, at festivals, on Sabbaths and songs marking historical events, such as the giving of the Copper Plates to Joseph Rabban. Many of these were written in the native tongue—Malayalam—others in Aramaic or Hebrew. One song used in all the synagogues, written in Malayalam, was translated for me by Josef Hai Isaac, formerly of Cochin and now Chief Librarian of Israel's Supreme Court in Jerusalem:

Prayer for the Royal Family of Cochin

To the King Who reigns supreme
Let us humbly be permitted Thee to praise
O Thou creator of twice seven that is fourteen
    worlds
Who holds unruffled sway
O Lord Who gives protection to kings
And ruling power to princes
Great Lord Who rules over the entire universe
May Thy name be blessed forever.

O Lord all glorious crowned ruler
Hasten to bestow upon our benevolent Rajah
All greatness and glory
O Lord Whose mercy is well known
Exempt him graciously from enemies and war
Let the Rajah be the head of all
Let him be saved from evil enemies
And may all blessings be showered upon his head.

Let his lot be to walk in goodness
And may his kingdom be saved from famine
Let the Most Merciful God vouchsafe
Mercy for us in the mind of the Rajah
And in the minds of all his ministers
Mercy to do good and render service to us.

May God our Redeemer bestow upon us
Greatness without constraint
To the humble nation
May God be merciful
And give peace to the sons of Israel
O Eternal, deliverer of Jerusalem.

But this seemingly idyllic community has had its problems, chief of which was the "color" issue, for in Cochin lived White Jews, Black Jews (not, in fact, black as are members of what the world calls the black race—but rather brown-skinned, as are the natives among whom they live), and a third group, also brown-skinned, the Meshuhrarim or Emancipated Ones. This being

India, caste played an important role in life, and caste distinctions were based on color.

Questions were raised as to whether Black Jews were "proper" Jews. About the year 1600, they appealed to rabbinic authority Rabbi Jacob Castro of Alexandria and again in 1882 to Rabbi Phanizel—the Sephardi chief rabbi of Jerusalem—to resolve the question. Each time the decision was in favor of the Black Jews, who followed rituals of the Oriental Jews and observed Talmudic laws. But the Black Jews continued to live in one part of Jewtown and prayed in their own synagogues, the Kadavumbhagam and the Thekumbhagam.

The problem of the Emancipated group was somewhat different. Slavery had once been practiced in Cochin, and the White Jews had also had their quota of slaves and offspring of women slaves by their masters. When these slaves were freed, they were, according to Jewish religious law, accepted into the Jewish faith in the prescribed manner. They and their children did not merge with the Black Jews, but preferred to continue their association with their former masters and so formed a third caste attached to the White Paradesi Synagogue.

They were recognized as Jews, but not fully welcomed into the White Jewish community. At services they were restricted to sitting on the floor, the pews being reserved "for whites only." Nor did they ever receive the honor of an aliyah, of being called to the Reading of the Torah—except on Simhat Torah. Marriage into the families of the White Jews was not permitted, and their children and children's children continued to be treated in like manner.

I was therefore astonished at my first service at the Paradesi Synagogue to see Avraham Baruch Salem, an Emancipated Jew, sitting on one of the pews. How had integration come to the Paradesi? Brown-skinned, frail, gentle-voiced A.B.—as he was affectionately known to all—told me the story of his one-man fight for integration as we talked and walked along Jewtown Road.

Educated at the Protestant-mission elementary school and the Santa Cruz secondary school (he had scholarships to both), A.B. became the first non-white Cochin Jew to matriculate for a college degree. He studied at Ernakulam and at Madras University under government grants. White Jewish leaders raised funds enabling him to complete his law studies.

After some government work, A.B. returned to his home town to enter the private practice of law. Law practice led to politics. Speaking his mind freely, he ran counter to the British colonials then ruling India. "The British didn't like me, neither did the Jews," Mr. Salem said. The Jews were afraid his outspoken stand against the British would be considered representative of the position held by the entire community.

Sitting on the floor of the Paradesi Synagogue did not suit university-trained A.B. He entered petitions, he made speeches on behalf of the rights of the Emancipated Jews to sit on the pews in full equality with the White Jews. Twenty-five years of petitioning went by, but there were no changes.

"The time for action is now," A.B. finally decided. Synagogue sit-ins were his next step. The following Sabbath he placed his two young sons not on the floor of the synagogue as usual, but on a pew. Immediately someone came to put them in their "proper" place. A.B. prevented their being moved. Mr. Hallegua, a communal leader, came up saying, "Wait until the close of the service. In the meanwhile let the children sit on my lap. Just have patience."

Another Sabbath, A.B. directed his sons to sit on the steps leading to the Ark, the most sacred spot in the house of worship—and no one dared to remove them.

The one-man struggle continued. Other Emancipated Jews pleaded with him to put an end to the fight. A.B. asked Elias Japhet, an Emancipated Jew who was respected because of his advanced age, to join in the war against second-class citizenship. But Japhet refused.

Then A.B. staged a one-man peaceful demonstration. It was Kol Nidre Eve and he prepared to pray at home facing Jewtown Road. As people went by on their way to the Paradesi, they were startled to hear him call out, "I'm not going to the Paradesi to pray with slaves. We were slaves unto Pharaoh in Egypt. Here I am a free man. No more sitting on the floor while the White Jews sit in the pews."

During the feast of Sukkot A.B. returned to the synagogue with his sons. Mr. Hallegua's grandson was to become Bar Mitzvah that morning, and the grandfather was anxious that nothing should mar the occasion. He suggested a compromise—let A.B. and the children be seated, not on the floor, but on the steps leading to the upper gallery.

A.B. refused. "That passageway is very narrow. We'll have to jump up to make room each time a man ascends the steps for the Reading of the Torah. No, we won't do it." Again Mr. Hallegua pleaded, "Don't make a scene now. Don't spoil my grandson's Bar Mitzvah. I promise you the whole matter will be settled before this evening."

Unexpectedly A.B. found adherents to his cause that day. Rebellious white youths spoke up. "Unless you settle this matter before the evening," they told their elders, "we will not take part in tonight's ceremonies. We will not carry the heavy Scrolls in the seven circuits around the synagogue in the Simhat Torah celebration."

The older generation surrendered. Since that Simhat Torah of 1932 there has been integration at the Paradesi Synagogue.

The problem facing Cochin today is the reduced number of the community. Since the Declaration of the State of Israel in 1948, when there were 2,500 Jews in Cochin, most of the Black and the Emancipated Jews have emigrated to the Holy Land, selling their synagogue property to pay for the cost of transportation.

The majority of those who have migrated to Israel have taken root in agricultural settlements or in development towns. They are to be found in Nevatim near Beer Sheba, in Mesillat Zion near Jerusalem, at Aviezer in the Adullam area, at Kfar Yuval in the Galilee, at Yesod Hamaaleh, at Hodaya. In the Haifa Bay area they are settled at Kurdani, where they work with the Ata textile firm as spinners and weavers.

One of the families I visited in Kurdani was that of David and Dina Yefet. For ten years before coming to Kurdani Dina and David had been "kubbutzniks." To the question, "Why did you leave the kibbutz?" came the reply I heard so frequently from other Indian families who had gone the same path—from kibbutz to town: "In India our family ties were very close. We could not stand the separation from our children who spent the nights at the kibbutz children's homes."

Supper with the Yefets was the typical Israeli light evening meal—salad, an egg, bread with tea. No more rice and curry for this former Indian family. The Yefet children, too, have become integrated into Israeli life. Thirteen-year-old Shoshanna played the accordion, and seven-year-old Miriam was already expert on the recorder—two musical instruments favored in Israel. The only difference I could see between these two dark-skinned children and other Israeli youngsters was their shy, reserved manner.

Ruby (now Rebecca) Daniel is one of the Cochin Jews who has remained at a kibbutz. The only non-white Jewish woman to attend university in Cochin, she was superior in education to the men of the Black Jewish groups, yet marriage to a White Jew had been impossible there. In Israel, her sister has married a blond European kibbutz member.

Only a few of the Paradesi White Jewish families have moved to Israel. Indian government regulations do not permit the transfer of funds out of the country, so they—the more affluent—remain in Cochin. Their number now is down to a mere forty or fifty. Dr. Julian Koder, one of the few White Jews who has settled in Israel functions as the Kupat Holim physician in Binyamina. Asked what had impelled him to make the change from Cochin—where he had operated a clinic with a staff of seventeen and a household with four servants—Dr. Koder's reply was, "There was no one my daughters could expect to marry in Cochin."

Thus has the wheel of fortune turned. Less than ten years before the Dutch took control of Cochin in the 1660s, a small band of refugees—twenty-three in number—escaped Portuguese power and persecution and landed in a locality under Dutch control in the New World. That community, New York, has grown to number almost two million Jews. And the Paradesi Synagoue, which marked its 400th anniversary in December of 1968, has only a handful of Jews.

From Cochin I flew north to Bombay, where I was astonished to find that the hotel in which I was staying was the Taj Mahal. I wondered, the Taj in Bombay, rather than in Agra where that wonder of the world—the real Taj Mahal is located? Bombay's Hotel Taj Mahal has an old-world Victorian charm and overlooks the Gateway of India, the waterfront arch erected in honor of the 1911 visit of Britain's King George V and Queen Mary.

From this Gateway of India arch I took a motor launch to the Elephanta Caves on an island six miles across the Bombay harbor to see the eighth-century rock-hewn sculpture dedicated to the worship of the Hindu god Siva, his consort Parvati and other Hindu divinities.

I rode along the Marine Drive through the exclusive residential area of Malabar Hill, past the Hanging Gardens, to reach the Tower of Silence. Within this five-story, grey-stone building are three stone slabs on which the Parsis place their dead. Within minutes, the flesh is devoured by a pack of vultures; then the skeletons are dried, pushed into a well and washed out to sea. The Parsis, a tiny minority of about 70,000 Zoroastrians among Bombay's population of 5,000,000, include many rich and powerful industrialists, bankers and traders.

Within the crowded bazaar streets of Bombay's Crawford Market I began looking for Jews. A number of the shops bore the Magen David. I could not assume that these were all Jewish-owned stores, for Hindus use the six-pointed star as a device for warding off evil. But when I came to a shop that displayed a sign reading "Closed on the Sabbath" in addition to the Magen David, I knew that I had found a Jewish shopkeeper. Moses David, an Iraqi Jew, welcomed me and immediately invited me to partake of Sabbath kiddush with his family.

The Maghen David Synagogue, where I attended Sabbath morning service, is a large edifice with colonnades and tower. At the close of the service the women came down from the gallery to kiss the Scrolls of the Law, suggesting that I do likewise for "If you ask for something as you kiss the Torah, your wish is bound to come true."

12

The Maghen David Synagogue in Byculla, once the center of Bombay's Jewish life, is named for David Sassoon, a member of a Baghdadi family which is reputed to have furnished Reshe Galuta ("Princes of the Captivity") in Talmudic and Gaonic times and later Chief Treasurers to the Governors of Baghdad. In difficulty with the ruler there and fearing for his life, David ben Sassoon (David, son of Sassoon) fled his home town for Basrah on the Persian Gulf. In 1832 he settled in Bombay with its untold possibilities for trade, a city in which there were already between twenty and thirty other Baghdadi Jewish families, as well as the Bene Israel and Jews from Surat and Cochin. Surnames being in use in this locale, David ben Sassoon became David Sassoon.

With a reputation for honesty and integrity, his firm for the import and export of textiles and yarn expanded. Soon he also had the monopoly of the opium trade, and branches of David Sassoon & Co. were established in Canton, Shanghai, Hong Kong, Japan, Calcutta and Mesopotamia. With a family consisting of eight sons and six daughters, it became a policy of David Sassoon & Co., "the Rothschilds of the East," to have a member of the family supervise each branch as it opened.

Tall, dignified David Sassoon, always dressed in a long, flowing Oriental robe and a turban, was a pious Jew who attended services daily. Business would stop for the Minhah prayers. And on Sabbath afternoons people would assemble in his home for study of the Talmud and the Zohar.

Assured of finding employment in the Sassoon enterprises, more and more Jews left Baghdad for Bombay. For their religious needs, David Sassoon had a synagogue built and established a Jewish Day School and a mikveh. Ritual slaughtering was taught in order to ensure continuation of the traditional way of life in those cities to which his firm was sending men to work in the newly opening branches of the company. When David Sassoon died in 1864, the Jewish community of Bombay had increased to 2,870.

Sassoon philanthropies had not been limited to the Jewish field alone, but extended beyond that to include gifts of a library, museum, hospital, monuments, a sailors' home and reformatory for juvenile offenders in Bombay.

Gateway of India waterfront arch erected in Bombay in honor of 1911 visit of King George V and Queen Mary.

Abdullah, later known as Albert (after Prince Consort Albert), the oldest son of David Sassoon succeeded his father as head of the business. Able son of an able father, Abdullah Sassoon expanded the firm's interests to include banking, insurance, industrial enterprises such as spinning and weaving, and the creation of Bombay's first modern dock facilities.

Albert-Abdullah Sassoon's home—Villa Sans Souci—with its woodwork inlaid with ebony and ivory and walls lined with silk, rivaled ducal palaces in magnificence. He continued the family tradition of philanthropic interest. For his aid to Persian commerce he was honored with the Persian Order of the Lion and the Sun; England made him a Companion of the Order of the Star of India and later "The Queen has been pleased to confer the dignity of a Baronetcy of the United Kingdom on Sir Albert Sassoon, Knight Companion of the Star of India." His coat of arms bore the Hebrew motto "Emet V'Emunah"—Truth and Faithfulness.

When the Sassoons and the rest of the Baghdadi Jews settled in Bombay they found the Bene Israel already living there. The Baghdadis looked down upon them and used the derogatory term "natives" for the Bene Israel—whose women dressed in saris, and whose men wore their shirts hanging loosely over their white trousers, with typical Hindu caps on their heads.

One religious rite observed by the Bene Israel seemed particularly strange to the Baghdadis. This was the sacrificial meat offering, the Zebah Todah or "Thanksgiving," also called "A Dish offered in the name of God." This was tendered upon recovery from illness, upon rescue from a storm, after a long journey or upon moving into a new home. On a sheet were placed a dish containing the liver and heart of a fowl, a cup of wine, unleavened rice-bread, meat and fruits. Frankincense burned; the Shema was recited and some of the wine poured on the ground as a libation. The officiating minister then took some of the offering for himself as had the High Priest in the days of old; the rest was shared by all present. A feature of the occasion was the well-known song "Elijah the Prophet" and the repetition of the Shema over and over, at least a dozen times.

Aside from the non-observance of Yibbum and Halitzah the calendar of holidays and the rituals of weddings, circumcisions and funerals were all faithfully carried out in a manner similar to that of the rest of the Jewish world. For the feast of Sukkot, booths were built of the green leaves of the coconut trees; for Simhat Torah the mantle of the Ark was covered with flowers.

The Sabbath was a holy day indeed to the Bene Israel. They abstained from work and did not smoke, kindle a fire or ride on this day. Food was prepared on Friday and eaten cold or warmed up over a charcoal fire. Kiddush was recited over grape juice as part of the synagogue service. Kashrut was strictly observed and to be called a "pork eater" was the grossest form of insult.

Who were these people who preferred to be known as Bene Israel (Children of Israel) rather than as Jews—a term not popular, according to some, among the Moslems of India—and who believed themselves to be descended, not from the tribe of Judah, but rather from those tribes that had formed the original kingdom of Israel.

Their tradition has it that in 175 B.C.E. in the days of the Second Temple (when Antiochus Epiphanes was seeking to impose his Greek religion upon the Jewish inhabitants of Palestine), a group of Galilean Jews emigrated to India via Egypt. There had long been brisk trading between Egypt and India, the route leading from the Red Sea via Aden to Arabia, the Persian Gulf, Karachi and on to India, for the Bible tells us that among the wares brought to the homeland by King Solomon's ships were peacocks and apes, their Hebrew names "tukki" and "kof" stemming from the Tamil and Sanskrit tongues of India.

The emigrating Galilean Jews were shipwrecked off the western coast of India. Most of the wayfarers, together with all of their possessions—including ritual objects such as the Scrolls of the Law—were lost at sea. Only seven men and seven women came safely to shore near Cheul—center of the Indian trade with Egypt—about thirty miles south of Bombay. They settled there holding themselves apart from the local population, and followed the same work they had pursued in Galilee—oil pressing. They came to be known as the "Caste of Shanwar Telis" or Saturday Oil Pressers, for they kept the Sabbath as their day of rest. Later the seaport of Cheul was closed to foreign trade, thus isolating the Caste of Shanwar Telis from communication with the outside world.

Thus separated from the mainstream of Jewry, certain practices were forgotten by the Bene Israel. Having left Palestine in 175 B.C.E., before the Maccabean War and the rededication of the Temple which followed in 165 B.C.E., the Bene Israel were not aware of the festival of Hanukkah. They learned of it only two centuries ago, on the arrival in their midst of a scholarly sage from Cochin.

Nevertheless, throughout the hundreds of years when they had no scholars, no rabbis nor teachers, they clung tenaciously to four ordinances—the Sabbath, kashrut, circumcision and the Shema. Prayers generally were forgotten, but the Shema Yisrael was recited on all occasions—at weddings, at circumcisions and at funerals. Whenever the Bene Israel gathered for a special event, always the Shema was on their lips.

Word of the existence of this Caste of Shanwar Telis filtered through somehow to the rest of the world. According to their tradition, David Rahabi, a learned teacher from Egypt, came to this area of India about 900 years ago. After some time spent among them he felt assured the Bene Israel were a lost colony of Jews. Rahabi determined upon one decisive test. He collected various species of fish and asked the women to cook them for him. The women began by separating the fish—those with scales and fins they put into one pile, all the rest into a second pile, saying, "We use only the fish that have scales and fins." Convinced now that he was among long-separated Jewish brethren, Rahabi stayed with them for some time bringing knowledge and learning of current Jewish life.

Then about two hundred years ago another David Rahabi, this time a man whose visit is authenticated by records in his home town of Cochin, came to the Kolaba district. He too was satisfied that he was in the presence of Jews and set about to teach the Bene Israel the liturgy, the Torah and the commandments.

Influenced by these two David Rahabis, a religious revival took place. Young men were trained to be "kajis" who would officiate at religious rites and ceremonies. And the celebration of the previously unknown festival of Hanukkah was inserted into the Bene Israel calendar.

From Cheul the Bene Israel had spread into rural areas of the Kolaba district, where they continued life as oil pressers, as farmers and as village artisans. By the middle of the eighteenth century, at the time of the second David Rahabi's stay with them, a new occupation was becoming popular with the young men. Many of them became soldiers in the forces of the British East India Company, participating in the fighting along the Malabar coast, and later on in Persia, in China, Abyssinia and Afghanistan. Nineteen percent of the Bene Israel were in the military service, where their record for gallantry and faithfulness was extraordinarily high.

Although they formed but a tiny minority within the total population, more than half of the native military officers were Bene Israel. Presentations of decorations to individual Bene Israel men included the following citations:

Of Sirdar Bahadur Moosajee Ballajee Oomer-dekar: "He possessed such abilities as are rarely if ever to be met with in a native. He was extremely zealous."

Of Sirdar Bahadur Haskeljee Issajee Zavlikar: "He evinced such zeal, energy and capacity as to call from every officer he served under the highest

*testimonials, many of which have been published
in Regimental Orders . . . . He received the Star of
the Order of British India, First Class on account
of his long arduous and loyal services [42 years]. . . .
To his example and the beneficial influence he has
exerted among the men is to be attributed in a
great measure the steadiness and loyalty of the
Detachment, whether in field or quarters."*

In both cases the title "Sirdar Bahadur," was the highest mark of
commendation that the Government of India bestowed on a
native officer. Their names Moosajee Ballajee and Haskeljee Issajee had the Indian suffix "-jee," as the Bene Israel commonly
attached it to their Hebrew names.

The popularity of military service among the Bene Israel
waned, however, when officer ranking came to be assigned on a
percentage basis of the enlistment from each caste.

With the early nineteenth century came further innovations in
the mode of life of the Bene Israel. There was a strong tendency to
move from the rural areas to urban centers, and communities
were founded in Poona, in Ahmedabad and Bombay. Craftsmen
became mechanics in the cities; and as the Bene Israel literacy
rate was high, many became white-collar workers or entered
government civil service. Some found their way into teaching,
law and medicine.

With the coming of the English and the Baghdadi Jews, knowledge of the Bene Israel was spread to the West. Rabbi David de
Beth Hillel, a Wilno Jew who left from Jerusalem on a tour of the
Jewish communities of Asia, spending 1829 to 1831 in Bombay,
gave the first eye-witness account of the Bene Israel in his book
The Travels of David de Beth Hillel. He tells that Christian
missionaries interested themselves in these Jews, bringing them
knowledge of the Bible and setting up schools to teach the
children Hebrew. Among them was the Cochin-born Jew Michael
Surgun who had become a convert to Christianity, but retained a
feeling of kinship with the Jews. From Rabbi David de Beth
Hillel we also learn how the first synagogue of the Bene Israel
came into existence.

Samuel ben Eliezer Ezekiel Divekar, a rich man and Commandant in "the Honorable Company's Army" (British East

India Company) was taken prisoner in the Anglo-Mysore War of the early 1780s. Through the intervention of the Jews of Cochin he was released and taken for a stay in their city. Out of thankfulness for his liberation he vowed he would build a synagogue in Bombay, and upon his return the Sha'ar Ha-Rahamim Synagogue was erected in 1796 on Samuel Street.

Later on the New Synagogue (Sha'ar Ratson), the Tiferet Israel at Jacob Circle, the Etz Hayim Prayer Hall and the Magen Hassidim Synagogue came into being.

Somewhat later, in 1882, Sir Julian Goldsmid and David Schloss, of the Anglo-Jewish Association of London, visited India to meet the Bene Israel. In the same year the Bombay branch of the Anglo-Jewish Association sent this report to London:

> On receipt of the news regarding the persecution against the Russian Jews and the outrages to which they were subjected, the Bene Israel community were aroused to give expression to their fraternal feelings for their suffering Russian brethren and subscriptions to the Relief Fund were raised among them.

The twentieth century brought further contact with the Western world and Western Jewry. Influenced by English Liberal Judaism while studying surgery in London, Dr. Jerusha Jhirad was instrumental in organizing a Liberal synagogue on her return to Bombay. This Jewish Religious Union or Rodef Shalom Synagogue, established in 1925 (and one of the founding congregations of the World Union for Progressive Judaism), holds worship services at 23 Sussex Street and has a membership of nearly three hundred.

Some years later Baruch B. Benjamin, then Under-Secretary of the Ministry of Commerce and Industry, attended a convention of the World Council of Synagogues (Conservative Movement) in the United States. Returning to India, Mr. Benjamin organized a branch of that movement, calling it the United Synagogue of India, which he hoped would follow a path "strictly in accordance with the teachings of the Holy Torah." While all this change was taking place within Indian Jewry the majority of the Bene Israel remained Orthodox.

For Friday evening service I joined the Rodef Shalom Congregation where a sari-clad woman recited the blessings over the Sabbath candles, and the prayer book used was that of the Union of American Hebrew Congregations. A special feature that Sabbath was the naming of a daughter born to one of the member families. The child was named Rebecca in honor of an aunt—Rebecca Reuben, venerated by the entire community, who until her death had been headmistress of the Sir Elly Kadoorie School. Opened in 1875, and renamed in honor of the man who had contributed generously when the school was being expanded, the school had an enrollment of 600 Bene Israel and 300 non-Jewish children.

The Reuben clan is a large one in Bombay, for the Bene Israel believe that many of them are descended from the Tribe of Reuben. Rebecca Reuben and her immediate family had been particularly gifted and distinguished. Her grandfather, Rebenji Isaji Nawgaonkar (Reuben, son of Isaac of the village of Nawgaon), was a well-known ballad singer and composer of religious poems in the Marathi and Hindustani tongues. Her father, Ezra Reuben, had a remarkable career as Chief Judicial Officer of the State of Junagadh. Her brother, David Ezra Reuben, was a member of London's Inner Temple and in India he became Chief Justice of the Patna High Court.

Other Bombay Jews have been distinguished in different fields of endeavor. There is David Abraham, the internationally famous character actor of Indian films. With his white hair worn long in the manner of an Indian philosopher, I found "David" (as he is popularly known) a charming, intelligent, gifted conversationalist with a mellifluous voice.

An active citizen, David Abraham was appointed to the State Welfare Board of Bombay and in 1952 he was a member of an Indian Goodwill Delegation to the United States. The film star was also a weight-lifting enthusiast and acted as referee for sports events.

The number of Jews that are attracted by the Indian film industry is out of all proportion to the size of this microscopic Jewish minority among the hundreds of millions of the Indian population. Among these was screen idol Ruby Mayers, known as

Sulochana, film director Ezra Mir, writer Joseph David, screen siren Nadira (Ferhet Ezekiel), stars Ramola (Rachel Cohen) and Elizer (Eddie Sopher) and young Levi Joseph who played Elephant Boy in "Tarzan."

In political life there has been the eminent Dr. Elijah Moses—Mayor of Bombay in the 1930s—for whom one of the city's streets has been renamed. The Iraqi wing of Bombay Jewry has also given two Mayors to the city—Sir Sassoon J. David and Meyer Nissim in the 1920s.

Relations between the two sub-castes of Bombay Jewry—the Iraqis and the Bene Israel—have not been happy. The Iraqis are white and the Bene Israel brown-skinned, and as we have noted, in India skin color makes a marked difference in social status. The Iraqis hold themselves aloof from the Bene Israel. As early as 1837 they had asked the government to supply a partition wall to divide the "Indian Jews' cemetery from that of the foreign [Iraqi] Jews," a request that the government declined to grant. A Bombay visitor in the 1840s said the Baghdadis "avoided" marriage with the Bene Israel.

The Iraqis say that the Bene Israel serve idols and pursue Hindu customs. At the stone villa of one of the Iraqi well-to-do merchants where I was being very graciously entertained, the daughters said vehemently, "The Bene Israel are idol worshippers. They henna their fingers and use rice during wedding ceremonies, just like the Hindus." Actually these are Moslem practices.

A unifying factor between the two groups is their common love for Zion. At a Hebrew class for adults sponsored by the Jewish Agency, Josef Grossman, the Agency representative who was conducting the lesson told me in 1961, "History is being made in this class. This is the first time that Iraqis have been willing to sit in the same room with the Bene Israel. And all L'ma'an Yerusha-layim—for the sake of Jerusalem."

That this love for Zion was not just idle talk is proven by statistics. In 1941 census figures showed there were 22,480 Jews in India, three quarters of whom were Bene Israel. Today, figures of the American Joint Distribution Committee reveal only 14,450 Jews in all of India, the largest concentration being in Bombay

and in the area around this city. This means that despite government restrictions on taking money out of the country which has
kept both affluent, as well as those receiving pensions from
leaving the country, more than one out of every three Jews who
lived in India before the Declaration of the State of Israel has
emigrated. The vast majority of this exodus has been to Israel.

In Israel the Bene Israel have become integrated in places
ranging from Eilat to Beer Sheba to Kiryat Shmoneh in the north.
At a weekend conference of their Executive Council on the shore
of the Sea of Galilee, I met 73-year-old agronomist Professor
Hayim Ezekiel, who had once stayed at an ashram with Gandhi.
Professor Ezekiel came to witness Israel's Independence Day
celebration in 1951, returned his air ticket and has remained as
instructor at Kfar Ofer. Also on hand that weekend in 1967 were
Nissim Samson, a former captain in the Indian army, who has
fought in Israel's War of Independence and is now a member of
Kibbutz Degania A; attractive Uriella Solomon, a psychiatric
social worker with the blind near Haifa; and Samson Samson
who is on the staff of the Hebrew University National Library.

Other Jews, neither Bene Israel nor Iraqi, have made their mark
on Bombay. I mention only two of these—one who was invited by
the Government of India, the other who came as one of the 1,300
refugees seeking freedom from Nazi persecution in India, a land
where anti-Semitism was unknown.

The first was Russian-born Dr. Waldemar Mordecai Wolf Haffkine, an Orthodox Jew, Hovev Tsion (Lover of Zion) and scientist
who left his homeland because as a Jew he could not be appointed to a responsible academic position there. After success-
fully preparing a vaccine against cholera in Calcutta he was
invited by the Government of India to help fight the dreaded
bubonic plague raging in Bombay. Within three months, Dr.
Haffkine inoculated himself with his newly discovered anti-
plague vaccine to prove its effectiveness.

When the small laboratory room proved too small for the
required production, His Highness Sir Sultan Shah Agakhan
offered his own bungalow at Mazgaon for Haffkine's use. Within
two and a half years of his arrival in Bombay, the Plague Research
Laboratory, with Haffkine as director, was opened. Today this
center, vastly enlarged and renamed the Haffkine Institute in his

memory, serves as a medical research institute in the fields of entomology, vaccines and antitoxins.

Polish-born Mr. Hersh Cynowicz, former lawyer at Wilno and Cracow, escaped just two days before the Nazis marched into Russia, and headed for Palestine by way of Moscow and Teheran, walking long distances enroute. He ended his flight in Bombay, entering the business world there and becoming an Indian citizen. Active in work among the Central European refugees, he has been elected and reelected to the presidency of the Central Jewish Board of Bombay on which are represented all local Jewish institutions. President of this Central Jewish Board at its founding in 1944 was Sir Victor Sassoon; later Bene Israel Dr. Elijah Moses was President; and now Mr. Cynowicz heads the Board that is the responsible, representative organ of Bombay Jewry in its dealings with the Government of India and its authorities.

No more is the Jewish community of India an island unto itself. The Jewish Agency encourages Jewish studies by training teachers and conducting classes in a number of the villages as well as in Bombay itself. The American Joint Distribution Committee includes India in its sphere of activity, supplying funds for needy children, orphans and the aged. Cultural and religious activities also benefit from the J.D.C., which in 1968 assisted a total of 1,700 individuals in India.

The ORT (Organization for Rehabilitation Through Training) School opened in Bombay in 1963 and gives technical training. The majority of its students come from the villages speaking only the native Marathi, whereas English is required for the jobs for which they are being trained. An electronic language laboratory helped solve this problem, and local industrial plants now compete for the services of the graduates of this school.

Bombay may well be the gateway of India, but today it has proved to be the gateway *out* of India for the large number of Indian Jews emigrating to Israel.

∽§ UNITY IN NEW DELHI §∾

New Delhi, declared India's capital by the English in 1911, is today a city of spacious boulevards, broad tree-lined avenues and parks, diplomatic enclaves and luxury hotels. Along majestic Rajpath are the imposing pink-buff sandstone government buildings—the Presidential palace, Parliament and secretarial buildings. Connaught Place is the place to go for a smart cafe or restaurant. Connaught Place is also a paradise for shoppers, for here are the "Emporia" selling such exquisite items as the soft, supple Kashmiri shawls, Benares brocades and handicrafts from all over the country. Near the old Imperial Hotel on broad Janpath Road is an open-air curio market. And Rajghat, the memorial marking the spot where Gandhi was cremated, is impressive with a paved road leading to the simple block of concrete set on a platform and surrounded by a garden.

But New Delhi is more than a creation of the twentieth century. It is a city with an ancient past. The site of the city was shifted seven times. Go to Old Delhi today and you will see what remains of that Delhi which was built by Shah Jahan, seventeenth-century Moghul emperor responsible also for the Taj Mahal. There in Old Delhi, behind red sandstone walls, still stands Shah Jahan's home—the Red Fort with its arcades and gardens, its marble and its precious stones. Facing the Red Fort is Jama Masjid, largest mosque in India, and near the mosque—a junk market. Old Delhi is a place of narrow pathways, of traffic jams, of teeming bazaars on Chandni Chowk, main thoroughfare in the days of Shah Jahan.

It was in the days of these Moghul emperors of the sixteenth and seventeenth centuries that Persian Jews emigrated to India in search of religious freedom. Emperor Akbar, grandfather of Shah Jahan, initiated open religious disputations among leaders of various religious groups, and some of the participants in these discussions were Jews.

But back to the broad boulevards of New Delhi—and at 2 Humayun Road one comes to the heart and center of today's Jewish community, the Judah Hyam Hall, named for the late Khan Bahadur Dr. Judah Hyam, a leader of Poona Jewry. A modest, yet dignified structure, its front elevation is trimmed with two rows of Stars of David superimposed on orange-colored glass and a menorah.

The Donors' Tablet in the entrance foyer lists contributors from all over India—from Cochin, Bombay, Calcutta, Ahmedabad,

Poona, Simla, Lahore, Nagpur, Gangapur, Junagadh and other places in addition to those of the local community. Kadavumbhagam Synagogue of the Black Jewish Community of Jewtown, Cochin, also added its contribution. Gifts came from London, from Canada and from the United States. American donors included the J.D.C. as well as Emanuel Celler, member of the U.S. House of Representatives, and Rabbi Ferdinand M. Isserman of Temple Israel of St. Louis, both of whom had been in New Delhi in the early 1950s.

Separated from the synagogue by a wall and with its own special entrance is the Jewish cemetery, a well-kept, garden-like plot in which all tombs face west, toward Jerusalem. One of the graves is that of Signalman Bernard Pruim, a British World War II casualty. When the Imperial War Graves Commission wished to remove his remains for reburial in one of its own cemeteries, the Jewish Welfare Association asked that the Jewish soldier's body remain in this Jewish cemetery.

Another grave is that of Baby Mitra, grandchild of Hannah Sen, the brilliant and talented Calcutta-born Jewess who was director of the Lady Irwin College of New Delhi, a representative of the All-India Women's Conference at international gatherings, a delegate to the U.N. Commission on the Status of Women and a member of the Indian delegation to UNESCO in 1951.

In 1931 when the British began developing New Delhi, two Jewish families went there on government service. They applied for and were granted this plot of land for use as a cemetery. More Indian Jews were posted to work there, and as it was the capital, Jews from other countries came with the staffs of foreign embassies.

In 1949, not long after India had become an independent nation, the Jewish Welfare Association of Delhi and Northern India was reorganized as a "non-political body for social, cultural and religious purposes." Prayer services were held in private homes. As numbers increased to about 125 in and around New Delhi, including those at the foreign embassies, the need was felt for a public center, and an appeal for funds was launched.

The cornerstone of the Judah Hyam Hall was laid on February 12, 1956, at a ceremony including the recitation of the well-known Psalm 121 beginning:

I will lift up mine eyes into the mountains;
From whence shall my help come?
My help cometh from the Lord,
Who made heaven and earth.

and the Hallelujah Psalm 150 containing the lines:

Praise Him with the blast of the horn;
Praise Him with the psaltery and harp.
Praise Him with the timbrel and dance;
Praise Him with stringed instruments and the pipe.

In September of the same year the dedication took place. During this rite the congregation ascended the steps of the synagogue chanting Psalm 30, used at the dedication of the Second Temple in Jerusalem, which begins:

A Psalm; a Song at the Dedication of the House;
*   of David.*
I will extol Thee, O Lord, for Thou hast raised me
*   up,*
And hast not suffered mine enemies to rejoice over
*   me.*

and Ezra Kolet, Honorary Secretary of the Jewish Welfare Association, opened the main door of the new place of worship with the benediction:

Blessed art Thou, O Lord our God, King of the
universe who has kept us in life and hast preserved
us and enabled us to reach this season.

Built on part of the plot originally allotted for cemetery purposes, the Beit Din of London ruled that since the whole piece of land had not been consecrated as a burial ground and in consideration of the dividing wall and separate entrance, the synagogue could be built on part of the original cemetery tract.

On a pleasantly warm Sunday morning in November 1961 I sat in on a meeting of the Jewish Welfare Association at the Judah Hyam Hall. The meeting had been moved out of doors to take advantage of the fine weather. Leaders of the community then included E.E. Jhirad, Judge Advocate of the Indian Naval Headquarters, who was president of the association; Baruch B. Benjamin, Under Secretary, Ministry of Commerce and Industry, a former president of the group; Colonel George Benjamin of the Indian Army, who was treasurer; Joshua Benjamin, a Senior Architect in the Government of India, who had designed the Judah Hyam Hall (the surname Benjamin is very common among Indian Jews and these Benjamins were not related); Ezra Kolet, then a Deputy Secretary to the Government of India (and now a Joint Secretary) who was honorary secretary of the association and Benjamin Jacob of the Delhi Safe Deposit Co.

Under discussion that Sunday morning in New Delhi were the plans for the forthcoming Hanukkah party for the children. Also on the agenda was a report on the plight of the half-dozen Jewish families living in Ajmer, almost 300 miles distant.

Some days after the meeting I went down to visit that lost corner of Indian Jewry at Ajmer. It was the period when all India was celebrating one of its major festivals—the Diwali—honoring among others Lakshmi, the Goddess of Wealth. Free for the holiday period, Ezra Kolet was also making the journey to his old home town where his parents were buried. Everyone else seemed to be on the move that night. The railroad station was full of clamor as hundreds of people converged there carrying their food—and their bedding.

Ezra Kolet had wisely warned me, "Don't travel first-class, for even there you must provide your own bedding for the overnight journey. Go air-conditioned class; it's more expensive than first class, but your berth will be supplied with bed linen." I followed his advice. I seemed to have not only a berth, but a whole air-conditioned car to myself for the night's trip, during which we passed the rose-pink stone city of Jaipur.

Promptly at six in the morning, at one of the stops, there was a knock at my door and morning tea was brought in. At nine that morning we were met at the Ajmer station by three local Jews.

Ajmer, a fair-sized city of Oriental charm encircled by hills in the state of Rajasthan, is a railway center with workshops for the manufacture, maintenance and repair of locomotives and railroad carriages. The Jews find employment in these railway workshops as artisans or fitters, their average salary being about 120 rupees ($25) a month. Ajmer has had Jews since the beginning of this century, for the earliest tombstone in the cemetery, in a quiet setting on the fringe of Lake Anasager, bears the date of 1905.

The Ezekiel family, first on my round of visits, lived in a thick-walled stone house with small barred windows and a tiny front lawn. The daughters were in native dress—one in a sari, the other in the popular trousered Punjabi dress. Handsome, dark-eyed, nineteen-year-old Raphael had a burning desire to settle in Israel. From the Jewish Agency office in Bombay he had received an application form and a book. Holding the book reverently with both hands, he brought it to me. It was *Elef Millim* (A Thousand Words) written by Dr. Aharon Rosen of the Hebrew University. To Ajmer's Raphael Ezekiel this book spelled a holy bond with Israel. But what could he do with it? He knew no Hebrew— "didn't know an aleph from a bet," and there was no one to teach him.

For in Ajmer there was no teacher to give any Hebrew instruction. In the 1920s and 1930s, when there were between fifteen to twenty Jewish families, Dr. Samuel Korlekar had conducted religious services in his home, following the Orthodox Sephardi ritual. Now there was no minyan, no public service, no Sefer Torah, no instruction. A Bar Mitzvah ceremony means only that the boy is supplied with a tallit. However, one rite that is adhered to is circumcision, with the mohel being brought from Ahmedabad or Bombay, hundreds of miles away. Whatever remains of Jewish consciousness in Ajmer is a result of home observance.

From the Ezekiels I went on to the Kerulkar home. This was a one-bedroom house. Five of the nine children of this family had gravitated to Bombay in search of better economic opportunities. There they had found work as mechanics or electricians, and were trying to maintain the family unit by living together in one apartment. At home, the father found it hard to support the rest of the family.

The Aaron Elias Isaac home was the typical tiny stone house, with the entrance door leading directly into the living quarters. "Living quarters" meant just one room which served as a dining room, living room and bedroom for the entire family of two adults and five children—ranging in age from seven to fourteen years. For sleeping there was a double bed and a window seat, the remaining children sleeping on blankets spread on the stone floor. A table, a few chairs and a simple glass-fronted cabinet completed the furnishings. Jewish touches in the room were a Book of Psalms and a brass Hanukkah lamp with glass containers for coconut oil.

Opening from the living room was a small space without any windows, used for general storage. A few steps and I was through this storage room standing in the doorway of the kitchen, talking to Nora and Malka, fourteen and twelve years old, as they rolled out the dough for the flat bread to be baked on the charcoal stove. The kitchen was a tiny cramped space, with room only for the two girls, the stove, a small table and a few jugs of water. What light there was came through the open door leading into the backyard.

As a guest (the first American Jew to visit the Ajmer community), I was invited to join the men, Mr. Kolet and our host, for the evening meal. Intended as an honor, it succeeded in making me thoroughly uncomfortable—for while we three were being served by the girls, the hostess sat at the far side of the room. When we finished, she and the children would, according to local custom, eat what remained.

That night all Ajmer was ablaze with lights—on rooftops, in windows, in doorways—to illuminate Goddess Lakshmi's way to one's home in the hope that she would bring good fortune to the family within.

I returned to New Delhi Jewry, itself a small community of Jews who carried on the age-old tradition "Kol Yisrael arayvim zeh lazeh" (All Jews are responsible one for the other). Some time ago they had aided brethren from Pakistan; at another time they had eased the way for Afghanistan Jews trying to reach Israel via India. Now they were coming to the assistance of the small group in Ajmer. How appropriate that the Jewish Welfare Association of New Delhi had taken for its motto, "Behold how good and how lovely it is when brethren dwell together in unity."

A fitting addition to this thought of unity is that at the first wedding celebrated at the Judah Hyam Hall (November 1969) the bride was native Rachel Roy and the groom, American Myron Belkind, Bureau Chief of the Associated Press, stationed in New Delhi.

• 7 •
AFGHANISTAN

⋖§ PURIM IN AFGHANISTAN §⋗

PURIM IN AFGHANISTAN—I HAD BEEN INTRIGUED WITH
the idea of spending this holiday with the thirty-five Jewish
families in Kabul and the thirty families in Herat, all that remained in 1966 of a once large Jewish community in this landlocked country bordered on the north by Central Soviet Asia, on
the east by China, on the south by India and on the west by Iran. I
came up from the south, from New Delhi—where there was an
Ariana (Afghanistan National Airlines) flight once a week on
Thursdays—to Kabul 6,000 feet high in the Hindu Kush Mountains. After hours of delay, I was glad to see the sign "Fasten Seat
Belts" which meant we were ready for take-off. Unable to make
the simple attachment work I called the steward for assistance.
His response was "Is it really necessary to have it fastened?"
Such was my first contact with the Afghan people.

I was armed with a letter of introduction to one of the Jewish
families, given to me by a native son of Afghanistan Jewry—now
a rug and gem dealer in Singapore—and I had been told, "Go to
the Serai Shazadeh—the Royal Marketplace—there you will find
the Jewish shopkeepers."

Scene near Kabul's post office; year-round snow-covered Hindu Kush Mts.; veiled women in the typical Afghanistan all-enveloping chadaries.

In any other place I would have asked at the hotel how to locate the Simantov family. But this was Kabul, in a country that is 99 percent Mohammedan, Islam being the official State religion. Two former kings (Amunullah and Nadir Shah), who were reformers and had advocated freeing women from the wearing of the veil, had been forced to abdicate by fanatic Moslems.

Life for Jews under such a regime was hemmed in by restrictions. Until a few years ago they had to pay a head tax. Military service for Jewish men meant only clean-up duties, and no training with weapons. Officially, Jews may not engage in the import and export trade, and are limited to petty business.

About forty years ago Jews living in the northern cities of Mazar i Sharif and Maimonne, near the Russian border, had been evacuated—for the government feared their trade with Russia was a cover-up for Communist activity. So now all the Jews are found either in Kabul or in Herat, a thousand kilometers (621 miles) to the west on the way to Iran. Emigration to Israel is forbidden.

With this background in mind, I limited my enquiries at Hotel

Three Kabul Jews, wearing Afghan caracul caps, in front of one of Serai Shazadeh's Jewish-owned shops; dilapidated and almost bare shelves, seemingly not to arouse envy of non-Jews.

Kabul to a request for directions to Serai Shazadeh and started out that Friday morning. All along the streets, paralleling the sidewalks, ran open ditches intended to drain off rain water, but serving also as fine repositories for orange peels.

Clop, clop went the horses drawing the ghadis, the two-wheeled carriages with one seat next to the driver and room for two more passengers sitting back to back with the coachman. Two men, yoked to a heavily laden cart, were pulling the burden while another man helped push it. Bent over from the weight of heavy cases on their backs, other men trudged by. Small-time "merchants" took up their sidewalk posts with trays of nuts and raisins, and I thought of the Yiddish folksong "Rozshinkes und Mandlen" (Raisins and Almonds).

Women looked like walking tents in their finely pleated, ankle-length chadaries with small open-work lattice frontispieces to enable them to see their way. Many of the men wore wide pantaloons and knee-length shirts, to which a waist-length jacket had been added on this cold February day. One man made a colorful picture with his green pantaloons, purple turban and brown robe thrown over his shoulders. Another man's robe of variegated stripes made me think of Biblical Joseph's coat of many colors. And some, the more sophisticated, were in Western suits and coats, and caracul caps. In front of the Ariana Airline terminal, was a line of men ready to start their pilgrimage to Mecca.

Lovely rugs were hung for display over the low mud walls lining the banks of the Kabul River running through the center of the city. On both riverbanks were numerous tiny stalls. As I crossed the bridge to the far side of the river, I noticed a donkey carrying two panniers full of oranges. His master was urging him to cross a ditch. But the not-so-dumb beast refused to jump across the ditch with those bags loaded with oranges. Despite the kicks of his owner, the donkey calmly continued along his own chosen path, followed by his dejected master.

Turning left, I continued until I came to a partly opened wooden door between two shops on the riverside thoroughfare. Stepping through this door, I found myself in the world of Serai Shazadeh, a block-square inner courtyard lined on all sides with small shops on three levels. Down the center of the extensive courtyard ran another row of shops. Most of these places were closed, for this was Friday, the Moslem Sabbath. Those places of business that were open were attended by bearded and turbaned Sikhs.

Apparently Friday was a bad day on which to have started my search for Jews. After some time an English-speaking man approached me. "Where is the shop of Mayer?" I asked. "Closed today." "And where is the shop of Musa?" "Closed today and tomorrow." And in an aside to another one of the group that surrounded us by this time I heard him say, "Yahoodi." "Where are the shops of the Yahoodim (Jews)?" I asked, following his lead. "Oh, they're all closed today and tomorrow. But come into my shop," he said opening the closed shutter of his store from whose dark interior he brought out a little notebook and gave me the house telephone number of Mr. Shalom, one of the Jewish shopkeepers. I had to be content with that. Then I discovered

Purim in Kabul—Reading the Megillah of Esther in the synagogue; men following the reading from individually owned scrolls.

why he had been so helpful. He was a Hindu—and Hindus don't feel any anti-Semitism.

Back in the street I meandered about in Kabul mud. Only the main streets were paved, and that with the aid of the U.S.S.R. I was observed by one and all, including the policeman. After all, a Western woman strolling about all alone was not too familiar a sight in Kabul. Later my steps brought me back to the wooden door shutting off the inner world of Serai Shazadeh. Some of the men who had surrounded me earlier were still there. From their excited babble, I somehow gathered the notion that one of the Jewish shopkeepers had come.

Word of my return must have spread rapidly, for in a moment, shiny-eyed, English-speaking young Mordecai dashed down the wooden steps from the second story to welcome a fellow Jew from abroad. He led me to his father's office, a tiny cubicle with a beautiful Turkoman rug and a small stove with its stack of wood in one corner.

Behind the desk, on which there was an abacus, sat dignified

Musa ben Mordecai Moradoff, of a family, which like many of Kabul's Jewry, had originally come from Meshed crossing the border from Iran into Afghanistan's western Herat. My quest had met with success—I had made contact with the Jews of Afghanistan.

That evening Mordecai ben Musa Moradoff guided me to the synagogue for the Sabbath service. Between one shop displaying rugs and another selling antiques, ran a narrow alley leading into a courtyard. In the rear was a small one-story house with a bay window, decorated with potted geraniums both outdoors and indoors. Two rooms had been combined and were being used as a synagogue. No inscription, no indication on the outside that this was a house of worship. An extra room leading off the narrow hallway served for the quarters from which the women could listen to, but not see, the service. But no matter, for Kabul's women do not attend Sabbath service. They come only on festivals.

The men sat on the narrow benches encircling the walls and surrounding the Reading Desk in the center. The ceiling was carved, the floor and benches covered with rugs. As the only woman in attendance, I was prepared to find a place near the entrance so as to make my presence inconspicuous. Instead, I was led close to the Ark, the place of honor, where three chairs had been placed facing the congregation—one for Mr. Shalom, the head of the community, another for Mr. Moradoff who was gabbai and one for me.

As the men came in, many removed their shoes. One man was in pantaloons and turban; most were in Western dress with grey or black caracul hats. The only man of the local group who had been to New York wore a fedora for the Sabbath.

A hasid of the Lubavitsher Rebbe of Brooklyn had been in Kabul the preceding year and taken the Jews to task for not having a proper house of worship. For despite the tiny offices, warped wooden floors, dilapidated furniture and the all but empty shelves, Kabul's Jewry was doing well financially. Means had been found to get around the official regulations and they were in business as importers and exporters, money-changers, dealers in rugs, tires, automobile spare parts, dried fruits and pistachios.

They took the hasid's admonition to heart. Later I was shown the new synagogue complex under construction for the use of these thirty-five families. This new house of worship would face directly on the street just a short distance from the American Embassy and had a Magen David design built directly into the wall. It would have place for the two congregations that were in existence—one whose membership had immigrated either from Bokhara or from the Afghanistan city of Balkh; the other composed of families who came to the capital from provincial Herat. In addition there would be classrooms for the children, a mikveh and space for the shohet to perform his duties.

Most of their homes, surrounding courtyards where chickens freely roamed about, gave the same feeling of being run-down as did the shops and offices. It was as if they were making a conscious effort to appear no better off than the Ishmaelim, as they called their Mohammedan neighbors.

After the Sabbath morning service I was invited to join the Mayer Simantov family for the Sabbath meal. This was the home of a well-to-do family that had upholstered chairs—an unusual sight in Kabul. A young Mohammedan servant girl sat on the floor in the corner—like Cinderella in the old tale—feeding the wood stove. Food had been kept warm overnight on the stove in a compartmentalized container. One receptacle was for meat and potatoes, a smaller pot above that for fish, and atop that one for hard-boiled eggs, all covered over to retain the heat.

By the time Purim approached I felt so much at home that I casually popped in for a chat at the Serai Shahzadeh shops. On the day before Purim—the Fast of Esther—one man said, "I must telephone home to see how the family is. My wife and both my sons, aged ten and twelve, are fasting this day."

Then came megillah night when the Scroll of Esther is read. This time the women and girls, dressed in gala clothes, were present in the room reserved for them. A two-year-old, dark-eyed girl was in Afghanistan national holiday costume, pantaloons and a bespangled knee-length dress. The women wore long loose gowns of brightly colored velveteen. They did not seem to resent my leaving them so that I could listen to the reading of the megillah in the synagogue proper with the men, while they stood in the doorway when they wanted to see the proceedings.

Among those in the synagogue was Yehezkel the Kalantar, whose duties had been to represent the Jewish community in all official matters with the Afghanistan government, including matters of passports and army service. Now sixty years old, he was considered too old to function. Out of respect for his age, however, he was permitted to retain his title, but the duties of his office were actually being carried out by David Moradoff, an intelligent, modest man in his thirties. This Moradoff not only performed the duties of Kalantar, but also acted as hazzan, shohet and reader. "He's our little rabbi," the people said of him fondly.

Everyone had brought his own megillah in which to follow the reading. The boys were well provided with "gragers." One young boy sported a toy gun in his hip pocket in true Western style. All were used at the appropriate times. But stamping one's feet to drown out the name of Haman lost its effectiveness on the rug-covered floor. During the evening a song with the following chorus was heard:

> *It's Purim, it's Purim*
> *Blessed be He Who chose us.*

Long ago it was customary to make life-size figures representing Haman and his children to be burned on Purim, but this practice is not followed any more.

Purim in Afghanistan is a two-day festival. This enabled me to spend the first day in Kabul and to fly down to Herat for Shushan Purim. My friends in Kabul tried to dissuade me from going. "Why do you want to go to Herat, a thousand kilometers away? It's such a primitive place. There are no trains; traveling by bus is long and arduous over a road that has not been completed; and the Ariana Airline, well, that is notoriously uncertain as far as fixed schedule is concerned." But I had not come all these thousands of miles to be diverted. Fortunately Ariana did not cancel its flight that day and off I went.

I reached Herat, with its mud-brick houses, with donkeys plodding along under heavy loads, and camels haughtily raising their heads into the air. The Jews lived in Bazaar Iraq, one of the oldest parts of this ancient city rebuilt by Alexander the Great, destroyed again by Genghis Khan and by Tamerlane, and whose minarets and mosque and old walls are a reminder of days of former splendor.

How could I find Bazaar Iraq? At the Park Hotel (recommended to me as Herat's best by the Royal Afghan Consulate in New York), which offered a tiny wood stove for a bit of comfort in my room, I had difficulty making myself understood. I decided to enquire at the local Ariana office. I asked for a taxi, only to discover there was no such thing in Herat. Here one traveled by ghadi, drawn by a horse in fancy trappings, so up I climbed to the rear seat and away we bumped on the rutted unpaved road. Arriving at the Ariana office, I had to wait for the English-speaking staff member. Yes, he was in the office, but at the moment he was on his knees, prostrating himself before Allah. When he was finished and his prayer rug carefully folded away, he directed me.

Past the Blue Mosque, down one bazaar street where the goldsmiths and silversmiths plied their craft, along another street where rugs were being woven I kept going. "Bazaar Iraq?" I continued to ask. Hands pointed to the direction I should follow. Clanging and banging in another bazaar told me I had reached the area where copper vessels were being formed. Then I came to the comparative quiet of a section of small drapery shops. I was in Bazaar Iraq.

Somewhere in the web of small shops owned by both Moslems and Jews, down narrow lanes no more than six feet wide, lived Herat's lone English-speaking Jew, Naftali Basal. I asked one shopkeeper sitting cross-legged on the raised platform of his little stall, "Naftali?" I got no response indicating any recognition of the name. I walked on. A patriarchal grey-bearded man in a fine robe came by. "Naftali?" I asked again. The expression of his eyes told me I had met someone to whom the name Naftali was known. I attempted a few words in Hebrew. "It's Purim today. I'm Jewish." While I was trying to establish communication, four young men came up. Shimon, one of the four, spoke Hebrew—so I had a personal guide to the Jewish community of Herat.

Naftali? He really existed, but did not turn up until late that evening, when he took me back to my hotel in his jeep. But before that, Shimon had guided me through a narrow passageway between two shops, into a courtyard and up narrow steep steps to a home where the Purim Seudah was taking place that Shushan Purim day.

Leaving our shoes at the entrance, we entered a room that had no chairs, no tables, no couches, no furniture as we know it in America, only exquisite rugs covering the entire floor. Along one side of the room sat the men, cross-legged on the rugs, in pantaloons and turbans. On the opposite side sat the women, some in Afghan costume: knee-length dresses over ankle-length pants, others in Western dress, but all with kerchiefs on their heads. I took my place on the women's side of the room, sitting down, not too gracefully, on the rugs.

Runners of white cloth were extended over the rugs, one in front of the men and another in front of the women. On these were platters with the special Purim delicacies—hard-boiled eggs dyed in fanciful design much like the Easter eggs common in the West, and halvah. The halvah—made of browned rice and sugar boiled in water until of a kasha-like consistency, then cooled and pistachio nuts added—made good eating. All this in addition to the usual fried fish, boiled chicken, raisins and pistachios. In true Herati fashion, the food was eaten with no other implements but one's hands. For that evening I, too, was a true Herati.

On my return to Kabul, Ariana lived up to its reputation. Three days in succession flights were canceled. Finally I made the return trip by hitch-hiking to Kandahar, and from there by taxi for the remaining five hundred kilometers, through an area where, with the exception of one tiny village, the sole inhabitants were the nomadic kuchis in their tents.

This time, Kabul seemed a sophisticated city.

◄§ THE YEAR ROUND IN AFGHANISTAN §►

Each holiday of the Jewish calendar is celebrated meticulously in Afghanistan, a country almost as large as the state of Texas, with a population of fourteen million. Among these Tajiks and Uzbeks, Pushtuns and Sikhs, and other ethnic groups, lived those few Jewish families, remnant of a community whose origin goes far back in history in a land that was on the caravan route of Central Asia. The late Itzhak Ben Zvi placed the coming of the Jews to Afghanistan between the sixth and fourth centuries B.C.E. Other scholars say there were 40,000 Jews in Afghanistan a century ago.

Had I remained there for the Passover I would have seen great preparations for that holiday. Rugs must be changed lest some bit of leavened bread has lodged in them; dishes are "kashered" in the courtyard; each family bakes its own matzoh from wheat which has been checked for purity and the milling of which is supervised by a religious leader.

For the Seder, the family sits on mattresses placed on the rugs, each one supplied with a hand-embroidered pillow, so that he may truly "lean" back. The haroset on the Seder plate is made of dates, nuts, raisins, pomegranate, lemon water and wine. Sugar is not used, for that is considered non-kosher for Pesach. The matzoh to be reserved for the afikomen is placed in a scarf and held over the shoulder of the youngest child during the entire Seder. He has been told, "This is how our forefathers went out of Egypt on this night" and the father recites the Four Questions. During the recounting of Dayenu they strike one another with leeks, to recall the Egyptian taskmasters' beating of the Jewish slaves. At the conclusion of the Seder, part of the afikomen is preserved in the firm belief it will bring good health.

The chickens which I had seen rambling about in the court-yards at Purim time now come to their intended use. For at Passover time, great quantities of food are prepared for guests and family.

A special ceremony takes place on the closing day of the Passover festival. After gathering wheat stalks in the fields, the people come to be blessed at the home of Musa Moradoff (of the first family I had met in Kabul) who is a kohen and gabbai. On a table, a mirror and water have been placed to which one adds some money and precious stones as one enters. They bow to Mr. Musa, as he is affectionately known to everyone, and he blesses them and the wheat stalks, invoking for each one a year of good luck, a year with money and gems. Before leaving, I was told, they take back the money and the gems which they had deposited on the mirror.

The day following the close of the Passover season is a day for picnicking in the gardens outside the city.

The period of Omer is observed as a time of mourning, as in the rest of the Jewish world. No weddings or other joyous occasions are celebrated during this time.

Shavuot time is the season for roses in Kabul. When the Sefer Torah is brought to the Reading Desk on this festival, it is decked with garlands of roses. After the reading the roses are again placed on the Sefer Torah and in this manner the Scroll is returned to the Ark.

On Tisha B'Ab, in addition to the customary fasting and sitting on the floor of the darkened candle-lit synagogue in poor clothes, a collection of money is taken. Formerly, this money was used for the purchase of sheep and cattle which were sacrificed on the day following Tisha B'Ab in the courtyard of the synagogue (in memory of the near-sacrifice of Isaac by Abraham) with the meat going to the poor. There being no poor Jews in Kabul, the meat was given to poor Mohammedans. Nowadays, however, this practice has undergone some change. In place of the sacrifice, the money raised for this purpose is sent to Israel.

Again for Rosh Hashanah a sheep or calf or chicken is slaughtered in memory of the sacrifice of Isaac, and the meat distributed to the poor. For the rite of tashlikh, all assemble at a home that has a large well, into which they cast their sins symbolically by shaking out their clothing. Holiday food includes not only honey with apples to wish everyone a sweet year, but also the lung and head of an animal to ensure good health all year, for, "So it is written in the Torah," they said.

On the day preceding Yom Kippur the following scene is enacted. A man, stripped to the waist, his face to the wall, leans against a wooden pillar jutting out obliquely from the wall of the synagogue, his hands outstretched above his head. The religious representative ties his wrists to the pillar. The following is heard:

My son, despise not the chastening of the Lord,
Neither spurn thou His correction;
For whom the Lord loveth He correcteth,
Even as a father the son in whom he delighteth.

*And thou shalt consider in thy heart, that as a man
chasteneth his son, so the Lord thy God chasteneth
thee.*

With a leather thong the rabbi scourges the man across the left
shoulder thirteen times, repeating quietly this verse:

*But He, being full of compassion, forgiveth
iniquity and destroyeth not;
Yea, many a time doth He turn His anger away
And doth not stir up all His wrath.*

Each lash accompanies one of the thirteen Hebrew words com-
posing this verse. The rabbi hands the whip to a man sitting
nearby and says:

*No weapon that is formed against thee shall pros-
per;
And every tongue that shall rise against thee
in judgment thou shalt condemn.
This is the heritage of the servants of the Lord;
And their due reward from Me, saith the Lord.*

Again the rabbi takes up the thong and lashes the man thirteen
times over the right shoulder, and thirteen times again over the
left shoulder—thirty-nine times altogether. The younger generation is now breaking away from the observance of this rite—the
Malkot.

The sukkot put up in the individual home courtyards for the
Feast of Booths are lined with lovely rugs, and the family's main
meals are eaten in these temporary homes.

For Simhat Torah, the Scrolls are clothed in especially beautiful mantles. Only one Sefer Torah is carried in the seven circuits
of the synagogue and the privilege of carrying it is determined by
auction—for which vegetables, fruit and wine have been brought
to the synagogue. "Who will buy vegetables?" asks the auctioneer. The bidding usually starts at thirty afs (75 to 80 afs equal one
American dollar) and has been known to go as high as two
hundred afs for the honor of carrying the Torah for one circuit of
the synagogue.

On Hanukkah affianced girls receive gifts from their future
in-laws, the present usually a dress or something made of gold.

Tu B'Shevat is marked by eating seven different kinds of fruit—apricots, melons, apples, plums, bananas, raisins and watermelons. This is easily arranged in a fruit-growing country such as Afghanistan.

The weekly Sabbath observance has for all practical purposes brought the five-day work week to Kabul Jewry. "On Friday one must prepare for the Sabbath," said Mayer, one of the leading importers in Serai Shazadeh. "One must shop [the men in Kabul do the family shopping—an outgrowth of the government restrictions ordering Jewish women away from public markets], one must bathe and anyway the Mohammedan shops are closed on Friday." And as schools are closed on this day, Friday has also become the time for family picnics and social gatherings.

At all times Jews here prefer to avoid contact with or jurisdiction of the civil courts of the country. Should any controversy arise between two Jews, a committee of ten or fifteen people will hear both sides of the case. The individuals involved must accept the judgment of this group. If any individual is not willing to accede to the committee's decision, he is free to take his case to the civil court. But I was told, "Our people prefer to assent to the settlement proposed by the Jewish group—and never go to court."

All year round, no matter what the day is, Afghanistan's Jewry holds fast to certain beliefs. In time of severe illness, the "brick preparation" is considered a panacea. Salt, an onion, garlic, a raw egg, cotton, coal and a coin are placed on a clay brick. A knife is thrust into the clay brick which is then set out-of-doors in front of the house. Whosoever helps himself to either the coin or the egg will thereby have the illness transferred to him. Said intelligent, Westernized David: "Of course I don't believe in all this process, but two years ago my young son was seriously ill. The doctor's prescriptions didn't seem to do the child any good. Every day the boy was growing weaker and paler. My mother-in-law kept insisting we prepare the brick. I didn't think it would do any harm, so finally I told her to arrange and place the brick. And the child recovered," David finished with a half smile.

Another cure used in time of illness is to give the sick person a drink of water over which a kohen or scholar has recited Psalms.

Amulets containing the Shema are worn, and necklaces of eye-shaped pebbles are considered a protection against the Evil Eye.

There are a number of remedies which are believed to be effective in curing a woman's childlessness. One is to rub the afflicted woman with soap which has been used in the purification of a deceased person. Another cure is to take a girdle from a dead person and place it around her abdomen. If she is given a drink of the wine used at a Brit Milah, she will surely bear a child, according to their conviction.

Heaven's gates are believed to be wide open on the first night of Shavuot and again on the seventh night of Sukkot. On these nights one's wishes and prayers ascend easily to Heaven, and will be granted. "As a child," Mrs. N. said, "I always looked up to see the heavens open on these two nights, but somehow I never succeeded in seeing the longed-for happening."

In time of calamity, when the community is threatened, Psalms are recited in the synagogue. Money is collected and a sheep or cow sacrificed and the meat given to the poor. This is held to be such a great mitzvah that the threatened evil must surely be averted.

But let us move on now to a happy event such as marriage. In Afghanistan marriages are arranged by the parents. The boy's parents send representatives to broach the subject to the girl's parents. It isn't proper to give an answer immediately. So the agents return on their mission a number of times. When the girl's parents finally agree to the proposed marriage, they signify their acceptance by sending a gift of sugar tied in a silken kerchief to the young man's parents. Then friends of both houses come to the girl's home, where each one receives a small dish of sweets tied in a kerchief or in decorative paper.

Two weeks later, the groom-to-be, his parents and some young friends are invited to a Shabbat meal at the girl's home. On this occasion it is customary to bring gifts made of gold. The groom brings a bracelet, his mother a necklace and his father a watch or ring. Other gifts may include clothing, shoes, lipstick or manicure sets—to the value of two or three thousand afs. Appropriately enough, the menu for this shiduchin evening (betrothal) features doves.

The girl must take no notice of the young man on this betrothal evening, but she sits with his mother or sister. Should he talk to her, she must not answer. After everyone has left, the couple is left alone in the room for a little while. "It was such an embarrassing time for both of us," said one man in recalling his betrothal.

Within six months to a year after the betrothal, the wedding is held in the synagogue. A tallit is held as a canopy over the groom and the bride, and everyone holds a lighted candle during the ceremony.

The first week of the honeymoon is spent at the groom's house, where for seven consecutive evenings different groups of friends are invited for dinner. At each dinner, the Sevenfold Benediction is recited. There is another round of dinners at the bride's home during the second week of the honeymoon.

Gifts? Of course. Close friends bring three meters of good cloth; a box of chocolates from others is considered proper. And the groom gives a money gift—from 10,000 to 30,000 afs.

"Are there any cases of divorce?" I inquired. "We have no Beit Din any more so no divorces can be granted. Should the marriage turn out to be an unhappy one, they just suffer."

Intermarriage with Mohammedans is practically unheard of. Girls always accompany their parents to cinemas or outings and are never left alone with young people of their own age. There was only one case in this generation of a Jewish girl marrying a Mohammedan. In that instance the girl had been abducted by the boy's parents.

I was with the tiny community of Herat in their joy and in their grief. The joyous occasion was the Shushan Purim Seudah held on the second day of that festival. On another day word came that Yosef Aharon, Rabbi of Kabul and the only remaining rabbi serving in Afghanistan, had died and was being brought for burial to Herat, his birthplace.

That was a venturesome undertaking, what with the casual twice-a-week flight schedule between Kabul and Herat, and the one paved road (and that not yet complete) going the long way round via Kandahar in the south, making the distance to be covered a thousand kilometers. But Rabbi Yosef had been highly respected and his wish to be buried in Herat would be fulfilled.

A bus was hired and the shrouded body placed on a braided cot in the rear of the bus; the widow and members of the Kabul community accompanied the deceased. Word reached us that the cortege was leaving at three-thirty that afternoon, and by driving all night, should reach Herat by ten the following morning.

Early the next morning a group went out by jeep to a point a hundred kilometers away to act as escort, and the rest of Herat's Jewry assembled at the cemetery. I joined the group waiting there.

Ten o'clock, eleven o'clock, twelve o'clock came and went. No sign of anyone approaching. People spent some time visiting the graves of their kindred. Over the graves were tumuli, the artificial hillocks of mud and straw erected over cement or stone slabs. Many had no inscriptions to indicate whose resting place it was. But the family members knew.

Then word came that the bus had broken down along the mountainous route. Repairs were made and they were on their way again. Everyone remained calm. The women, most in chadaries—which they wore only when leaving their homes (so as not to differ from their Mohammedan neighbors)—settled down inside the entrance gate of the cemetery. The caretaker brought out small rugs on which one could rest. In view were the remains of the ancient city walls of Herat.

Soon the women began whiling away the time by smoking the chillum—the hubble-bubble water pipe—which was passed from one to another. Graciously it was offered to me, and I had a hard time turning down the friendly offer. The men, in the meanwhile, were resting outside the cemetery wall.

Someone on a bicycle served as liaison between the homes and cemetery and brought the flat pittah (bread) to allay any pangs of hunger. People talked quietly, or walked about or smoked the chillum. Not a word of impatience did I hear.

At four-thirty in the afternoon the cortege arrived, after a full night and day on the road. With its sad burden shrouded and concealed by a white cloth on which had been placed flowers and greenery, now wilted, the rug-covered cot was borne from the bus into the cemetery. Psalm 91 was recited as the cot was carried to an open area.

Woman smoking the chillum (water pipe) in Herat's Jewish cemetery during six-hour wait for arrival of body of deceased rabbi being brought by bus from Kabul, a thousand kilometers away.

The white cloth cover was raised somewhat for final inspection to ensure that everything was in order after the long arduous trip, and a small bag of Jerusalem soil was placed on the eyes of the deceased.

The honor of acting as pallbearers was decided by auction. The eulogy, in the Persian tongue, included a request for forgiveness and pardon for all from the departed one. Recitation of Psalm 137: "By the rivers of Babylon, there we sat down; Yea, we wept, when we remembered Zion," set a still more solemn mood.

All this time the widow sat on the ground, to one side, surrounded by the women. At times she was quiet, but then spells of chanting in a sing-song air would follow, the widow beating herself with both hands. Twice she ran to the open grave, wailing and throwing soil over her head, and had to be forcibly brought back.

As the body was being lowered into the grave, there were recitations from the Prophet Elijah and from the Zohar. With the saying of the Kaddish, the grave-side service ended.

I called one evening at the local home being used as the house of mourning. The men, including those who had come from Kabul and were paying their last respects by staying on for the entire shiva week in Herat, were in one room sitting on narrow mattresses spread over the rugs. Some were in the Oriental pajama-like costume, others in Western suits; some wore turbans, others the caracul caps.

Following the Afternoon Service, a section of the Zohar was recited. Then tea was served. Now the reader, in pajama outfit, bare feet and caracul cap, rose to lead the Evening prayers. Following this service, a pewter pitcher and bowl were passed around for the ritual washing of hands. A cloth runner was spread on the rugs in front of the men, bread and salt for the "motzie" placed and fried fish served. Again Zohar selections were read and the Kaddish repeated. Once more food was served, this time dried peas, raisins and salad greens. The men sitting near me said, "It is not so much an interest in eating so many varied foods, but rather the opportunity to recite the different berakhot for each type of food."

The Zohar selections following now were listened to with great attention. The words Gan Eden (paradise) and neshama (soul) were repeated over and over in this section and at the close Kaddish was recited again. Now came the main dish of food—rice and chicken, followed by oranges as the last course.

All this time, the widow sat in another room, surrounded by women. In taking leave of her one said, "May you remain in life; his place is now in paradise with the patriarchs."

What does the future hold for the Jews of Afghanistan, now left without a single rabbi and no Jewish schooling for the children? Herat's children—among whom I met Ibrahim, Sion, Daud, Amin, Zaolon, Bobojohn, Esther and Blura—were getting two hours' daily instruction in Persian and English from Danish Saljugi, an Afghan teacher. Fearing assimilation, their parents did not permit them to attend the government school. As to Jewish learning—there was none at all for these children. And the rooms where once the men gathered daily to imbibe some Hebrew learning, stood unused. Herat's four synagogues with their Sifrei Torah topped by ornate silver crowns and rimonim made by the

Mohammedans (for the Jews here are no silversmiths or crafts-men) were a reminder of the Jewish life that once throbbed in this ancient city. I found that weekday services were being held in only one synagogue, but all four open for Shabbat services for Herat's thirty families.

In Kabul the children did attend the government schools. Therefore the boys could not attend Shabbat services, for the schools are in session then. Only in the winter were they free to come to the synagogue, for then the schools are closed for the annual long vacation. Afghanistan cannot afford to heat its school buildings, so education takes a holiday in the winter of the year.

As for Jewish learning, I found none in Kabul. But the parents were hoping, in the near future, to reach an understanding with a former teacher so that Jewish instruction could start again.

How was it that under these circumstances most of my com-munication with the Jews of the older generation had been in Hebrew, I wondered. "Oh, we remember it from our youth, when we did have Jewish instruction in Jewish schools," I was told.

Members of these communities are finding their way to Israel. The government of Afghanistan does not permit emigration to Israel—but "a Jew finds a way." Suffice it to say that since the Declaration of the State of Israel, 3,800 Afghanistan Jews have settled in Israel. More are leaving, but not all. Said one of Kabul's well-to-do importers when I questioned him about the possibility of his taking up life in Israel, "I can't hope to compete with all those clever Jews in Israel. I guess I'll stay on here among the Afghans."

• 8 •

IRAN

IRAN—LAND OF THE PEACOCK THRONE—A NAME SUF-
ficient to excite the romantic imagination. When in Teheran, go to
see this Peacock Throne—and the rest of Iran's Crown Jewels in
the vault of the Melli Bank. You will be amazed at the resplendent
sight! The throne originally belonged to the kings of Delhi, from
where it was brought at the close of a military expedition.
Adorned with a fully expanded peacock's tail, all of solid gold
and gems, the throne is but one of the glowing sights in the vault.

There is also the globe with land and sea areas defined by
different-colored jewels. Crowns, tiaras, necklaces, watches—
everything gleaming with emeralds, rubies, diamonds, pearls and
sapphires. The mind reels at the sight of all this beauty and all
this splendor, which is on view twice weekly at the vaulted room
of the Melli Bank on Ferdowsi Avenue (named for a poet so
called because he was "the poet who came from Paradise").

Turning from all this radiance I went to another part of Teheran—the mahalleh, or ghetto, where the majority of Teheran's
50,000 Jews live, although since 1925 they have been free to live

wherever they choose. Streets were narrow and unpaved. Behind six-foot walls were the homes of mud-dried brick, each family having one or two rooms in which there was little or no furniture except for a rug on the stone floor.

As earning one's living through the crafts or the work of one's hands was looked down upon, most of the men made a meager living for their large families as peddlers or petty merchants. Their whole stock in trade consisted of a mere basket or two of fruits or vegetables. With their stock they sat cross-legged on the raised platform which served as the floor of the shop open to the street.

The mahalleh is what remains of an ancient Jewish community dating back more than 2,500 years, as recalled in II Kings 17:6:

> In the ninth year of Hosea, the King of Assyria
> took Samaria and carried Israel away into Assyria,
> and placed them in Halah and in Habor by the
> river Gozan and in the cities of the Medes.

The Jews spread out from Babylonia to other provinces including that of Persia, whose inhabitants were an Aryan people which had come down from the Black Sea to the north.

Cyrus, a Persian chieftain and vassal of King Astyages of Media, overthrew that king and himself became king of all the Median dominions; then he went on to conquer Lydia and the Babylonian empire. It was this Cyrus, founder of the largest empire the world had known, who permitted the first return to Zion less than fifty years after the destruction of the First Temple:

> Thus saith Cyrus, King of Persia: All the kingdoms
> of the earth hath the Lord, the God of heaven given
> me; and He hath charged me to build Him a house
> in Jerusalem, which is in Judah. Whosoever there
> is among you of all His people—His God be with
> him—let him go up to Jerusalem, which is in
> Judah, and build the house of the Lord, God of
> Israel, He is the God who is in Jerusalem. And
> whosoever is left, in any place where he so-
> journeth, let the men of his place help him with
> silver and with gold, and with goods and with
> beasts, beside the free-will offering for the house of
> God, which is in Jerusalem. [Ezra 1:2–4]

Because there was a strong element in Babylon that disapproved of the religious innovations of the last Babylonian king, Cyrus found it good politics to pose as the restorer of the religious status quo—and perhaps some prominent Jews were able to persuade Persian officials to advise Cyrus to extend this policy to Judah.

Cyrus's proclamation was later reinforced by Darius, who succeeded to the throne in 522 B.C.E. and in the following year issued this decree:

> . . . Moreover I make a decree concerning what ye shall do to these elders of the Jews for the rebuilding of this house of God; that of the king's goods, even of the tribute beyond the River, expenses be given with all diligence unto these men, that they not be hindered. And that which they have need of—let it be given them day by day without fail; that they may offer sacrifices of sweet savour unto the God of heaven, and pray for the life of the king and of his sons. [Ezra 6:8–10]

About eighty years after the first return, another group left for Jerusalem under the leadership of Ezra, in the reign of Artaxerxes; and thirteen years later Nehemiah received permission from the same Artaxerxes to go up to Jerusalem to rebuild the walls of the city. But it was true then, as it has been so many times since then, that it was the poorer class that made the return to Zion. The wealthier preferred to stay where they were, sending funds and gifts for the Temple in Jerusalem.

The Jews found life agreeable among the Persians as long as the ruling dynasty was Zoroastrian, as Cyrus had been, for Zoroastrians felt a close kinship with Judaism: They believed that mankind was descended from a single couple—Mashya and Mashyani (Adam and Eve)—and that God had appeared to Zoroaster on a mountain top and had given him a law for human behavior. There were no pictures in their temples, only a constantly burning fire. Prayers were recited three times daily: in the morning, before sunset and after dark. Feasts of the New Year and the New Moon were observed. Priests drank the juice of an intoxicating plant before the temple fire. Laws of uncleanness and purification after contact with the dead or unclean matter were strictly adhered to.

Zoroastrians believed it was the duty of man to fight for the powers of Good or Light headed by Ahuramazda, and to struggle against the powers of Evil or Darkness, chief of which was Ahriman. If he does so, a man would be rewarded with paradise; otherwise he would be punished with hell. The Jewish belief in the resurrection of the dead and in the doctrine of the Olam Haba (world to come) is considered by many Jewish thinkers to have resulted from contact with the Zoroastrian faith.

The tide of invasion and conquest moved over the land. Alexander the Great swept over Asia, across the Persian Empire as far as India. The Greeks were followed by the Seleucids and then the Parthians. Not until the third century C.E. did a Persian dynasty, the Sassanids, gain control once more. Making Zoroastrianism the state religion again, they held sway for four centuries. They in turn were overthrown by Arabs who brought Mohammedanism into the country. Throughout all these changes of rulers and dynasties and religions, Jewish life went on.

Benjamin of Tudela, visiting there in the twelfth century, reported that four of the tribes of Israel dwelt in Persia—the tribes of Dan, Zebulun, Asher and Naphtali. At times Jews reached positions of importance, as did Saad al Daulah in the thirteenth century. A physician, he became controller of finance and eventually the grand vizier. (For his part in uncovering corruption among government officials, Saad al Daulah was assassinated.)

During the sixteenth century there took place an event of such magnitude that it molded the character and condition of Persian Jewry for centuries to come. This was the time that Shiite Mohammedanism was made the State religion by the Safavid dynasty. The Shiites, followers of Ali (son-in-law of Mohammed) and of Husain and Hasan (grandsons of the prophet) introduced the tenet of Ritual Uncleanness, making anything touched by an infidel, by an unbeliever, ritually unclean for the Mohammedan.

As a result no Jew could leave his home on a rainy day lest the rain rolling off his garment touch a "believer" and make the Mohammedan "tref." Jews were not permitted to shop in the local markets, for fear their hands would defile food that might be used in a Mohammedan home. New coins were not minted lest an unbeliever's fingers touch the Mohammedan confession of faith engraved on one side of the coins. Jewish homes had to be of low elevation, and a Jew could not ride a horse—for an infidel's head must be lower than that of a "true believer." Special clothes and headgear were to be worn by Jews to make it easier for the Shiite to steer clear of contamination. The result—Jews were confined to ghettos shut off by gates.

Life for the Jews became humiliating and degrading. Economically poor, there was hunger and squalor. Culture declined and superstition grew. At the conclusion of the Yom Kippur services, men would crowd around a synagogue official who passed out bits of the candles that had been lit in the synagogue for the holy day. These were taken to childless women who ate the wax on the spot, for this was believed to be a remedy against barrenness. Visiting holy sites, such as the supposed tomb of Queen Esther, was widespread. They put faith in the efficacy of amulets and charms, and sold love potions.

As one writer has put it, "The soul departed, only the broken and decaying body remained." They had no strength or spirit to fight against their conditions, believing rather that their suffering would earn for them a greater portion in the world to come.

Another form of discrimination was the inheritance law—the Law of Apostasy. This gave a Jew who converted to Mohammedanism the right of inheritance from a relative, no matter how distant the relationship, if nearer relatives remained Jewish. Shah Abbas II in the seventeenth century tried forcible conversion, but eventually gave that up when he came to the conclusion that "Jews could not make good Moslems." The Qajar dynasty, in power until 1925, continued the policy of Ritual Uncleanness introduced by the Shiite Safavids.

A picture of what life was like for the Persian Jews is found in the reports of venturous explorers who undertook the hazards of travel in a country where robbers and marauders were on every road. Rabbi David de Beth Hillel, on his tour of Asian Jewish communities in the nineteenth century, tells how he was received in Persia:

I arrived one night near Bashkala. Nobody would receive me into their houses for any money I offered to them saying that the house would be de-

filed by my coming in because they knew me to be a Jew; and the same night was a very cold one and abundance of snow had fallen and it was impossible to sleep in the street. After many supplications I gave half a rupee to be allowed to sleep in a stable among their cattle.

Christian missionaries who reached the country in the nineteenth century thought they would find fertile soil for their work. Schools were opened in the ghettos and the London Missionary Society published the Old Testament in a Persian translation with Hebrew characters. Eventually, however, this Society had to admit:

The close connection of the Jews with the Jewish world outside Persia and the munificent donations of the French Alliance Israelite make the Jews less accessible to missionary influences.

For it was in this century that the bonds between the Jews of Persia and the Jews of the Western world became close. In 1858 Sir Moses Montefiore urged that the British and the French intervene through diplomatic channels with the government of Persia. He wanted to undertake the trip to Persia himself and use his own best efforts on behalf of the Jews there, but he was dissuaded from doing so by the British because of the perils that such a venture entailed and because of his age (he was in his seventies at the time).

Sir Moses then appealed directly to the Shah himself. Although a progressive man, the Shah was unable to effect a change in attitude on the part of provincial officials.

When in 1871 the Persian Jews appealed to their brethren, "Bring us forth out of this burning furnace of Iran to the Holy Land or cause us to emigrate to other countries," funds were raised in the United States and in England for their relief.

Three Jews—Bachshi ben Simon, Ismail ben Suleiman and Fettoulah bin Eliah—came from Teheran to London to report to the Anglo-Jewish Association. Included in this report was the story of a Jew who owed a Mohammedan the sum of £1. Unable to repay the £1, the Jew was killed by the Mohammedan. The

Jewish community petitioned the Shah to punish the murderer. The Shah referred the matter to a minister, who in turn submitted the case to a court of Mohammedan clergy. Since the testimony of a Jew was not accepted in Mohammedan courts, and as no Mohammedan was willing to testify against a brother believer, no redress for the crime could be found. Even if two witnesses had testified, the maximum sentence the murderer could have received would have been a fine of £12.

When Shah Nasir ad Din visited Europe in 1873 he was presented with petitions on behalf of the Persian Jews by the communities in London, Berlin, Amsterdam and Brussels. The Alliance Israelite Universelle in its petition said:

> *Sire—all the Jews know the history of their ances-*
> *tors. The Persian people brought the Jews back to*
> *their beloved Palestine, under the protection of the*
> *immortal Cyrus. . . . In the books of the Prophets,*
> *only Cyrus is called by the title of Messiah. . . .*
> *Cyrus broke the chains of the Jewish captives.*

And the French community, headed by Adolphe Cremieux, asked for permission to start a Jewish school in Persia. The Viennese Jews said, "Sire, be the Cyrus of our day."

The reaction of the Shah was a favorable one as indicated in the letter addressed some time later to Sir Albert Sassoon and other representatives of the Anglo-Jewish Association, by the son of the Shah, H.I.H. Prince Zil-us-Sultan:

> *I received your letter during my stay in Teheran*
> *and was made aware of its contents. I brought the*
> *letter in original to the sacred sight of His Gra-*
> *cious Majesty (my august Lord and benefactor and*
> *may my soul be sacrificed for him). His Majesty*
> *was much pleased for the manner in which you*
> *had expressed thankfulness. I am also highly*
> *obliged for your declaration of appreciation and*
> *satisfaction for the comfort and security enjoyed*
> *by Jews under my government.*

When the Shah made a second visit to Europe in 1889, Jewish deputations again met with him. This time the leader of English Jewry's representatives was Sir Albert Sassoon, head of David

Sassoon & Co., on whom the Shah had conferred the Persian Order of the Lion and the Sun, first class, in recognition of his assistance to and encouragement of Persian commerce.

Despite the benevolent attitude of the Shah and the effort of the central government to improve the system of justice, however, the mullahs (religious leaders) in the provinces continued to stir up religious hatred. The restrictions, the insults, the scorn, the contempt, the conversions and the massacres continued. The mention of the word Jew by a Moslem was considered an insult to the listener, so that the speaker would immediately add "saving your presence" or "excuse the term."

"We can no longer allow this poor Jewish population to stagnate in ignorance," said the Alliance Israelite Universelle in 1897 and the following year the first Alliance school for Jewish children in Persia was opened. The school received the patronage of the Shah:

> *I have learned with satisfaction that a number of Israelites desiring to procure for their children instruction they cannot acquire in other schools which are closed to them have decided to open an educational establishment where poor children and orphans will learn to bless my name according to the principles of the Law of Moses and to pray for me and for my kingdom. I consider the Israelites as my faithful subjects and the school which they wish to found in order to give instruction to a portion of my subjects as being useful and profitable to the entire kingdom. I have therefore ordered Nizam Es-Sultanah to remit for this undertaking a subvention of 200 tomans.*

Finally the conscience of the world was aroused by the situation in which Persian Jewry found itself. Diplomatic intervention was made in the closing years of the nineteenth century. The ministers of England, France and Turkey made representations to the Shah. The United States also showed its concern. Alexander McDonald, American consul in Teheran, intervened with the grand vizier.

In 1918 an amount of $15,000 was deposited with the State Department in Washington by the Joint Distribution Committee, and Secretary of State Lansing told the U.S. Minister at Teheran to render relief. In 1921 President Harding appointed Rabbi Joseph Saul Kornfeld as Envoy Extraordinary and Minister Plenipotentiary to serve in Persia, a post which Rabbi Kornfeld held for three years.

Not until the coming to power in 1925 of Shah Reza Pahlevi, father of the present Shah, did conditions take a turn for the better. Rising from the ranks as a soldier in a Cossack brigade in the Persian army, Shah Reza broke the power of the clergy, secularized and Westernized the country, permitted the Jews to leave the ghettos and to elect one of their group to represent the Jewish minority group in the parliament.

But so ingrained was their way of life, that when I visited Iran thirty-six years later the vast majority of the Jews were still living in the old mahallehs, with the narrow unpaved streets and tiny homes of mud-dried bricks.

In Teheran I met Rabbi Itzhak Meir Lewi. A Tarnower hasid born in Cracow and a member of Jerusalem's Beit Din, Rabbi Lewi had been sent to Teheran on a mission during World War II. That mission was to aid the Jewish refugees fleeing Russia and coming through Iran on their way to Israel.

What Rabbi Lewi witnessed in Iran came as a violent shock—the crushing, appalling life of the local Jews, a community where girls of nine or ten years of age were permitted to marry. Birth records were non-existent; all that was required was a statement by two witnesses that the girl was of a marriageable age, and this was easily arranged.

"What we need is a mission to the Jews in the Orient," thought Rabbi Lewi. He traveled through the country speaking in synagogues against early marriage, gathering the children who were receiving no schooling, renting buildings to serve as schools, appealing for funds. Isaac Shalom of New York was the first to respond.

Rabbi Lewi came to New York in search of collaborators for his mission to the Jews in the Orient. The Joint Distribution Committee allocated $100,000 for a three-year program. And Rabbi Lewi, with the formal permission of the Iranian Ministry of Education, organized the Otzar Hatorah, schools with a religious orientation, and a Teachers' Seminary. Many girls now continue

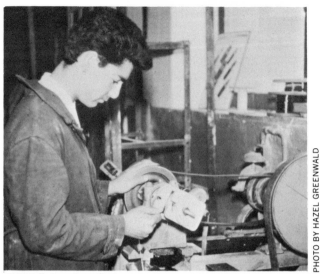

ORT School in Teheran, Iran—providing vocational and technical training in addition to academic education for boys and girls.

their education through the age of seventeen or eighteen.

After World War II the ORT opened a school for vocational training in addition to academic studies. To do so was no small accomplishment, for it had to overcome Persian Jewry's aversion to work with one's hands. Today the curriculum includes courses in toolmaking, automobile mechanics, electro-mechanics, refrigeration, radio and TV mechanics and drafting for the boys; office skills, cutting and dressmaking for the girls.

In 1967 ORT added a Basic Educational Center aimed at "salvaging lost children from the lowest depths." Dormitory facilities in the school compound have attracted students such as Aroni, of a Kurdish family. When he reached the school, Aroni was fifteen years old, penniless and dressed in a goatskin robe, the costume worn in his native Iranian Turkestan, isolated in place and remote in time. Upon his graduation four and a half years later, Aroni was awarded a scholarship to the university, the first-prize winner in a field of 2,300 applicants, and the Shah pinned the medal of his award on Aroni.

First in the field of general education for the Jews of Iran had been the Alliance Israelite Universelle, when it opened a boys' school in Teheran in 1898. Then followed a school for girls.

Gradually schools were established in other cities. Now there are Ettahad Schools (as the Alliance Schools are known in Iran) in Isfahan, Hamadan, Yezd, Kermanshah, Broudjerad, Nehavand, Senandadj and Shiraz.

Curriculum in these schools follows the Iranian Ministry of Education syllabus. Time for religious study is allotted, the term "religious" being elastic enough to include study of Hebrew as a language, Bible stories, songs, ceremonials and religious laws. At the Alliance School of thirty-eight classes, on Teheran's Avenue Jaleh (purposely placed outside the mahalleh), were (at the time I visited this institution) ten teachers who had received their professional training at L'Ecole Normale Israelite Orientale, a four-year central teacher training institution conducted by the Alliance in Paris.

Of 700 Jews in the universities of Iran, 500 are former students of Ettahad. Devoted Director General of the network of Ettahad Schools is Andre Cuenca, of a well-known Sephardi family tracing its lineage back to Spain.

A large part of the budget for all the schools—Alliance, Otzar Hatorah and ORT—is provided by the Joint Distribution Committee, which began operating on a regular basis in Iran in 1949. The J.D.C. spends 30 percent of its budget on education for the 13,000 children in thirty-eight schools in seventeen communities, including nursery schools and kindergartens as well in Teheran, Shiraz, Isfahan and Hamadan.

Another important sphere of J.D.C. activity has been in the field of health. When the J.D.C. came on the scene, disease was rampant. Eighty percent of the Jewish children were suffering from trachoma; sanitation was lacking and malnutrition was extensive. The medical program in the schools involves examinations, keeping of health records, immunization, weekly baths. Hot meals are provided daily for 7,000 children. Preventive health work includes inspection of sanitation installations and water in the mahalleh.

Pride of the community is the Jewish hospital and health center—the K.K.K. (Khanoun Kheir Khan)—erected as a memorial to young Dr. Ruachala Sapir, a doctor who early in the 1940s started a clinic to serve the Jews. Located in an old synagogue courtyard on the edge of the mahalleh, it did wonders during a typhus epidemic which raged in 1942. Dr. Sapir himself was a victim of the epidemic at the early age of thirty-one.

The K.K.K. focuses on coordinated family health care, with prevention of illness a main concern. There are mother and child clinics, out-patient and dental clinics and a surgical unit. A Nurses' Training School attached to the K.K.K. is important not only because it provides a health service, but because it has made nursing an acceptable profession for Jewish girls.

Medical programs in Teheran and provincial centers account for another 30 percent of J.D.C.'s budget in Iran. Its programs in health, education, culture, welfare, care for the aged and summer camping serve almost one out of every three Iranian Jews.

Of outstanding significance in this country which had been accustomed to "take and not to give" was a meeting in 1947 of ten young women who determined to "wash off the rust of ignorance, disease and poverty from the innocent faces" of the children of the mahalleh and to that end formed the Jewish Ladies' Organization of Iran.

They have helped erect five day care centers for children in Teheran, Isfahan, Shiraz and Hamadan and have fostered the Nurses' Training School. The Ladies' Organization has taken the Jewish women out of the ancient mold and has brought about their participation in community work. Courses in social work are given for the board members and two women have studied in the United States under a grant from the Council of Jewish Women. Representatives of Iranian women have participated in International Jewish Women's Conventions in Jerusalem and in Switzerland. One of the ten present at the 1947 founders' meeting, Mrs. Shamsi Hekmat, has been invited to speak in the United States for a U.J.A. campaign. Mrs. Hekmat has also been a delegate to the meeting of the U.N. Commission on the Status of Women held at Teheran. Branches of the Ladies' Organization now exist in Abadan, in Arak and Khoramshahr, as well as in the cities where the day care centers operate.

At the first Congress of Iranian Jews in 1955 the Ladies' Organization broached the subject of women's rights. According to the rigid religious interpretation clung to by the Iranian rabbis, a woman could not inherit from her husband nor could a daughter inherit from her father. The women's continued stress on the matter brought no amelioration in the interpretation.

Then religious authorities came from Israel, and finally in 1966, Chief Rabbi Nissim himself. After long discussions a decree was issued, signed by religious officials, community leaders, Israeli representatives and duly confirmed by the Minister of Religion and rabbis of Israel. An Iranian Jewish woman now has the right of inheritance from her husband and a daughter can participate in a legacy left by her father.

Other changes are taking place in Iran's Jewish community, now numbering about 75,000. People, particularly the younger members, are beginning to move out of the ghetto and into better homes (some surrounded by gardens with fountains) with a refrigerator in the living room as a status symbol. A very small number have become rich; there are a few merchant princes and bankers, rug traders and antique dealers. But the overwhelming number remain poor.

Iran, as the Shah has requested this country be called (in preference to Persia)—to stress the Indo-European or Aryan origin of its people—has no formal diplomatic relations with Israel. However there is "de facto" recognition including trade relations. Israeli agricultural experts, engineers and technicians work in Iran, and the Jewish Agency sends personnel to work there in the field of education.

From this Land of the Peacock Throne, nearly three times the size of France, about a hundred Jews leave each month to start life in Israel.

✑ BEHIND THE WALLS OF ISFAHAN ☞

As the plane swooped down to a landing at Isfahan, in the center of the Iranian plateau 200 miles south of Teheran, the city began to exert its charm. The blue of the airport terminal building was echoed in the blue dome of a nearby mosque. The same turquoise blue was repeated in the domes and minarets of the city's many palaces and mosques with their breathtakingly beautiful mosaic tiles, relics of days of ancient glory that was Persia. No wonder the inhabitants of this magnificent city, enveloped in a mantle of beauty, once said, "Isfahan is half the world."

Along Chehar Bagh—originally intended as a promenade to be lined with garden pavilions of the nobility, and now Isfahan's main boulevard—is the site of one of these pavilions, occupied by Madressah Mader-i-Shah (Religious School of the Mother of the Shah). This Islamic yeshiva has a facade of colored tile, two-story arcades with over a hundred study halls and two minarets rising above the great blue dome of its mosque.

Not far from the Madressah I came to the famous Maidan-i-Shah or Imperial Square, an open space of vast proportions, around which are many jewelers' shops. Two mosques face each other on the square—the Mosque of the Shah, with a gateway of blue tiles in geometric patterns, and the Mosque of Sheikh Lutfullah, with its sixteen grilled windows in the dome, and mosaic faience with inscriptions of Koran verses covering its interior.

On the third side of this square is Ali Qapu, Lofty Gateway, a six-story-high administrative center of the court, with a spiral staircase from whose high terrace Shah Abbas watched polo being played in the square which still retains the stone goal posts used in this sport.

Isfahan's side streets seem to be nothing more than narrow avenues hemmed in by two long stone walls with an entry gate every so often. The stone walls enclosed private homes. The passerby was shut out. Each street crossing brought more walls of stone seeming to say "thus far and no farther may you encroach."

I found my way to the Masjid Jami, Congregational Mosque, holiest of Isfahan's places of worship, with its pillared cloisters, domed chambers and architecture of various periods. Surrounding this mosque was a large enclosed dim bazaar with high vaulted ceilings. Here was a street with all its craftsmen pounding out the brass and copper pieces for which Isfahan is famous; there a street given over to carpenters and another for tinsmiths; a section for silversmiths, and another area where spices and dried fruits were sold. Many more winding streets made up this veritable city within a city.

Out again into the sunlight, and a mere block away, I entered the mahalleh where three out of every four of present-day Isfahan's 4,000 Jews live. The Jewish presence in Isfahan has a long history. Local tradition, both Jewish and Persian, claims that the Jews taken into captivity by Nebuchadnezzar carried with them samples of the soil and water of their beloved Jerusalem, vowing to settle only at a spot where earth and water equaled those of the old home. Both were found at this site, and so originated Isfahan, known at first as Al-Yahudiyyah (City of the Jews). Centuries later some Arab geographers, speaking of the large number of Jews in the city, said, "Investigate the genealogy of the noblest families of Isfahan and you will find that their origin is—from Jews."

But trouble came to Isfahan as well as to the rest of the country. Two magis, members of a priestly caste, were slain in the fifth century. The Jews were charged with the murders and half of the city's Jews were put to death.

Messianic hopes and beliefs ran strong in Isfahan, especially in the eighth century, when a simple illiterate tailor, Ishak Ben Yakub Obadiah Abu Isa al-Isfahani, was proclaimed first as the herald preceding the coming of the Messiah, and later as the Messiah himself sent to free the Jews from foreign rule and to make them politically independent. His followers, known as the Isawites, abstained from eating meat and drinking wine, forbade divorce and prayed seven times daily.

Although Abu Isa was unable to read or write, his disciples maintained that he had written books—with divine inspiration. When he headed an insurrection against the caliph, an army was sent against him, and he and his followers were routed. As to Abu Isa's fate there are a number of versions. According to one account he fell under his horse and died. But there were some among his adherents who claimed that during the course of the battle Abu Isa had hidden in a cave, later to wander into the desert to bring the word of the Lord to the Bene Moshe, mythical Jews believed to be descended from Moses.

When Benjamin of Tudela came this way, he spoke of Isfahan as:

The great city and the royal residence. It is 12
miles in circumference and about 15,000 Israelites
reside there. The Chief Rabbi is Sar Shalom, who

has been appointed by the Head of the Captivity to
have jurisdiction over all the rabbis that are in the
kingdom of Persia.

A traveler in the nineteenth century recorded finding only 400 Jewish families, three synagogues and eight hahamim (rabbis) in Isfahan.

As I walked in the autumn of 1961 through the mahalleh so steeped in history, it seemed as if I could almost touch the enclosing walls lining the streets by merely stretching out my arms, so narrow had the lanes become.

I opened a door in one of the walls and found myself in a compound—a bare, stone-floored yard encircled by "apartments," one windowless room to a family, the floor raised somewhat above the yard level. In the plastered walls were a few niches holding a lamp, a kerosene cooking stove, a tea kettle and a few dishes. Worn rugs on the stone floors and some blankets piled in a corner made up the balance of the household possessions. A few tiny holes above the wooden doors provided the only ventilation.

It was midday and all doors were open. The women, wearing kerchiefs over their braided hair, stood about in the open courtyard. Near the entrance a single toilet (a hole in the ground surrounded by door and walls) served all the families of the compound.

Relieving the drabness of the ghetto was a small but architecturally beautiful synagogue, its arches, dome and walls of blue mosaic tiles in harmony with the style of Moslem places of worship in Isfahan. In the center was the Reading Desk with carved wood decorations bearing the inscripion, "The labor of Isaac and Abraham Sasson." Overhead hung a crystal chandelier; rugs were spread over the entire floor. Around the sides were low tables, no higher than footstools, on which fruit, flowers and spices had been placed.

Upon entering the synagogue the men leave their shoes in cubicles in the entry before sitting down on the rugs behind the low tables. The women watch the service from behind wooden lattice work.

A Jewish National Fund folder hanging on the wall seemed a bond between the Isfahan ghetto and Israel.

Another pleasant oasis in the dingy ghetto was the nursery school for 200 children, among whom were little Soraya, Jehanshah, Manije and Kurosh, as well as others bearing the more familiar names of Rivkah, Daoud, Ibrahim and Shimshon. Around a small playground area were the light, clean, cheerful rooms with pictures of Israel and photographs of the Shah and Empress. The day began with the singing of Hatikvah and Iranian songs, followed by free play, dancing, rhythm play and Bible stories. Once a week each child received a bath, and when necessary a haircut. Before partaking of lunch, the children chant the blessings for the washing of hands and for eating of bread.

Isfahan was one of the first Iranian communities requesting aid from European Jewry in order to establish a school. The Alliance School had 900 pupils. But not all Jewish children attended this school, as I learned when visiting with a family living outside the ghetto.

"Come and you will see that not all Jews live like those in the mahalleh" was the invitation. Their street, too, was lined with the inevitable walls; but once inside the gate, I passed through a large garden before reaching the house itself. A bowl of roses, fresh from the garden, was on the table around which we sat chewing cashews, eating cake and drinking tea. Featured in the furnishings of the cheerful living room was the status symbol, a refrigerator.

The daughter of this household did not attend the Alliance School. She studied at a private school run by Christians. "It's closer to home," said the parents who had made the move out of the ghetto. Did she receive any Jewish religious training? I asked. The answer was no.

I went back to the mahalleh another evening for a meeting of the Hechalutz youth group. Unusual was the presence of girls, aged thirteen and fourteen, clothed in chadaries, the long robes enveloping them from head to foot. The word "Israel" had such a magic pull that the Hechalutz meeting was the only evening activity these girls were permitted to attend away from parents in a mixed group of boys and girls.

Fifty young people ranging in age from nine to twenty were present, reading *Lamathil* (the Israeli newspaper intended for those with only an elementary knowledge of Hebrew), singing, dancing and talking of going to Israel. It was a spiritual break in the walls surrounding the Isfahan ghetto.

◦§ CITY OF ROSES——SHIRAZ ﮯ

Shiraz, City of Roses and poetry 430 miles south of Teheran, has been exalted by its poets. In turn the city has honored two native sons, Hafez and Sa'adi—bright jewels of Persian poetry— with statues and a tomb set in a beautiful formal flower garden.

Just thirty miles north of the city are the remains of Persepolis, one of the mightiest cities of the ancient world. One is lost in wonder at its soaring columns, its mythical winged animals (supposed guardians of the palace) and its superb sculpture depicting royalty and court ceremonies. What was once the audience hall is approached by stairs 300 feet long, on whose sides are portrayed in relief long lines of officials and tribute bearers from twenty-three nations who converged on Persepolis, the capital of ancient Persia. Not far away are the tombs of Darius, Xerxes, Artaxerxes and Darius II.

But Shiraz, the City of Roses, was not always a bed of roses for its Jewish population, which numbered 10,000 in the days of Benjamin of Tudela. Closer to our own day, in 1844 twenty-six-year-old Romanian Jew Israel Joseph, who called himself Benjamin the Second in remembrance of Benjamin of Tudela, left his home on a search for the Lost Ten Tribes in Asia and Africa. Travel in Persia then was a perilous undertaking, what with the bandits and highwaymen abroad. Not being foolhardy, Benjamin joined a caravan of two thousand. But the going was slow, for he related that the journey from Isfahan to Shiraz took twenty-two days of travel—a distance I was to cover in 1961 in a one-hour flight.

Benjamin's book *Eight Years in Asia and Africa* is a record of his search. Benjamin had been aided by a British consul who:

> . . . *made arrangement himself with Caravan-Baschi* [*leader of the caravan*] *respecting my journey and made him in writing responsible for my safety.* . . . *Our road led us through regions in-*

*fested by hordes of robbers. . . . Every morning at
daybreak I retired before the caravan proceeded on
its way in order to pray. One day when I was on
the point of putting on my tephillin I heard with
terror the words, "A Jew is amongst us". . . . A
Persian pointed his gun at me and fired, but the
bullet whistled by me. The Caravan-Baschi
wrested the weapon from the hands of the per-
petrator who cried out in rage, "A Jew is daring to
contaminate our company." The Caravan-Baschi
turned pale, but answered, "Perhaps you are mis-
taken; but be it as it may, Jew or Musselman, I
answer for his safety with my head and must deliver him up unharmed at the house of the consul
of Shiraz." Nobody dared to dispute the authority
of the commander.*

And Benjamin was delivered safely to this British consul at
Shiraz who had him escorted to the leader of the Jewish community, Mullah Israel.

Soon the Jews came to call on the visitor from Europe. Amazed
that the women were veiled in white (Jewish women being
permitted only black veils), Benjamin was told the story: Twenty
years earlier, when there were 3,000 Jews in the city, persecution
had started and 2,500 of its Jews had been forcibly converted to
Islam and their synagogues laid waste. Secretly, however, they
preserved their Jewish faith. And, added the "apostates":

*Our brethren know under what fearful circum-
stances we were compelled to apostatise; we did it
to save ourselves from tyranny and death. We
acknowledge, however, that notwithstanding our
apparent apostasy, we still cling with all our hearts
to the faith of our fathers.*

Confirmation of this situation in Shiraz at that time came in a
report made by American missionary Henry A. Stern, who said in
1849, "All the silk merchants in the Wakil bazaar are Jews
converted to Islam."

My Sabbath in Shiraz was a memorable one. Services held at
the Kowsar Otzar Hatorah School started at an early hour, for in
Shiraz one does not eat before the service. The Torah reading was

Jewish Day School in Shiraz, Iran; much of the budget supplied by the J.D.C.

from a scroll encased in silver. As each man who was honored by being called up to the Reading of the Torah returned to his place, he acknowledged the congregation's greetings by making a wide, all-encompassing gesture with his tallit or by touching it to the head of one congregant and then bringing the tallit to his own lips and kissing it.

By ten o'clock, following kiddush at home, women were already returning to the Girls' School for their weekly Oneg Shabbat. Led by a woman, they discussed the weekly portion of the Bible which had been read earlier at the Morning Service.

What was unusual was that here were shy, reserved women, many of them wrapped in the full length chadaries—women whom it was hard to imagine away from home and kitchen—yet here they were, all on their own, conducting a cultural program equal to anything the well-dressed clubwomen of the West might carry out.

• 9 •
TURKEY

✑ BURSA ❧

TURKEY HAS HAD A LONG HISTORY OF ONE POWER AFTER
another gaining supremacy and leaving its mark on the land and
the people. The Ottoman Turks took over from the Seljuks, and
after an eleven-year siege, Bursa—nestled at the foot of Mount
Olympus—became the Ottoman capital in 1326. About forty
years later, Sultan Murat transferred the capital to Adrianople,
now Edirne, on the edge of the Thracian plain where the Turkish
armies could easily be grouped for expeditions to Eastern Europe. When Constantinople, now Istanbul, fell to the Ottomans in
1453, that legendary and fabled city became and remained Turkey's capital for almost five centuries. Ankara was proclaimed the
capital after Turkey's War of Independence in the twentieth
century.

Throughout the centuries, and for long periods before the
coming of the Ottomans, Jews have lived in each of these capital
cities—in Bursa, in Edirne, in Istanbul and in Ankara. In the
spring of 1966 I visited with Jews living in each of these capi-
tals—past and present.

A two-hour boat ride, starting from Istanbul's Galata Bridge on the Sea of Marmara, to Yalova and then a dolmus (shared taxi) ride brought me to Bursa, fifty-four miles south of Istanbul. A city of great natural beauty at the foot of Ulu Dag—8,000 foot-high Mt. Olympus of Mysia—believed to be the abode of Zeus, it is a ski center and favorite spa for the Turks who take its hot sulphur baths to cure their rheumatism.

Said to have been founded in 350 B.C.E. by King Prusias of Bithynia, Bursa is an open museum, rich in antiquities and relics of the Roman, the Byzantine, the Seljuk and the Ottoman periods. Bursa is sacred to the Moslems, for within it are the tombs of the first six conquering sultans.

That Jews have been in Bursa many centuries is confirmed in the Epistle of St. Peter, who recorded finding there an old tombstone with Jewish symbols. Later the Mishnah speaks of the quality of the cheese sent to Palestine from Bithynie, of which Bursa formed a part. Bursa's oldest synagogue, the Etz Haim (now destroyed to make room for street widening), dated back to Byzantine times. When in the fourteenth century the Ottomans besieged the city, the civil population was evacuated. But the Jews returned and under tolerant sultans, Jewish communal life was resumed.

Following the Inquisition of the fifteenth century, many of the Spanish Jews seeking shelter in Turkey, settled in Bursa, whose beauty and gardens and palaces reminded them of Granada and Andalusia in their old home. Bursa's two existing synagogues, the Mayor and the Gerush, were built in those days to accommodate the large numbers of Spanish Jews. Among their rabbis was Abraham Ben Yaeche, descendant of Don Yahye Ben Yaeche, treasurer to the first king of Portugal.

"The Jews have all the commerce of Bursa," said Le Sieur Paul Lucas, visiting the Orient on order of Louis XIV, for it was a well-known fact that the Jews had introduced the silk cocoon industry here. At one time Bursa's leading bank, the Ottoman Bank, was generally known as "Yahoudi Bankassi"—the Jewish Bank—when its director was Isaac ben Sasson and all its employees were also Jewish. Other Jews led in the various professions and held government posts early in the nineteenth century under Sultan Mahmoud II.

All seemed to be going well until natural calamities struck: The city was shaken by an earthquake, three times it suffered through epidemics of cholera and then fire consumed a large part of the Jewish quarter.

Economically, too, the Jews were affected so that by the end of the nineteenth century, Bursa's 600 Jewish families (3,000 souls in all) had become small shopkeepers, peddlers, tinsmiths and silk weavers. Only twelve families were wealthy.

But their interest in education remained great. "The Jews of Bursa incur great pecuniary sacrifices for the education of the children of the poor," reported F.D. Mocatta to the Anglo-Jewish Association in 1885.

And all the normal Jewish communal activities continued to function there. The Ozer Dallim assisted the poor, the Bikkur Holim Society visited the sick, the Hevrah Kaddisha (to which practically all belonged) rendered necessary service in case of death, Hakhnassat Orhim welcomed and aided any needy Jew passing through the city. The women provided trousseaus for orphans and assisted needy young women of marriageable age.

Jews turned to the local Beit Din in cases of any litigation. Even non-Jews who had any dispute with Jews preferred to have their case heard by the Beit Din and would accept its decision as binding.

Bursa Jewry was known for its patriotism. When a Greek army occupied the city in the early 1920s the Jews would not display the Greek flag over their homes and shops, thereby incurring the anger of their Greek and Armenian fellow-citizens. At a civic meeting a suggestion was made that Bursa declare itself autonomous and no more a part of Turkey. Silence reigned. Only Kemal Levi, president of the Jewish Community Council, had the courage to speak up, saying, "I will not be a party to this commission and I will never consent to the autonomy of the province of Bursa, which is Turkish and so will remain—always Turkish."

Later at a court martial of the persons who had favored autonomy at that meeting, Kemal Levi was cited as the only citizen who had had the courage to protest Bursa's breaking away from Turkey. The representatives of the "Israelite Community" at the meeting were declared innocent and Kemal Levi's "patriotic sentiments and services rendered to the country" were praised.

When free of his duties as shohet, Izak Beyo, religious head of Bursa for the last two decades, showed me around the city he loved so well. We went to what was formerly the Jewish quarter, with its typical narrow streets and two-story houses, the second story protruding over the ground floor. Here are located Bursa's two remaining synagogues.

One wall of the Gerush, Synagogue of the Expulsion, is covered with photographs of eminent rabbis and scholars, both Ashkenazi and Sephardi. Center place was given to Maimonides. Among the surrounding pictures were those of the Ashkenazi Gaon of Wilno, Akiba Eiger of Posen, the Hatam Sopher of Bratislava, Ezekiel Landau of Prag, as well as the Sephardi Don Isaac Abarbanel of Madrid, Isaac Abouab Hasefardi and Isaac Alfasi. Now that the community has shrunk to number only eighty families, this Gerush Synagogue is open only for Sabbath services.

Weekday activities are centered at the Mayor Synagogue, an architectural gem. Six columns surround a center oval of seats in addition to the usual row of seats placed around the walls. A magnificent crystal chandelier and other lamps are suspended from the decorated ceiling, windows are arched and a staircase leads to a small gallery where one of its twenty-four Sifrei Torah is brought for the reading. The lattice work shutting off the women's gallery reminded me of the harem apartments I had seen that very morning at the city's famed Green Mosque.

"Do the children get any Jewish instruction?" I wanted to know. I was told a school would need a special government permit, and licenses for new religious schools of any denomination are not being granted in the country—now a secular country. So "officially" the children gather at the Mayor Synagogue every weekday afternoon in order to recite their prayers. Before prayers start, they read from a Hebrew text—and it was evident that the Hebrew, which they read with fervor, and its modern Jewish historical references, had much meaning for them.

Men gathered for the Afternoon and Evening Services, and we joined them. During the service a plate was passed around for small contributions. "To provide oil for the lamps of the synagogue," I was told. Among those present at the weekday services were Nathan Bahar, head of the kehillah, and Chayim Palacci, of a

Bursa's Mayor Synagogue, built after influx into Turkey of refugees from Inquisition in Spain.

family that had provided a number of rabbis for the community.

Adjoining the Mayor Synagogue, to the right and to the left, were two buildings of interest. One was a little cafe used as a clubhouse by the Jewish men, the other was the bakery where the community had formerly prepared its matzoh for Passover. This bakery was rented to a Moslem Turk, but its facade still retained the old Hebrew inscription.

The bakery is one of thirty shops owned and rented by the community. The rental income from these stores is sufficient to provide for all communal needs, to maintain the synagogues— and Haham. As no local Jew wishes to be a butcher, the kosher meat slaughtered by Haham Beyo is on sale at another one of these thirty shops operated by a Moslem butcher.

Marriages are arranged by the parents. It has been found necessary to look to Jewish families in other communities of Turkey for marriage partners. Intermarriage is very rare. About fifteen years ago, a Jewish man did marry a Turkish girl for whose sake he became a convert to Mohammedanism. Now very influential, he quietly continues to render aid to the Jewish community.

Jewish holidays are celebrated with great devotion. On Shavuot, the synagogue is decked with flowers, blossoms adorn the Ark and the Scroll of the Law and its silver trimmings. On the first days of Pesach and Sukkot, a special holiday kiddush is provided for all at the synagogue. The Grace After Meals concludes with a verse in Ladino that I have never heard in any other place.

But changes are taking place. Services on the Sabbath are now held at an early hour so as to enable the men to open their shops after the prayers. Bar Mitzvah celebrations are fast becoming "Western" style. Formerly the high point of the occasion had been when the boy put on his tefillin in public for the first time. Nowadays the stress is on the aliyah, a speech given by the boy, and a big evening celebration to which the entire Jewish community is invited as well as Turkish friends.

Other changes illustrate how the Jew feels in this Republic of Turkey. When the Jews lived close to one another in the Jewish quarter of town, each family would build its own sukkah. In those days, I was told, "The Turks would be afraid to go by our area, for they knew the Jews could take care of themselves." Despite the country's constitution, according to which Jews have all rights as Turkish citizens, it is now considered "better not to make too much of an outward display of religion" in this secular country. Today one community sukkah in the courtyard of the Gerush Synagogue suffices for the entire group.

And although the practice of Tashlikh on Rosh Hashanah continues, again one does not go to the river symbolically to cast one's sins into the waters. That would be too public a demonstration. The water of a well is used instead for the purpose.

And so life continues for this small Jewish community in a city typically Turkish, adorned with magnificent monuments of the past.

᛫ᠥ EDIRNE ᠊ᠥ᠊

Leaving Bursa, I headed for the Ottoman Empire's second capital city, now Edirne, going via Istanbul and from there proceeding northwest for 140 miles by a bus which was far from deluxe. Villages along the way had unpaved roads and thatched-roofed homes, horses were in the fields pulling plows and shepherds followed their flocks. Children were dressed in black smocks and women wore black skirts covering their pantaloons. With long black stoles wrapped about their heads, the women's faces reminded me of nuns peering out from their hood-like coverings.

At Corlu we halted and made a grand exit from the bus to buy sandwiches. These were of the "hero" type—half a loaf of bread cut in half lengthwise and filled with meat and slices of onion, all nicely wrapped in newspaper. With my fellow passengers thus fortified, we continued on our way.

I was not traveling as a tourist to see the Turkish landscape and the Turkish people, but rather to see a city where there had once been a large flourishing Jewish community, a city of scholars and scribes, a city where one yeshiva alone had boasted a hundred Scrolls of the Law and a library of 15,000 books.

Edirne, better known by its former name Adrianople, was home to many famous men. "L'khah Dodi" ("Come, My Beloved"), the song with which Jews all over the world welcome the Sabbath, was composed by a sixteenth-century son of Adrianople, Solomon Alkabetz. An intimate friend of his was Joseph Karo, who is famous for the Shulhan Arukh, the last great codification of Jewish law and practice, and whose earlier Beit Yoseph was published in this city.

Four hours out of Istanbul we reached Edirne and passed Hotel Kerwan, at which I was to stay. Not being able to speak Turkish, I had not been able to communicate with any fellow travelers on the bus. My English jabbering—and especially my busy assembling of all my paraphernalia—made the bus driver finally understand that the foreigner wanted to descend. Then I walked back to small, clean Hotel Kerwan, where a bit of German helped me to get settled.

Then out I went to find Yuda Romano, leader of the Jewish community of Edirne. I had no street name, no house number to go by. But the Turks were friendly and helpful, and the name Romano seemed to be well known. I went past the Selimeye Mosque with its lovely faience tiles and minarets as impressive as those of many a famed Istanbul mosque, then down a narrow cobblestone street lined with shops, until I came to a "Goodyear" sign in front of one of these. Inside this shop with Goodyear tires and Mobiloil cans on its shelves, I found Yuda Romano—a silver-haired, fine-looking gentleman. Hebrew, which he had learned in his youth at a local yeshiva, was our means of communication.

"Things are very different from what they were in my youth," said Mr. Romano. He had studied at an Alliance Israelite Universelle School, and in addition had attended a yeshiva three hours daily. In 1905 when the Talmud Torah was combined with the Alliance schools, the Boys' School had 1,236 students and the Girls' School (with 560 pupils) had a reputation for being one of the most progressive in the East, providing dressmaking and cooking courses for its pupils. The Jewish community, which then numbered 20,000, was known for its generous support of educational institutions.

Today in Edirne there is no Alliance School, no Talmud Torah, no yeshiva, no seminary for training rabbis and teachers. Today's youth attends the government schools, which are in session on Saturday mornings. For the adults there is the Circle Israelite, which meets on Sundays, but meets only for social purposes. B'nai B'rith and Zionist groups which had formerly been active there have gone out of existence, for any affiliation with organizations based outside the country is forbidden by law.

I asked Mr. Romano how he accounted for such a decline in the size of the Jewish community here from 20,000 in 1905 to a mere 300 souls. The answer was a complex one. The nineteenth and twentieth centuries were hard ones for all the people of Edirne. First of all there was a plague of cholera and then the fires. In September of 1905 half of this city of wooden homes was consumed by fire. All thirteen synagogues and the fifty yeshivot of the Jewish community were burned down.

And then there were the wars. During the nineteenth century's Russo-Turkish wars Edirne was occupied by the Russians. Edirne's position—only four miles from the Greek border and twelve miles from the Bulgarian frontier—brought actual fighting to the streets of the city during the Balkan and Greek wars in this century.

After a siege of five months in 1913, Edirne fell to the Bulgars in the First Balkan War and was retaken the same year by the Turks in the Second Balkan War. In 1920 the Greek army, commissioned to restore order to Thrace (European Turkey), entered the city which had been ceded to Greece. A few years later the Treaty of Lausanne restored Edirne to Turkey.

With the tide of war surging back and forth it was no wonder that many of the inhabitants, including the Jews, left the city. After the State of Israel came into existence, over 8,000 more Jews left Edirne to start life again in Israel.

I located a few of the remaining members of today's small Jewish community in Edirne's Covered Bazaar, a large, roofed-over shopping area, several blocks long and wide. Some of them had small shops selling yard goods; one had a tiny stall selling notions such as thread, buttons and tape; another had a cigarette stand. Soon I was presented with an "Evil Eye" charm made of glass the size of an eye and colored blue and yellow, to be worn under or over one's clothing. The belief is that should anyone look at you with evil intentions, the "eye" will shatter and the wearer will thus be saved from harm.

But these small shops are deceiving. The owners may not be rich, but most are doing well. Only ten families, including those with widowed mothers, were in need of financial assistance, which the Jewish community provided through its charity arm— the "Matan B'Sayter"—which distributed aid anonymously.

Most of the Jews I met in the Covered Bazaar wanted to send greetings to a brother or sister or an uncle who had emigrated to the United States, the address usually being either in Brooklyn or Queens, New York.

Many of the families bore the name of Mitrani, which seems to be as common in Edirne as the Smiths are elsewhere. The Mitranis are descended from the prominent Spanish family di Trani that had left Castile during the Inquisition period and reached Edirne in 1502 by way of Italy. Through the generations this family had produced numerous noted Talmudic scholars. Among these were Aaron di Trani, founder of the Edirne branch of the family, and Joseph di Trani whose Responsa (answers to questions on Jewish law and observance) earned wide renown.

Another member of this illustrious family, Moses di Trani, was sent from Edirne at the age of sixteen to complete his studies in Palestine, afterward serving for ten years as rabbi of Safad there.

I wasn't at all surprised when one of the present-day Mitranis told me that his son was a Roberts College graduate who had taken his Master's Degree in engineering at the University of Pennsylvania and was continuing there for his doctorate.

In another part of the city—formerly the Jewish section—I saw the shingle of Dr. Sami Haras, on a characteristicly narrow Turkish wooden house, with the second story extending out beyond the first story. Dr. Sami, as he is affectionately called, is beloved by his patients. On a drive one day with the Haras family we passed the railroad station, at which the famed Orient Express (in which so many tales of mystery are supposed to have taken place) makes one of its stops. We came to the Greek border just four miles out of town. There the guards greeted Dr. Haras with great warmth. "Don't ever use a Turkish doctor," said one, and another quietly added, "Dr. Sami saved my daughter's life." No wonder that I, as the guest of Dr. Sami, was given freedom to photograph at the border as I pleased.

Sabbath Day in Edirne began with a visit to "The Great Synagogue," the only synagogue now in the community, constructed after the great fire of 1905 had burned all the then existing thirteen synagogues. The Great Synagogue is a commanding structure seating six hundred, with many impressive chandeliers and a velvet parokhet (the Ark's curtain) with medallions embroidered in silver.

A plaque on the synagogue wall reminds one that "This structure was completed in the spring of the year 5669 after the creation of the world," and that ". . . in the great conflagration of Elul 5665, fire ravaged the holy sites and halls and all the precious abodes for a whole day."

To heat a building seating six hundred was too expensive for a community that numbered only a hundred families, so services that Sabbath and all through the cold season were held in the nearby, small Beit Midrash. Preceding the Friday Afternoon Service the Song of Songs was recited, and before the Evening Service L'khah Dodi was sung. Hearing this familiar hymn at a

Interior of the Great Synagogue in Edirne, only house of worship in the community; built after conflagration of 1905 burned half of the city including all existing thirteen synagogues.

Sabbath service in the very town in which its composer had lived was quite a moving experience.

I took Sabbath dinner with the family of Dr. Haras. Mrs. Haras, an Oriental beauty with olive complexion, dark eyes and dark hair, is a university graduate. We began with "borekas," a hot pastry filled with cheese, and served with a hard-boiled egg, then came artichokes surrounded by potatoes and carrots. The main course was lamb with rice and peas. Fresh fruit and good Turkish coffee brought the delicious meal to a close.

On Sabbath morning I was again at the Beit Midrash, a simple unadorned room, but the curtain in front of the Ark was of velvet with medallions and a Magen David embroidered in silver thread, and the shamash on duty looked like a naval officer in his navy blue suit with gold buttons. The Sefer Torah was prepared for the reading with great ceremony, its velvet mantle removed and a very special cover put on it for the procession around the house of prayer.

Following the service I was invited for kiddush by 82-year-old vintner Israel Raytan. I walked through his cool, dark wine cellar with its many casks and out into the bright sunshine in the garden space at the rear. Yuda Romano was there, too, for it was a weekly rite for these two men to meet on Sabbath morning. We sipped red wine, munched nuts and enjoyed oranges. "Wine gladdens the heart," said my stooped host, most of whose customers were the Moslems, despite their religious scruples. But it was clear that Israel Raytan's real interest lay in his books and papers in Hebrew, Turkish, French, Spanish and Arabic, all of which languages he spoke as well. As we talked, he would scurry into the cellar and return with a book or pamphlet kept in some drawer or odd place among the wine casks.

We talked of the long association of Jews with Edirne. Jews were there during Greek days, for well into modern times there was a synagogue using the rites of the Gregos, or Greek-speaking Jews, and some of today's family names show a Greek origin. Recalling chapters from the community's long history, my host told me of persecutions during the rule of the Byzantines, when reading from the Scroll of the Law was banned and recital of the weekly portions was permitted only in Greek or Latin translation. A blood libel incident occurred in Edirne. According to the story a church sexton was said to have substituted blood for the wine in the havdalah cup left overnight in the synagogue and all was set for bringing the accusation of ritual murder. That same night, the legend continues, the entire scheme was unfolded to the synagogue shamash in a dream. It was the shamash who then emptied the cup and refilled it with wine, thus saving the Jewish community.

When Edirne became the capital of the Ottoman Empire and residence of the sultans, conditions became brighter for the Jews. The sultans often chose Jewish physicians for their own personal use. A rabbinical college attracted students not only from Turkey, but also from Russia and Poland. Jews of Hungary and France, expelled from their native countries as a result of the Black Death ravaging Europe in the fourteenth century, found refuge there as did Spanish and Portuguese Jews later on. So strong was the influence of this latter group that they imposed their language and customs upon the native Jews.

Newcomers from a particular place stayed together in one synagogue in the new home, so that among the thirteen synagogues that existed in Edirne until the 1905 fire, there were congregations known as the Aragon, Catalonia, Majorca, Toledo, Portugal, Italia, Apulia, Sicily, and Buda synagogues.

Our talk turned to famous sons of Edirne who had lived closer to our own time. There was Joseph Halevy, born in the early nineteenth century. He taught in his native town before moving on to Bucharest and Paris. A keen student, he was sent by the Alliance Israelite Universelle to make a study of the Falashas in Ethiopia. Later, Halevy was sent by the French Institute to Yemen to study the Sabean Inscriptions there. He became professor of Ethiopic at the Ecole des Hautes Etudes in Paris and taught at the Sorbonne.

Israel Raytan and Yuda Romano talked with especial pride of Abraham Danon. Born in Edirne in the middle of the nineteenth century, Danon headed the local theological seminary. He was a prolific writer, translating Virgil and Victor Hugo into Hebrew, and published a collection of fifty-five Judaeo-Spanish ballads sung throughout Turkey, each with its French translation. The Alliance Israelite Universelle invited him to direct its seminaries in Istanbul and later in Paris. Abraham Danon's influence was wide, for he also acted as Consulting Editor for the Jewish Encyclopedia.

In spite of Raytan's love for his literary collection, I was able to persuade him to part from some material about Abraham Danon. Now it is available for researchers on the shelves of the Ben Zvi Institute in Jerusalem.

What of today's youth in Edirne? For years there have been no schools, no classes where a youngster could be given some measure of Jewish knowledge. For the Bar Mitzvah ceremony the appropriate blessings were written in Turkish letters and the boy learned them by rote.

To help improve the situation, David Azuz, a member of the Mahazikei Hatorah Movement, came to Edirne from Istanbul, dedicated to bringing youth closer to Jewish knowledge and observance. Within two weeks young David had organized three Saturday afternoon classes, which attracted fifty young people.

I watched him with a group of seventeen- and eighteen-year-old boys and girls, to whom the Hebrew alphabet was strange. But David Azuz succeeded in involving the group in song, and they were lustily singing "Hevenu Shalom," "We bring greetings to you."

What of the future? Who can foretell? I left town—accompanied to the bus by Yuda Romano—with mixed emotions. But one thing was certain, the Jewish will to live was strong in Edirne.

◄§ LEGENDARY ISTANBUL §►

Istanbul——fascinating Istanbul with its skyline of domes and minarets of five hundred mosques; fabulous Istanbul with the treasures of the Topkapi Palace; alluring Istanbul with its vast bazaars, obelisks, fountains and towers; incredible Istanbul as the meeting place of Europe and Asia with its legendary waters of the Bosphorus, the Golden Horn and the Sea of Marmara; Istanbul—the captivating capital of the Ottoman Empire for almost five centuries.

All true—long ago. Today the glory of Istanbul has departed. True, the mosques, the Topkapi Palace, the bazaars, the waters remain. But today thoughts of legendary Istanbul are shattered by the sight of ugly, dark, hilly cobblestone streets ascending and descending, by taxis racing crazily and parking on the sidewalks. Gone are the sultans and their courts.

So, too, has the story of the Jew in Istanbul been transformed. In the days when Istanbul was in its glory—then, too, Istanbul Jewry was at its zenith. The story of today's Jewry is a different one.

The link between the Jews and Istanbul is a long one. That Jews were living there during the Roman period is attested to by a document dated in the year 390, signed by the emperor of the time. During the time of the Byzantine period the Jews suffered religious and civil persecution. Forced into a ghetto, they were forbidden to celebrate Passover before the Christian Easter of any year, no matter what the Jewish calendar said. The economic power centered in Constantinople of the day, however, was such that the Jews returned to it again and again.

Benjamin of Tudela reports that on his visit there:

> *The number of Jews at Constantinople amounts to*
> *2,000 Rabbanites and 500 Karaites. They live on*
> *one spot (Pera) but a wall divides them. Many of*
> *the Jews are manufacturers of silk cloth; many*
> *others are merchants, some of them being extreme-*
> *ly rich. But no Jew is allowed to ride upon a horse*
> *except R. Solomon Hamitsri who is the King's phy-*
> *sician and by whose influence the Jews enjoy many*
> *advantages even in their state of oppression. . . .*
> *The hatred against them is enhanced by the prac-*
> *tice of the tanners who pour out their filthy water*
> *in the streets and even before the very doors of the*
> *Jews who being thus defiled become objects of ha-*
> *tred. . . . They are exposed to beatings in the*
> *streets and must submit to all sorts of harsh treat-*
> *ment. But the Jews are rich, good, benevolent and*
> *religious men who bear the misfortunes of exile*
> *with humility.*

With the overthrow of the Byzantine Empire and the Ottoman capture of Constantinople, things took a decided turn for the better for Jewry. The system of "millets" was introduced, whereby each non-Mohammedan minority group was left autonomous under the supervision of its own religious leader. The Haham Bashi became the official Jewish representative to the government. As Chief Rabbi of the country he apportioned and collected the taxes, appointed the local rabbis and administered Jewish affairs. He had a seat in the Divan (the Council of State) next to the mufti. The Jews felt free in this state within a state. Synagogues and schools were built freely and no restrictions were placed in the path of any who wished to engage in trade or commerce. This period of prosperity lasted for over two hundred years.

So free and happy did the Jews feel, that Isaac Zarfati, who had settled there, sent a circular to the Jewish communities of Germany and Hungary saying:

> *Turkey is a land in which nothing is lacking. Is it*
> *not better to live under Moslems than under Chris-*

*tians? Here you may wear the finest stuff. Here
everyone may sit under his own vine and fig tree.
. . . In Christendom you may not venture to dress
your children in red or blue without exposing them
to the danger of being beaten blue or flayed red.*

Isaac Zarfati's advice was followed and many Ashkenazi Jews
came to live under the Ottoman rulers. Forty-four synagogues
served the needs of Istanbul's 30,000 Jews during the fifteenth
century.

Sultan Bayazid, in welcoming the Spanish and Portuguese
refugees who had found sanctuary in the Ottoman Empire said,
"Ye call Ferdinand a wise king—he who makes his land poor and
ours rich?" The Jews of Turkey received their persecuted brethren cordially. Moses Kapsali, the most noted rabbi of the time,
went from congregation to congregation, levying a tax on the
native Jews for the "liberation of the Spanish captives," for many
of the Spanish Jews came in ships whose captains claimed them
as their slaves, and for whose freedom a ransom had to be paid.

The sixteenth century was Istanbul Jewry's Golden Age. The
Spanish Jews, with their high degree of culture, energy and skills,
brought new life into the fields of commerce, philanthropy and
diplomacy. The Jews became the middle-class commercial agents
of the country, for the upper-class Turks were busy in the pursuit
of war and conquest and the lower classes were concerned with
farming. It was easier for the Turks to trust the Jews as business
agents in preference to the Christians, for the Turks feared the
latter might have sympathy with the foreign powers, whom
Turkey was then in the process of subduing.

Nicolo Nicolai, Chamberlain to the King of France, who accompanied the French ambassador to Istanbul, said:

*. . . It may be said truly that the greater part of the
commerce of the whole Orient is in their [Jewish]
hands. In Constantinople they have the largest bazaars and stores with the best and most expensive
wares of all kinds . . . . There is no Turkish family
of importance which has not in its employ a Jew to
estimate merchandise, to judge of its value, to act
as interpreter, or to give advice on everything that
takes place.*

In addition the Spanish Jews taught the Turks how to manufacture new firearms, cannon and gunpowder, and this at a time when the Turks were laying siege to Vienna.

In the field of medicine the Jewish doctors brought with them the aura of having trained at the schools of medicine at Salamanca in Spain. Every sultan had his own special Jewish physician. Prominent among these was Joseph Hamon, physician to Bayazid II and then to Selim I, the sultan whose conquests brought Mesopotamia, Syria, Arabia and Egypt into the Ottoman Empire. Moses Hamon, son of Joseph, was physician to Suleiman, that Suleiman whose conquests included Belgrade, Rhodes, Hungary, Baghdad, Persia and Cyprus. The Ottoman Empire was at its highest power in this era. And physician Moses Hamon was in great favor at the court and wielded considerable influence.

Most influential of the 10,000 Marranos who found asylum in Turkey—where they could be Jews openly once more—was Don Joseph Nasi, adviser to the sultans on political affairs. Of a Marrano family coming from Spain, Joao Miguez (in reality Joseph Nasi) was born in Portugal, then moved to Antwerp, where the family continued to profess Christianity. The family had large banking and commercial interests, and was held in great esteem by the nobility and royalty. Desiring to practice Judaism openly, Joseph Nasi decided to emigrate to Turkey. Through the intervention of Moses Hamon the Nasi family was enabled to proceed to Istanbul, where Don Joseph Nasi soon was close to the court of Sultan Suleiman. The sultan made his adviser a gift of the city of Tiberias and its surroundings in Palestine.

A Zionist of his day, Don Joseph hoped to resettle Tiberias with Jewish refugees. He had the walls of the city rebuilt and mulberry trees planted, to provide employment in the silk industry for the expected newcomers. Then Don Joseph issued a proclamation inviting Jews, particularly those who had been banished from the Papal States in Italy, to start life again in Tiberias, offering them free transportation in his ships. Over 300 Italian Jews decided to emigrate to the Holy Land. But one of the ships was seized by pirates who sold the people into slavery. This put a halt to the project.

Don Joseph's influence reached its peak at the court of Sultan Selim II, who succeeded his father Suleiman. It was Selim who showed his affection for his counselor and adviser Don Joseph by presenting him with six islands and naming him Duke of Naxos (one of the islands). The Duke continued to live in Istanbul, but governed the islands through a Christian-Spanish nobleman.

Don Joseph urged Selim to carry out his long-time plan to conquer the island of Cyprus. The sultan agreed and, so goes the story, promised to make Joseph king of Cyprus. The island was conquered, but there is no record of Joseph's having been named king.

The sixteenth century was the Golden Age of Jewry in Istanbul in yet another sense, for it was then that literature flourished and scholarly accomplishments were at their highest point. Rabbis and scholars immigrated from Spain, schools and academies were built, commentaries on the Bible and poetry were produced. Among Hebrew printing presses set up, was one by Gerson Soncino.

The widow of Joseph, Duke of Naxos, had printing presses at her palace to aid authors who needed financial assistance. Esther Kiera, wealthy and powerful at court as a protégée of Sultana Baffa, wife of Sultan Murad III, was a patron of learning. She paid for the cost of publication of various works, including a translation of a chronicle by astronomer Abraham Zacuto, whose astrolabe had been used in Vasco da Gama's expedition, and who himself found shelter in Turkey.

The sixteenth century was also the age of goodwill, when Rabbanite scholars instructed Turkish Karaites in the rabbinical literature, a field unknown and unstudied by them. The Rabbanites followed the traditions of the rabbis of the Talmud as well as the laws of the Torah, whereas the Karaites were members of that Jewish sect that had rejected observance of traditional rabbinical laws in favor of loyalty only to Biblical laws.

From this high point of security, prosperity, influence and learning began the decline of Istanbul Jewry in the seventeenth century. The year 1666 was believed, by Cabalistic computation, to be the year heralding the Messianic Era. So strong was the faith in and desire for the Messiah that people in many parts of Europe, as well as in Istanbul, were in a mad frenzy. Business was at a standstill. Many sold their possessions, packed their bags, took apart their homes, awaiting the signal to follow their

"King and Messiah" to the Holy Land. In Istanbul the Greeks and Armenians stepped into the economic positions previously held by the Jews.

When the year 1666 came, the pseudo-Messiah, Izmir's Sabbatai Zevi, appeared in Istanbul expecting to lead his people. Instead he was thrown into prison, and eventually converted to Islam to save his life.

With the debacle of the Messianic movement all energy and enterprise seemed sapped from the community. Istanbul ceased to be the center of Jewish learning. Ignorance, misery and poverty set in. In the nineteenth century the Alliance Israelite Universelle stepped in to assist the community in the education of its children. One of the schools started was a kindergarten intended to keep the young children away from missionary influence.

A study of the community made in 1889 by Reverend A. Lowy for the Anglo-Jewish Association found the mass of Istanbul's 48,000 Jews so poor that they lived from hand to mouth. Twenty-five hundred boys were getting religious instruction in Talmud Torahs in poor physical surroundings, and 2,200 boys and girls were attending thirteen Alliance schools where they were being prepared for apprenticeship in various vocations.

Of the Istanbul Jewry, Reverend Lowy said:

> [It] was devoid of energy; rigid in religious observance with no elevation in its orthodoxy. It had no Haham Bashi. That rabbinical office was filled by a kaimakan [a substitute] who doesn't claim to possess qualification for spiritual leadership.

One local contributor to the educational life was Count Abraham Camondo, Istanbul-born member of a family originating in the Spanish-Portuguese peninsula. Banker to the government before the founding of the Ottoman Bank and one of the richest landowners in Istanbul, the Count (whose title was conferred on him by King Victor Emmanuel for his gifts to Italian institutions) played an active role in communal life. In 1858 he had established a school in the poorest section of the city which provided free vocational training in addition to the usual curriculum. For his furtherance of vocational training, Count Camondo was excommunicated by certain rabbis of the community.

When I reached Istanbul in the spring of 1966, the Ottoman period was long past, the empire crumbled. Gone at last, too, was the age of capitulations when foreign countries had extraterritorial rights over their citizens living in Turkey, keeping them exempt from Turkish law. The 1923 Revolution had taken place and Kemal Atatürk was the hero of a people to whom he had given a feeling of strong national unity. The Jews, under the Treaty of Lausanne, had renounced their status as a minority. Under the constitution, "Every individual who is bound to the Turkish state by ties of citizenship is a Turk." The Jews had become full and equal citizens of the country.

The spirit of Turkish nationalism is so strong that it has led to what we have already described as xenophobia, a fear of foreigners and a fear of control by foreigners—as that which had existed in the period of capitulations. No organization that has headquarters or a sister movement in a foreign country may function within the country unless special government permission at *Cabinet* level has been granted (under the provisions of the Law of Associations of the 1940's). Such organizations as the Lions and the Rotary had to receive this Cabinet permission in order to have local units within Turkey.

To the Jews this means no official contacts with Jewish organizations abroad: The B'nai B'rith, the Zionist Organization, the Jewish Congress, the Alliance Israelite Universelle may not have affiliated lodges or chapters within the country. Nor may Turkish Jews attend international Jewish conferences without government sanction. Permission was requested a few years ago for the Haham Bashi to attend a conference of Chief Rabbis at London. The government granted the request.

The Jewish community of Istanbul numbers 30,000 including 300 Ashkenazi families who came to Turkey after the Russian pogroms and have their own synagogue on Galata's Street of the Steps. More than 37,000 had left for Israel between May 1948 and the end of 1956. It was the poorer class—the porters, the peddlers, the petty tradesmen—who left, so that today the community has a larger proportion of people in a higher economic bracket. Now the Jews are importers, exporters, bankers, professionals; the Karaites, of whom there are between a hundred and two hundred, are goldsmiths, jewelers and money changers; the Georgians from the Soviet Union are manufacturers.

The decline of Jewish scholarship was noticeable in the schools. The Rabbinical Seminary, with thirty students, was actually only a high school and any graduate who wanted to become ordained had to complete his rabbinical studies outside the country.

The former B'nai B'rith School, started by the local B'nai B'rith Lodge, was now known as the Beoglu Private Jewish Lycée. Time devoted to Jewish studies at this school meant five hours a week for pupils in grades 4 and 5; four hours a week for those in grades 6-7-8. In the high school grades, only two hours a week were set aside for Jewish content. With a total enrollment of only 270, the first three grades had already closed for lack of pupils.

Three primary grade schools in the Ortokoy and Galata districts, with a total of 600 pupils, completed the list of Jewish educational institutions. Children were sent to these schools not so much for the quantity or quality of the Jewish instruction, for to all intents and purposes they are Turkish schools, but to enable the children to be among Jews in a school that will be closed on the Sabbath and Jewish holidays.

Only 10 percent of children of school age—and these from the poorer families—attended the Jewish schools. All the rest study at private schools, for it has become a matter of status to do so.

An attempt to fill this void in Jewish education has been taken by the Mahazikei Hatorah. This is in large measure the result of the drive of one man—Nissim Behar. He spent some years studying in Israel and upon his return to Istanbul encouraged young men to study at the yeshivot in Israel, particularly at the Porat Yosef, a Sephardi yeshiva in Jerusalem. He has thus created a cadre of knowledgeable young men to act as youth leaders and instructors in the various communities of Turkey.

I sat in at a Sabbath-afternoon youth gathering at the synagogue in Shishli in a newer, better-off section of Istanbul. The room was crowded to overflowing with boys in their early teens, all of whom regularly attended non-Jewish private schools. The Mahazikei Hatorah leaders, university students themselves, were leading the boys in song. For about an hour the singing con-

tinued, interspersed with stories of Jewish content. Then came
the Minhah service led by the boys themselves. The procession
around the room with the Scroll of the Law was headed by one of
the boys who walked backward all the time so that he would
continue facing the Scroll. The service was followed by a light
Seudah Shelishit. Then came Maariv and the havdalah, signify-
ing the conclusion of the Sabbath.

At the Knesseth Israel Synagogue in old Shishanay that morning, the Mahazikei Hatorah members had led the regular services
with fervor and zeal.

On another Sabbath morning I went to the Neve Shalom, the
large fashionable synagogue in old Shishanay. This place of
worship has stained-glass windows, a large rose window over the
Ark and a gold-embroidered velvet cloth on the Reading Desk.
Two large decorative metal bowls placed on either side of the
pulpit held the yahrzeit lights.

When the moment came for the priestly blessing, the shamash,
in gold-braided cap and a tallit over his dark blue suit with gold
epaulets and a gold girdle, gave a long drawn-out call for
kohanni——m (priests). Only two kohannim responded to the
call. One was a young boy, the other the rabbi—old, ashen-pale
and frail, wearing a white turban and a white robe similar in style
to a sultan's costume I had seen at Topkapi Palace.

While the three Scrolls were being carried around the synagogue, everyone threw kisses at the Torah, with two fingers
pointing from an outstretched arm, and then touched their eyes
and lips with the same two fingers. Each man called up to the
Reading of the Torah saluted his successor to the honor and
kissed the hand of the rabbi before leaving the Reading Desk.
Upon returning to his seat, each one was congratulated by the
congregation with a loud "Hazak U'varukh"—"Be strong and
blessed."

Two services were held each Sabbath. The early, short one at
seven accommodated those men who desired to open their shops
for business.

Here, too, as in Afghanistan, Purim is celebrated for two days,
and on Shavuot the Torah is decorated with flowers. When a boy
becomes Bar Mitzvah and has lived according to all traditional

observances, he is permitted to read from the Torah. Otherwise he may only recite the blessings, while someone else does the actual reading from the Scroll. One custom that is changing is connected with the Brit Milah. Formerly the infant was kept awake the entire night preceding the rite and passed from one to another of those present who spent the night praying and singing. This custom is now dying out.

And whereas in former days marriages were arranged by the parents, nowadays two out of five young people choose their own partners. All marriages in secular Turkey are civil. After the civil ceremony a permit for the religious ceremony is granted by the Beit Din, which supervises all matters of marriage, divorce and conversion.

The Haham Bashi represents Jewry before the government. Not necessarily an ordained rabbi, but one who is knowledgeable in Jewish matters, he is nominated by Lay Councils of all places where Jewish communities exist, and if approved by the government, he then serves for life. In addition to his other duties, he also supervises kashrut, the making of matzoh and wines.

The present Haham Bashi, Rabbi David Asseo, completed his studies at the Rhodes Theological Seminary. Upon his return to Istanbul he became secretary to the former Chief Rabbi Rafael Saban, was a member of the Beit Din and director of the local Seminary.

I found the Haham Bashi to be a dignified man, wearing a black robe of office with a royal purple band. When he entered the Neve Shalom Synagogue for a special community-wide service one day, a long gold chain was added to his robe of office and a black hat, also with royal purple band. Preceded by two aides, he ceremoniously advanced to the pulpit. As the cantors came to the pulpit, they kissed his hand.

Jewish youth of Istanbul has some opportunity to meet and work together. There is the Culture and Art Organization, successor to the former Kadimah Zionist Society (now outlawed), numbering eighty members between the ages of seventeen and twenty-three, the great majority of whom are students. The Amical or Friendship Society, a somewhat older group, has cultural meetings of a general nature. The Kardeshlik Klub, with strong

Haham Bashi David Asseo, Chief Rabbi of Turkey in his headquarters at Beyoglu, Istanbul.

national feelings, has choral and dance groups, cultural sessions and Jewish holiday celebrations. A small group of teenagers, the Or Hayim Group, raises funds for the Jewish hospital.

The B'nai B'rith had been the most active group in Istanbul in former days. Now that affiliation with the world organization is forbidden, the lodge has become the Fakirleri Koruma Cemiyeti—Association for the Protection of the Poor. Its membership of 250, chiefly professional and industrialist, is the most dynamic unit within the community working for all—for solidarity and harmony among the Jews. It is a center for all communal activities.

Nor do the women lag behind in communal work. One of their chief interests is the Musevi Hastanesi, the Or Hayim Jewish Hospital. Built on classic Greek lines with columns, it was constructed in 1898 by Eliahu Kadoorie as a memorial to his wife Laura who had died in a fire in Japan, trying to save her children. The hospital synagogue has Venetian glass and crystal lamps. Located on the Golden Horn in the Balat area, once the center of a rich Sephardi community, it is now far from where Jews live.

Sarah Gueron near Hotel Hilton, Istanbul; a lawyer, she was first Jewish woman to graduate from a Turkish university; has represented Turkish women at many international gatherings; encourages cultural relations between Turkey and Israel.

Staffed by Jewish physicians, the patients in this 120-bed hospital are of all faiths. Its nurses are graduates either of the Red Crescent or the American Hospital School for Nursing. By tradition, no Jewish girl trains for the profession of nursing.

Another charitable institution is the Home for the Aged, housing fifty people in what was once an Alliance School in a neighborhood of wooden homes in Haskoy, also on the Golden Horn, but directly opposite Balat, again an area from which the Jews moved on to the Galata district. One of the features of which the committee is proud is the Turkish bath provided for the residents.

And then there is the orphanage, housing children of broken homes as well as actual orphans. Twenty-seven boys, whose ages ranged from four to sixteen, roomed in one large dormitory on one floor, while twenty-three girls, also of different ages, slept on another floor, again in one huge dormitory.

Although the Istanbul community is almost completely (97

Karaite Synagogue in the Haskoy district of Istanbul; this sect numbers between 100 to 200 people in Istanbul.

percent) Sephardi, there is a division and separation in the cemetery. There is a separate plot for Ashkenazi graves, and another one over the hill and behind the wall, for Karaites.

Just as they do not mix with the Karaites in death, so also in life. Though everyone spoke in the highest terms of the Karaites and of their generosity and philanthropy, the Rabbanite Beit Din does not permit marriage between Karaites and the main body of Jews who are Rabbanites (Talmudic Jews). In such cases, the couple has only a civil marriage.

The Karaite synagogue in Haskoy is small but jewel-like. The place of worship is built lower than street level, as is common with Karaite synagogues, so as to conform with the phrase, "From the depths I cried unto the Lord." The curtain of the Ark is of gold-embroidered velvet, the Reading Desk in the center, Oriental rugs on the floor, three rows of crystal chandeliers, and rug-covered seats around the walls. The particular service I attended was in observance of the shloshim, the memorial marking the thirtieth day after a death—in this instance, of Joseph

Hacohen, one of their tiny community. All the usual customs
common to Jews in relation to death were observed here—the
shiva, the shloshim and the yahrzeit.

As for the Istanbul Jewish community as a whole, it didn't take
long to become aware of a singular characteristic of the Jews
there. They took great pride in their full and equal rights of
citizenship in a country that was not anti-Semitic—and yet they
felt insecure, apprehensive and timorous.

When I noticed that leaders of the community, talking with me
in my hotel lobby, were constantly looking over their shoulder as
if fearful of being overheard, I shifted our meeting place to a
private room of the hotel. One man, evidently accustomed to
authority, power and position, said loftily, "Jews have all rights
as Turkish citizens." Yet, when four others joined us in the
private room, the same man asserted, "This doesn't look good. Six
people—it looks too much like a conference with a foreign
journalist." A leader of women's activities told me of a group that
met at different homes—but no more than twelve or sixteen
people at a time, a number that might ordinarily gather for a
social afternoon of cards—and, to use her own term, "clan-
destinely" had a Jewish study hour. I have avoided naming any of
these people, for one after another pleaded, "Don't use my
name."

And yet I did hear from others that if the people were really
concerned about Jewish education, if they truly wished it, they
could find a way to "transfer" a school that had been closed
because Jews had moved away from the area and have it reopened
in the new neighborhood as a transferred institution.

I met with two persons who did not suffer from this dichotomy
of spirit, two persons who felt themselves at home in the two
civilizations, who felt secure both as Turks and as Jews. These
two were Sami Kohen and Sarah Gueron.

Sami Kohen was Foreign Editor and chief political writer for
the leading Istanbul newspaper *Milliyet* (*The Nation*) and the
only Jew in the Turkish press. Said 37-year-old Sami Kohen,
"The Jews isolate themselves. They have a fear of mixing with the
Turks. As a result, the Turk looks on the Jew as a Jew, not as
another Turk."

Sarah Gueron, a descendant of Chasdai Ibn Shaprut, is by profession a lawyer. The first Jewish woman to study at a Turkish university, she was Secretary of the Turkish Association of University Women and was active in the Women's International Alliance. She was the Turkish delegate to an International Conference on Criminology, held in Israel. "I consider myself a bridge between my ancestors and the Turks," said this one-woman center for encouraging cultural relations between Israel and Turkey. Billboards all over Istanbul confirmed this interest of Sarah Gueron:

DON PASQUALE
Istanbul Municipal Opera
Israel woman conductor
SOFIA LIDJI

Sofia Lidji, protégée of Sarah Gueron, had been brought to Istanbul and was a great success. Don Pasquale had a phenomenal run and the house was always full.

This is Istanbul's puzzling Jewry of today—on the one hand a feeling of insecurity and a hush-hush attitude; on the other, public announcement of an Israeli opera conductor.

◄§ ANKARA §►

Two hundred and fifty miles east of Istanbul lies smog-covered, drab Ankara, capital since 1923 of the new Republic of Turkey. High on a hill overlooking all of Ankara, and approached by traversing long sculpture-decorated avenues, is the city's new shrine—Anit Kabir, the red sandstone mausoleum for revered Kemal Atatürk, Father of the Turks. Said the taxi driver who drove me there, "Atatürk good, like your Abraham Lincoln." There are many new statues around the city, all colossal and all showing heroic figures fighting for the fatherland.

Ankara is a new city with an ancient past. Shrines of the new mingle with relics of former days. In the Hittite Museum, built originally as a caravanserai or covered bazaar, are a cauldron and tripod with bullhead decoration dating back to the eighth century B.C.E., when the city was said to have been founded. Alexander the Great was here; Ankara's citadel, with its remaining twenty towers, is believed to have been constructed by the Galatians; the Temple of Augustus, 45-foot-high Column of Julian, Caracalla's Baths—all are reminders of the days when the Romans reigned here. Then in turn came the Byzantines, the Turks, the Crusaders, the Seljuks and finally the Ottoman Empire.

In old Samsun Pazari district with its narrow cobblestone lanes, street-corner shoe cobblers, open-air stalls where one can get squirted with a perfumed liquid, or buy halvah or Turkish sweets, I found a strong survival of the Moslem faith. Kemal Atatürk may have outlawed polygamy, and forbidden the wearing of the veil and the fez, but still observed is the Korban Bayram Festival with its sacrifice of sheep in memory of the day a ram was substituted for the son whom Abraham was prepared to sacrifice.

It was in Samsun Pazari that I saw many sheep brought in from the countryside all nicely painted and decorated with gay bows. After the usual process of bargaining the purchaser slung a sheep over his shoulder, to be taken home ready for the holiday sacrifice.

Here in Samsun Pazari, too, was the former Jewish ghetto. Off Anafartalar Street down narrow Birlik Sokhagi I came to the synagogue. Separated from the lane by a fence of metal bars and barbed wire, the synagogue bears a Hebrew inscription above its doorway, "My House shall be a House of Prayer for All Peoples."

Jews have been in Ankara a long, long time. Antiochus transferred two thousand Jewish families from Mesopotamia and Babylonia to Asia Minor; St. Paul's Epistle to the Galatians (as inhabitants of this inland province in Asia Minor were known) would indicate the existence of Jews here in his day; Rabbi Akiba spoke of Galia, usually identified with Galatia.

At the Samsun Pazari Synagogue, Sabbath services were scheduled for 7:00 o'clock in the morning, again in order to enable the men to go back to their shops at the conclusion of prayers. The reading of the Torah was done with great ceremony, a silver crown being placed on the Scroll for the ceremonial parade from the Ark to the Reading Desk. In place of the "shnodering" for the honors in connection with the reading, the men contribute an annual sum to the synagogue each in accordance with his ability. Here, too, the Sephardi congratulatory call of Hazak U'varukh greeted the men after their portion of the Torah had been read.

Leader of the service was another one of the "missionaries" of the Mahazikei Hatorah. Twenty-six-year-old, personable Avraham Cohen had studied in Istanbul at the Rabbinical Seminary and at the Wolf Gold Institute in Jerusalem. He returned to his home town Istanbul and opened a yard goods shop, but at Nissim Behar's insistence he left all that and came to Ankara, a community of 800 Jewish souls which was without any spiritual leadership.

Avraham Cohen introduced sermons in Ladino, the everyday language of so many of Turkey's Jews, and hoped to follow this up with a Ladino translation of the prayers, for he realized that his people did not understand the meaning of the prayers they repeated in Hebrew.

But Avraham Cohen did more than this. Aware that Ankara Jewish youth knew nothing of its heritage, Mr. Cohen (he is not an ordained rabbi) organized a discussion group of young adults that met weekly at his home. He also started Sunday morning classes that had an attendance of sixty boys and girls. He did this on a voluntary basis, in which he had the assistance of David Halido, a student at the Middle East Technical University, who, like Cohen, was a product of Istanbul's Mahazikei Hatorah. Jewish history, Hebrew, benedictions and religious laws were being taught.

One of the Sunday-morning classes I observed had only three pupils: Uri, Albert and Izet (the Turkish form for Isaac), and each was eighteen years old. All three attended Ankara College and all three were learning their Hebrew "Aleph Bet," this being their first step in any formal Jewish education. Their admiration for Mr. Cohen shone out of their eyes. Uri, Albert and Izet told me they had Turkish friends, but preferred to be among Jews, "so we can talk freely and feel more at home."

Although the synagogue is in Samsun Pazari that was not where I went to meet the Jews in their homes. Most have moved away from the old ghetto area. Many are now living in the heights, near Embassy Row in Kavaklidere, away from the smog that envelops the lower city. The apartments I visited were large and well furnished.

Most of the men are in business, although a few of the Jews are doctors and there are some engineers. The majority of the 260 families of Ankara that left to settle in Israel were of the lower-income group and now work in the factories of Petach Tikvah there.

As elsewhere in Turkey, the Jews of Ankara exhibit a sense of insecurity. Although Turkey was the first Moslem country to recognize the State of Israel, the Jews of Ankara were afraid to approach Israel's diplomatic representatives, a whole year going by before the local Jews got up enough courage to talk with Israel's first emissaries.

As to politics in general, the attitude is "Better be quiet and stay out of politics." Most of the Jews vote the ticket of the Justice Party, a right-of-center peasant-class party, which has been giving more and more power to the religious elements in the country, and is pro-Islamic and pro-Arab, according to reports. Ever since this party has gained power, Turkey's relations with Israel have cooled. Today's diplomatic exchange between the two countries is not on an ambassadorial level, a Chargé d' Affaires heading the delegation.

How does it happen that Jews who in other countries are usually associated with liberal movements, here in Turkey vote with the conservative Justice Party? To understand this one must go back over a quarter of a century, to the days when the Varlik Vergisi—the Tax on Wealth—was put into effect in November of 1942. This income tax was placed on property owners, on business people, merchants, on anyone who had since 1939 engaged in any commercial transactions, even if on only one occasion. Farmers were exempt from the tax, and as 85 percent of the Turkish population were farmers, those affected by the Varlik were the minority groups—the Greeks, the Armenians and the Jews—who acted as the country's middlemen. Assessments were fixed by local committees of government officials and their determination was final, for there was no appeal. If a person was unable to pay his assessment his furnishings were removed from his home and sold at public auction. If the amount of money raised by such auction was still insufficient they were sent to forced labor camps in the mines and on the roads of Anatolia in Asian Turkey.

Wherever I went in Turkey I came across Jews who had been affected by the application of the Varlik Vergisi. In Istanbul there was the white-haired man who was taxed £T 700. When it was realized he was a Jew, the assessment was raised to £T 7000. What hurt this courtly "gentleman of the old school" most was that in his youth, when the sultan was still in power, he had worked side by side with Atatürk to bring on the Revolution. In Izmir Jews had lost their factories, their furniture, their rugs and were left only with mattresses. One worker whose weekly salary was £T 5, was assessed £T 500. One of the men present at the Mayor Synagogue service in Bursa told me he had worked at a labor camp in the interior of the country for nine months because he had been unable to pay his tax.

Although the law was abrogated in March 1944 (at a time when the Turks began to realize Germany was losing the war), the memory of those years and the name Varlik has left a searing effect upon Turkey's Jews.

The People's Party, with Ismet Inonu at the head, was in office at the time the infamous Varlik Law was put into effect. The Jews therefore joined the opposition party—the Democratic Party. Following the 1960 *coup d'état* the Democratic Party was liquidated by court order. In reality the present Justice Party is a continuation of the outlawed Democratic Party. And the paradox of the Turkish Jews' voting the conservative pro-Islamic Justice Party continues.

Paradoxical, too, are the relations between Turkey and the State of Israel. So strong is the spirit of nationalism in Turkey, that Israel's fight for nationhood has caught the fancy of the Turks. Israeli courage and strength is highly admired and respected by the people. But Turkey wants the support of the Arab countries on the question of Cyprus. So commerce between Turkey and Israel continues, but political relations are in the deep freeze.

As one Ankara woman put it, "Sometimes it's difficult being a Jew here."

I spent the Seder nights in Izmir, the old Smyrna. The first night, my host, Rabbi Eshkanazi, head of the local Beit Din, wrapped the afikomen in an antique Turkish cummerbund, embroidered in gold thread, and held it suspended over his shoulder during the entire reading of the Haggadah. The Seder Plate, covered with another gold-embroidered cloth, was held for a moment over the head of each one at table. Together, all of us, children and grownups, recited the "Four Questions."

Rabbi Eshkanazi, scion of a family which has had a rabbi in each of the last seven generations, lived in the 130-year-old family home, with rooms opening off from both sides of a large central hall. The Seder was held in the raised section of this central hall, settees surrounding a low table where formerly men had studied Holy Writings. Sitting thus around the low table there was actually no need for any further attempt at mesubin (reclining). We were all reclining as we chanted the Haggadah in Hebrew and repeated part of it in Ladino.

Izmir itself, on the Aegean Sea, 285 miles south of Istanbul, gave me a spiritual lift after experiencing smog-filled Ankara. The palm-lined promenade along the waterfront and the white buildings seemed washed clean in the bright, clear air. This had been the Greek quarter of Izmir until their expulsion by Atatürk in 1922. Before retreating the Greeks set fires which destroyed more than half of the city. What I was seeing was a new, clean city risen from the ashes of that fire.

Grand Hotel Efes, many of its rooms with individual terraces facing the bay, looks out on a plaza with an imposing equestrian statue of Atatürk. Nato's COMLAND (Commander Land Forces) Southeast Headquarters are in Izmir, and the U.S. Air Force had a hospital there. Hotel Kismet seemed to be a little bit of America, so many American military men and their families were staying there. At night the lights twinkling on the hillside leading up to the heights of Kadifekale, where the Turks had always lived, remind one of another port city—the city of Haifa.

Izmir is an old, old city with thousands of years of history.

Native son Homer is said to have composed poems in a cave here; Alexander the Great had the city rebuilt after war's devastation; Marcus Aurelius raised the city anew after an earthquake. Arabs attacked it in the seventh century, Crusaders took it, Tamerlane sacked it in the fifteenth century, the Barbary pirates recruited crews there. The Ottomans held it until after World War I, when the Greeks were empowered to inhabit the area, marking their entry in 1919 with atrocities against the civilian population.

Reminders exist of the various conquerors and peoples who ruled there. Columns of an ancient market place and a statue of Poseidon are among the remains of the agora. From Izmir one goes south through villages of mud-brick homes and unpaved streets, to old Ephesus—where Cleopatra was once welcomed, where the apostles John and Paul preached and where the house in which the Virgin Mary is said to have lived until carried to heaven by angels is pointed out to the visitor.

Passover season happened to coincide with the Moslem Korban Bayram, and even on the streets of sophisticated Izmir, people were buying the beribboned and painted sheep. Without any religious ceremony, the sheep are slaughtered and the meat distributed, supposedly, among the poor. It was a gay holiday period.

My particular interest in Izmir was to see the city where pseudo-Messiah Sabbatai Zevi had lived. Born here on Tisha B'Ab of 1626, he was the son of Mordecai Zevi, an agent for an English merchant house. Fascinated by the study of mysticism and the Cabala, and accepting the belief then held, by Christians and Jews alike, that the Messianic Era was soon approaching, young Sabbatai Zevi revealed himself, when only twenty-two years old, as the expected Messiah who would redeem the Jews and lead them back to the Holy Land.

Excommunicated and banished from his native city when he was twenty-four, he moved on to Salonica, to Cairo and to Jerusalem. His fame and followers grew throughout Europe, Asia and Africa. Shortly before the year 1666, believed to be the beginning of the millenium and the Messianic Era, Sabbatai Zevi returned to his native city of Smyrna—fifteen years after being banished—"infinitely desired by the common people."

At the beginning of the year 1666 Sabbatai Zevi went to

Istanbul, fully expecting a miracle to happen—that the Ottoman Empire which then ruled over the Holy Land would be overthrown, that the sultan's crown would be placed on his head, and that the sultan would then do homage to Sabbatai Zevi as the Messiah, highest of kings on earth.

Instead he was arrested and thrown into prison for plotting to overthrow the Ottoman rule and later brought before the sultan in Edirne. Ordered to choose between conversion to Islam or dying at the stake, Sabbatai Zevi threw off his Jewish headgear and donned the white turban, symbol that he was embracing Islam.

Despite this denouement, the anniversary of his death continued to be marked by the local Cardozo family well into the twentieth century. Sabbatai Zevi's home in Lambat Sokhagi, a narrow lane near the Ergat Bazaar, is still to be seen. Believing that a great man once lived in the house, the inhabitants (non-Jews) light candles in his memory.

Although Alexander the Great is said to have transported some Jews from Palestine and to have settled them in Smyrna, and there is evidence of early inscriptions on tombstones, there was no organized community there until 1605. By that time Turkey had become a haven for refugees from the Spanish Inquisition, and when Sabbatai Zevi was born to a family of Spanish descent, Izmir numbered 7,000 Jews.

Normally one would expect that such a community would continue to grow in numbers. Instead, Izmir Jewry followed an unusual pattern of growth and decline. Ten thousand Jews were there in 1788. Only twenty-four years later the number was cut in half—down to 5,000. A generation later the number had risen—this time to 13,000.

Cause of this fluctuation is found in the misfortunes that beset Izmir. Six times during this period earthquakes had almost destroyed the entire city. In one of these upheavals of nature, 400 Jews died. The city had also been plagued by cholera epidemics and by fires. Near the end of the eighteenth century flames destroyed every synagogue. In 1841 another conflagration destroyed 1,500 Jewish homes and 5,000 people were made homeless. After this the community grew again and by 1910 there were 35,000 Jews there.

The Declaration of the State of Israel brought about an exodus

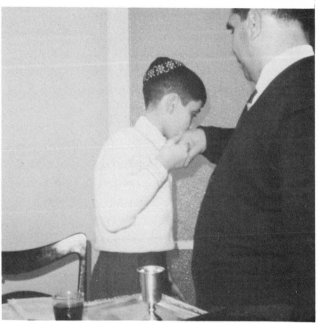

At close of Seder, children kiss father's hand, and he in turn blesses each one.

from Izmir. Fifteen thousand emigrated—including beggars, maids, peddlers and the porters, of whom it was said, "They appear to have the veritable strength of a Hercules." One Izmir matron complained, "You can't find a Jewish maid nowadays. They've all gone to Israel—and have done very well for themselves there." Some of the former Izmir Jews settled in Jerusalem's Yemin Moshe, literally within a stone's throw of the walls of the Old City. Today in Izmir—the second-largest port and the third-largest city in Turkey—there are 4,000 Jews.

Some of these are in commerce and industry. No one could miss seeing the large displays advertising Pe Re Ja Perfumes (associated with the well-known Roger and Gallet firm). The name Pe Re Ja puzzled me until I discovered that in good Hebrew fashion it stood for the initial letters of the three Jews who headed the business, Pepe, Rebecca and Jaques.

Edwin Cohen exported dried fruits under the brand name of "Lion"—a brand which I bought later at Jerusalem's Supermarket. Other Jews dealt in cottonseed oil and the jute business.

Certain business preferences exist. Jews do not operate beauty parlors or barber shops. University students study engineering, but do not go into the teaching profession in the government schools.

The old Caratache district along the waterfront had once been the area of Jewish concentration and the communal institutions were still there—the Home for the Aged and the Jewish Hospital. Chief of Staff Dr. Abouaf said, "There is no discrimination as far as studying medicine is concerned; in Izmir alone there are ten Jewish doctors. Getting a hospital post is another matter." Nearby was a Youth Group Center housed in inadequate quarters with a leaky roof, operating under a charter granted forty years ago.

The Jewish schools were also in Caratache. The B'nai B'rith School, opened in 1914, had been renamed the Caratache School in order to comply with government regulations of no affiliation with groups existing outside the country. Originally a private home, the rooms retained the high carved ceilings, the glass-fronted wall cabinets and fireplaces of a family dwelling. But floorboards were warped and cracking and the tiny classrooms had space for little more than the old-fashioned wooden benches. For over half a century Dr. Albert Yahyah was principal of this primary school whose enrollment numbered only seventy pupils.

Almost a century ago the Alliance Israelite Universelle opened a school in Izmir which counted Baron Edmond de Rothschild and Baron de Hirsch as benefactors. Known as the Talmud Torah, it was a primary school with 160 students.

In both of these schools the regular school curriculum was followed with the government paying the bill, and the Jewish Council providing additional instruction in prayers, Hebrew language and religious law five hours a week.

The Ortar Middle School (Junior High) was opened twelve years ago. Its staff is Turkish, the Jewish Agency supplying an Israeli religious teacher for one hour's daily lesson in the Hebrew language.

It was in Caratache, too, that I attended Sabbath morning service at 55-year-old Beit Israel Synagogue. From the women's gallery I watched as the sun's rays bounced off the prisms swinging from the fifty lights of the huge crystal chandelier and made a rainbow-like effect on the tallit of one of the men. Prayer shawls were drawn up over their eyes as the men recited the Shema. When the congregation began reciting the Eighteenfold Benediction, they stretched their arms wide. To me it seemed as if they desired to include the entire scattered brotherhood of Jewry in their prayer.

Time came for the Reading of the Torah. The Haham and hazzan, robed in black, with white ties and high black velvet hats, ascended the marble steps covered with fine rugs that led to the Ark of highly polished carved wood. Drawing aside a parokhet, inner doors were opened, then a second parokhet was seen before the Torah itself was revealed. Embroidered on its mantle were the silver crescent moon and five-pointed star, emblem of the Turkish flag. My neighbor, one of the three Izmir women present that morning in the large women's gallery, kept throwing kisses at the Torah as it was paraded around the synagogue. Not satisfied with that, she kept urging me to do likewise.

On Friday evening I had gone to Alsancak, the fashionable new district to which the more prosperous Jews were moving. Surely here, I thought in my innocence, the synagogue would be a "grand" one. The case was quite the contrary. I was led along a quiet street of homes, around to the rear of one of the houses, up a flight of steps into an ordinary apartment—and there was the shul. My surprised query brought the answer, "The government is a secular one and does not permit construction of any new religious institutions, which includes synagogues. This is the best we can manage. We don't know when the government will close this down, too."

On Sabbath afternoon I returned to this "shtiebel" to see youth study groups in action. Aware that only 30 percent of Izmir's children of school age attended a Jewish school, men had volunteered to lead groups aimed at reaching the rest. Three sections were in session simultaneously in separate corners of the shul, learning how to read Hebrew by repetition of prayers aloud. At the close of the session every boy received a bag of sweets.

At dawn of the day ushering in the Passover of that year of 1966, I left my hotel—the Kismet—and glided through silent, unawakened streets so as to be at the Alsancak shul in time for the day's special 6:00 o'clock morning service for behorim (first born). Attendance at this ceremony would release them from the duty of fasting that day, incumbent on every first-born man. All assembled around a table at the conclusion of the prayers (I was the only woman present), and one man read the closing portion of a tractate of the Talmud—the complete reading of which he had voluntarily undertaken during the preceding months. This was followed by a kiddush and breakfast of hard-boiled eggs, rolls, cheese, raisins, candied almonds and Turkish pastry.

The Behor Levis (every first-born son is named Behor) included me in their second-night Seder celebration. Here, too, as at Rabbi Eshkanazi's, the Seder Plate was passed around the table to be held over each one's head for a moment, and the afikomen suspended over Mr. Levi's shoulder to indicate the hurried departure of the Jews from Egypt.

The Seder meals included neither gefillte fish, nor matzoh balls nor chicken. Instead we ate very well both evenings of spinach baked with eggs, matzoh mixed with sliced leek and eggs, then fried, *bakli* (the large Italian style beans) cooked in olive oil with lamb's liver and meat balls, and a pudding made of matzoh with meat and eggs. At the end of the meal we drank Turkish coffee. Had Gadya (One Only Kid), sung in Ladino, concluded both Seder nights in old Izmir.

When I left Turkey (some time after the Seder) I flew directly to Israel—but that is another tale.

~§ GLOSSARY §~

Hebrew and Yiddish words used in the text

ADON OLAM. . . . . "Eternal Lord"; familiar hymn in Jewish liturgy

AFIKOMEN. . . . . Piece broken off from middle one of three matzot on Seder table and eaten at end of meal

ALEPH BET . . . . Alphabet; first two letters of the Hebrew alphabet

ALIYAH . . . . Being called up to the Reading of the
(pl. ALIYOT) Torah; also ascent or immigration to Israel

ALTER REBBE . . . . Founder of Habad, the Lubavitsher Hasidic Movement

ASHKENAZI . . . . Jews of middle and north European
(pl. ASHKENAZIM) origin; Jews of the West

AYN KELOHENU. . . . . . . Hymn: There is none like our God

BAR MITZVAH . . . . Ceremony inducting thirteen-year-old boy into adult membership of the community with full religious responsibility

BAT MITZVAH . . . . Ceremony inducting a girl into religious majority

BEIT DIN . . . . Rabbinical court

BEIT ISRAEL . . . . House of Israel

BEIT MIDRASH . . . . House of study of the Law

BEIT RIVKAH . . . . House of Rebecca

BENE ISRAEL . . . . Native Jews in and around Bombay who preferred to be called by the name "Israelites"

BENE MOSHE . . . . Mythical Jews believed to be descended from Moses

BERAKHOT . . . . Prescribed blessings or praises of God recited on various occasions and before eating, a different benediction used for each type of food—for bread, fruit, etc.

BETAR . . . . City where Bar Cochba made his last stand; name of a Revisionist Zionist Organization

BETH EL . . . . House of God

BETH ISRAEL . . . . House of Israel

BIMAH . . . . Elevated platform from which Scroll of the Law is read

BRIT MILAH . . . . Circumcision; covenant of Abraham

CABALA . . . . Mystical doctrine concerning God and the universe

CHESED EL . . . . Grace of God

CHOLENT . . . . Food, mainly meat and beans, placed in oven Friday afternoon and baked overnight; eaten at Sabbath midday meal

DAYAN . . . . Judge of a rabbinic court

DAYENU . . . . Song listing many Divine favors performed for Israel, each of which "Would have sufficed"; sung at Passover Seder

ELUL . . . . Hebrew name of the month preceding Rosh Hashanah

ETROG . . . . Citron; used in ceremonies during Feast of Booths (Sukkot)

ETZ HAIM . . . . Tree of Life

FLEISHIGE. . . . . Meat foods

GABBAI . . . . Warden of synagogue

GAN EDEN. . . . . Garden of Eden; Paradise

GAON . . . . Person endowed with extraordinary scholarship

GEMARA . . . . Talmud; the commentary of the rabbis from circa 200 to about 425 C.E. on the Mishnah; sometimes the Mishnah and the Gemara together are said to make up the Talmud

GOMEL . . . . Benediction recited upon escape from danger

GRAGER. . . . . Noisemaker used when name of Haman is mentioned during the reading of the Scroll of Esther

HABONIM. . . . . The Builders; a Zionist youth movement

HAFTORAH . . . . Portion from the Prophets chanted immediately after the Reading of the Torah

HAGGADAH . . . . Recounting of the story of the Exodus on eve of Passover

HAHAM . . . . A wise man; in Sephardi communities
(pl. HAHAMIM) a rabbi is officially designated by this title

HAHAM BASHI . . . . Chief Rabbi (Hebrew and Turkish language); official Jewish representative to the government

HALITZAH . . . . Ceremony releasing man from Biblical injunction to marry widow of his brother who died childless

HALLAH . . . . Loaves of white bread used on Sab-
(pl. HALLOT) bath and festivals

HALUTZ . . . . Pioneer who settled on the land of Israel

HAMETZ . . . . Leavened bread; any food containing leavened cereal

HANUKKAH . . . . Feast of Dedication lasting eight days, commemorating the rededication of the Temple in 165 B.C.E. by Judas Maccabee; also known as the Feast of Lights

HAROSET. . . . . Mixture of apples, nuts, spices and wine, symbolizing the mortar used by the Jews during slavery in Egypt; used at Passover Seder

HASHOMER HATZAIR . . . . The Young Guard; a Zionist youth movement

HASID . . . . Devotee of sect emphasizing devotion
(pl. HASIDIM) to God through song, dance and joy

HASIDISM . . . . Religious movement emphasizing devotion to God through joyous song, dance and happiness in a mystical ecstasy

HATAN TORAH and
HATAN BERESHIT . . . . . . Bridegroom of the Torah—honorary title for person reading final portion of Deuteronomy; Bridegroom of Bereshit —honorary title for person who follows immediately with reading of first portion of Genesis; this occurs on the Festival of Rejoicing of the Law

HATIKVAH. . . . . The Hope; national anthem of Israel

HAVDALAH . . . . Ceremony at conclusion of Sabbath indicating separation between the Sabbath and weekdays

HAZAK U'VARUKH . . . . . . Be Strong and Blessed; Sephardi congratulatory expression greeting person who has read portion from the Law

HAZZAN . . . . Cantor

HEHALUTZ . . . . Pioneering movement

HEKHAL . . . . The Temple proper; separated by curtains from the Holy of Holies

HESHVAN . . . . A month in the Jewish calendar, occurring in October–November period

HEVRAH KADDISHA . . . . . Holy Society; a group giving voluntary service in burying the dead

HOL HAMOED . . . . Intermediate days between the first and the last sacred days of week-long Passover and Feast of Booths; considered semi-holy days

HOSAN. . . . . Young man of marriageable age

HOSHANAH RABBAH . . . . "Oh, Save"; Seventh day of Feast of Booths; synagogue ceremonies make use of willow branches; Bible is studied at night

HUMASH . . . . The Pentateuch; Five Books of Moses; first part of the Bible; also known as the Torah

KABBALAT SHABBAT . . . . Welcoming the Sabbath; chants preceding Friday Evening Service

KADDISH . . . . Sanctification and glorification of God's name; recited by cantor at close of certain sections of prayers; also recited by mourners although no mention of death is contained in it

KADIMAH. . . . . Forward! Onward!

KARAITES . . . . Jewish sect advocating strict observance of Biblical laws and rejection of traditional rabbinical laws

KASHERED. . . . . Made ritually fit

KASHRUT. . . . . Ritual fitness, according to Dietary Laws

KEHILLAH . . . . Community

KETUBAH . . . . Marriage contract, in which the groom
(pl. KETUBOT)   assumes certain responsibilities towards the bride

KIDDUSH . . . . Ceremonial ritual over wine, ushering in holy days, Sabbaths and festivals

KNESSET ISRAEL . . . . Assembly of Israel

KOHEN . . . . Male descendant of Aaron; functioned
(pl. KOHANNIM)   as priest in the Temple; gives the priestly blessing and is called up first to Reading of the Torah

KOL NIDRE . . . . "All Vows"; opening prayer recited before sundown on eve of Day of Atonement

KOSHER. . . . . Ritually fit; prepared in accordance with Dietary Laws

KOSHER L'PESACH. . . . . . Ritually fit for Passover

KREPLACH. . . . . Boiled dumplings, filled with meat or cheese

KUPAT HOLIM . . . . Sick Fund

LANDSMANSCHAFTEN ... Associations of newcomers to a place, hailing from same area in the "old" country

L'HAYIM .... A toast: "To life (or health)!"

LULAV.............. Palm branch used during ceremonies of Feast of Booths

MAARIV .... Evening Service

MAFTIR .... One who chants a portion from the Prophets, following the reading from the Scroll of the Law

MAGEN DAVID .... Shield of David; six-pointed Star of David

MAGEN HASIDIM .... Shield of the Pious

MAGHAIN ABOTH....... Shield of the Forefathers

MAGHEN DAVID........ Same as Magen David

MAHAZIKEI HATORAH ... Those who hold fast to the Torah

MARRANOS .... Jews of Spain and Portugal who outwardly converted to Christianity, but secretly practiced Judaism at home; also applied to Jews anywhere who converted only outwardly

MASHIV HARUAH
UMORID HAGESHEM..... "Who makes the wind blow and sends down the rain"; a phrase included in the daily prayers during the rainy season of the year

MATZOH .... Unleavened bread; eaten at Passover
(pl. MATZOT)   to recall hurried departure from Egypt (See Exodus 12:39)

MEGILLAH........... Parchment scroll; in particular, the Megillah of Esther, which is read on Purim

MENORAH .... Eight-branched candelabra used during Hanukkah; seven-branched lampstand used in Temple

MEZUZAH .... Doorpost; parchment scroll inscribed
(pl. MEZUZOT)   with two sections of the Shema, affixed to the doorpost

MIKVEH............. Ritual bath; must be of a certain minimum size and the water must come from a natural source—spring, river, rain water or melted ice

MINHAH	Afternoon Service
MINYAN	Ten males, thirteen years old or over, forming minimum quorum for public worship
MINYAN MEN	Men paid to attend service, so that required quorum for public worship will be present
MISHNAH	Traditional doctrine or Law transmitted orally and compiled by Rabbi Judah HaNasi at beginning of third century C.E.
MITZVAH (pl. MITZVOT)	Commandment; also used to express an act of human kindness
MOHEL	Man religiously qualified to perform circumcision
MOTZIE	Benediction recited before partaking of bread; (*see* Berakhot)
MUSMEAH YESHUAH	(God) Who brings about salvation
NEILAH	Closing; concluding service of the Day of Atonement
NEVE SHALOM	Abode of Peace
NEVE ZEDEK	Abode of Righteousness
OHEL LEAH	Tent of Leah
OLAM HABA	The World to Come
OMER	A sheaf of grain offered on second day of Passover in Temple days; from that day seven weeks were counted and fiftieth day celebrated as Feast of Pentecost; a period associated with misfortunes
ONEG SHABBAT	Delight in the Sabbath; a gathering on the Sabbath for religious or cultural purposes
OR HAYIM	Light of Life
OTZAR HATORAH	Storehouse of the Torah
PALMAH	Striking force of the Hagana (self defense organization) before the State of Israel came into existence
PAROKHET	Curtain over Ark containing Scroll of Law

PASSOVER—PESACH. . . . . Festival commemorating the Exodus from slavery in Egypt; word Passover recalls that when the Angel of Death slew first-born of every Egyptian house, he "passed over" the houses of the Israelites

PIDYON HABEN . . . . Redemption of the first-born; first-born, if a son, was to be dedicated to service of God in return for sparing of first-born during night of Exodus; father redeems his son, when thirty days old, by payment of ransom of five shekels to a priest

PORAT YOSEF . . . . Fruitful Vine of Joseph

PURIM . . . . Festival in remembrance of deliverance of Jews of Persian Empire from plan of Haman to annihilate them; story told in the Book of Esther

RABBANITES . . . . Main body of Jewry who follow traditions of rabbis of the Talmud as well as the laws of the Torah

RAHAMIM . . . . Mercy

RASHI . . . . Acronym of name of Rabbi Solomon Yitzhaki who wrote famous commentaries on Bible and Talmud

RIMONIM . . . . Pomegranates; silver or gold ornaments on top of rollers of Scrolls of Law, originally made in shape of pomegranates

RODEF SHALOM. . . . . . . Pursuing peace

ROSH HASHANAH. . . . . . Beginning of the year; a day of judgment

SEDER . . . . Order; home service for first night of Passover, enacting the Exodus from Egypt

SEDRAH. . . . . Arrangement; weekly portion of Pentateuch read in synagogue

SEFER TORAH . . . . Parchment strips, sewed and rolled
(pl. SIFREI TORAH)   into a scroll; contains the Pentateuch

SEPHARDI . . . . Jews of Spain; now also used to de-
(pl. SEPHARDIM)   note Jews of any Oriental country—
North Africa, Asia Minor or Jews of
any place who follow the rites of the
Spanish Jews

SEUDAH. . . . . Feast

SEUDAH SHELISHIT . . . . . "Third Meal"; light repast on Sabbath
afternoon

SHAAR HARAHAMIM. . . . . Gate of Mercy

SHAAR RATZON . . . . Gate of Favor

SHAARE ZEDEK . . . . Gates of Righteousness

SHABBAT. . . . . Sabbath

SHAHARIT . . . . "At Dawn"; morning prayer

SHAMASH . . . . "Servant"; sexton

SHAVUOT. . . . . Feast of Weeks or Pentecost; held on
fiftieth day from the second day of
Passover; first fruits were offered in
Temple days; also commemorates giv-
ing of Ten Commandments on Mt.
Sinai

SHEARIT YISRAEL . . . . . . Remnant of Israel

SHEHEHEYANU . . . . Benediction thanking God "Who has
kept us alive and sustained us to this
season"; (*see* Berakhot)

SHEHITA . . . . Ritual slaughtering of animals and
poultry

SHEMA . . . . Hear, O Israel (Deuteronomy 6:4–9),
which is recited, with two additional
paragraphs, at every morning and
evening service

SHEMA YISRAEL. . . . . . . Hear, O Israel, the Lord is our God,
the Lord is One; considered the Jew-
ish confession of faith

SHEVA BERAKHOT . . . . . . Sevenfold Benediction; recited at marriage ceremony and at Grace After
Meals on seven days following marriage, if there is a minyan (*see* Minyan)

SHIR HASHIRIM . . . . Solomon's Song of Songs

SHIVA . . . . Seven days of mourning

SHNEIDER . . . . Tailor

SHNODER . . . . To pledge a contribution when one is called up to the Reading of the Torah

SHOFAR. . . . . Ram's horn; sounded in synagogues during period of High Holydays, also on singular ceremonial occasions

SHOHET . . . . One qualified to perform the ritual slaughter of cattle and poultry

SHTIEBEL . . . . Room in a private house used for religious purposes

SHUL. . . . . Synagogue

SHULHAN ARUKH. . . . . . . "Prepared Table"; codification of Jewish law and practice by Joseph Karo in sixteenth century; the standard code

SHUSHAN PURIM . . . . Purim celebrated in Shushan (Susa, ancient capital of Persia) and in all walled cities, on fifteenth day of month of Adar—the day following the festival's celebration elsewhere

SHUSTER. . . . . Cobbler

SIMHAT TORAH . . . . Rejoicing of the Law; a day of gladness; dancing permitted in the synagogue; in the morning the annual cycle of Torah readings is completed with Deuteronomy chs. 33–34 and immediately recommenced with reading of Genesis 1:1–2:3

SLIHOT . . . . Penitential prayers; recited after midnight. Western Jews — on Saturday night preceding Rosh Hashanah; Oriental Jews—for thirty nights preceding Rosh Hashanah

SUKKAH. . . . . During the Feast of Booths, Jews directed to live in temporary shelters
(pl. SUKKOT) allowing sun and stars to shine through roof covering in recollection of the wandering through the desert after the Exodus from Egypt (Leviticus 23:39–44)

TALLIT . . . . Fringed prayer shawl

TALMUD TORAH . . . . An elementary religious school maintained by the community; some private religious schools use same name

TASHLIKH . . . . A symbolic "casting of sins" into a body of water on first day of Rosh Hashanah (or on second day if the first falls on a Sabbath)

TEFILLIN. . . . . Phylacteries worn during weekday morning services by males thirteen years old and over

TIFERET ISRAEL . . . . Glory of Israel

TISHA B'AB . . . . Ninth day of month of Ab; the day on which the Second Temple was destroyed in 70 C.E.; observed as a day of mourning

TORAH . . . . Religious teaching; particularly the Pentateuch or Five Books of Moses; the most sacred part of the Scriptures

TREF. . . . . Forbidden by dietary laws; not kosher

TU B'SHEVAT. . . . . Fifteenth day of month of Shevat; the New Year for trees; trees planted that day in Israel, others send money for tree planting in Israel; fruit of trees eaten

UNTERFUEHRERS . . . . . . Persons accompanying bride and groom to wedding canopy

YAHRZEIT . . . . Anniversary of a death

YANKEL. . . . . Yiddish diminutive of the Hebrew name Yaakov (Jacob)

YARMULKE . . . . Skull cap

YESHIVA . . . . Religious academy of higher learning
(pl. YESHIVOT)

YIBBUM . . . . Levirate marriage; Biblical ordinance that a man marry widow of a brother who has died childless (Deuteronomy 25:5–6)

YOM KIPPUR . . . . Day of Atonement

ZOHAR . . . . Mystical commentary on the Bible with Cabalistic conceptions of God and the universe

✌ BIBLIOGRAPHY ✍

BOOKS

Abrahams, Israel. *Jewish Life in the Middle Ages.* London: E. Goldston, 1932.

Adler, Cyrus. *Jacob H. Schiff, His Life and Letters.* New York: Doubleday Doran, 1928.

Adler, Elkan Nathan, ed. *Jewish Travelers.* London: G. Routledge & Sons, 1930.

———. *Jews in Many Lands.* Philadelphia: Jewish Publication Society, 1905.

Alexander, Michael. *Offbeat in Asia.* New York: David McKay, 1960.

Auckland Hebrew Congregation. *75th Anniversary Commemorative Booklet.* Auckland 1960.

Australian Jewish Historical Society. *Journal and Proceedings.* 6 vols. Sydney 1939–1969.

Barish, Louis, ed. *Rabbis in Uniform.* New York: Jonathan David, 1962.

Baron, Salo W. *A Social and Religious History of the Jews.* New York: Columbia University Press, 1937.

Benjamin, Israel Joseph. *Eight Years in Asia and Africa.* Hanover: The author, 1859.

Benjamin of Tudela. *Itinerary of Rabbi Benjamin of Tudela.* Translated and edited by Adolf Asher. London: A. Asher, 1840.

Ben Zvi, Isaac. *The Exiled and the Redeemed.* Philadelphia: Jewish Publication Society, 1957.

Bergner, Herz. *Light and Shadow.* New York: Thomas Yoseloff, 1963.

Beth Hillel, David de. *Travels of David de Beth Hillel from Jerusalem through Arabia, Koordistan, part of Persia and India to Madras.* Madras: The author, 1832.

Brasch, R. *The Star of David.* Sydney: Angus & Robertson, 1955.

Burdon, Randal Mathews. *The Life and Times of Sir Julius Vogel.* Christchurch: Caxton Press, 1948.

Burnell, Arthur Coke, ed. *The Voyage of John Huyghen Van Linschoten to the East Indies.* London: The Hakluyt Society, 1885.

Burns, Sir Alan. *Fiji.* London: H.M. Stationery Office, 1963.

Canterbury Hebrew Congregation. *The First One Hundred Years of the Canterbury Hebrew Congregation.* Christchurch: The author, 1963.

Carmel, Josef. *A Reyse zu Farshtoisene Brider.* Tel Aviv: I.L. Peretz, 1959.

———. *With the Scattered in the East.* Jerusalem: Israeli Publishing Institute, 1960.

Cohen, Israel. *A Jewish Pilgrimage.* London: Vallentine, Mitchell, 1956.

———. *The Journal of a Jewish Traveler.* New York: Dodd, Mead, 1925.

Cook, James. *Journals of Captain James Cook on his voyages of discovery.* Edited by J.C. Beaglehole. London: Cambridge University Press, 1955.

Cowan, James. *The Caltex Book of Maori Lore.* Wellington: A.H. Reed, 1959.

Dicker, Herman. *Wanderers and Settlers.* New York: Twayne, 1962.

Douglas, William O. *West of the Indus.* Garden City: Doubleday, 1958.

Elbogen, Ismar. *A Century of Jewish Life.* Philadelphia: Jewish Publication Society, 1944.

৩৬ BIBLIOGRAPHY ৪৬

Elias, E. and E. Isaac, eds. *Jews in India with Who is Who.* Ernakulam: Indo-Israel Friendship Publications, 1963, 1964.

Emanuelson, Abraham. *The Remnant of the Jews.* New York: The author, 1929.

Encyclopaedia Britannica.

Encyclopaedia Judaica. Berlin: Eschkol, 1928. 10 vols.

Encyclopedia of Religion and Ethics. New York: Charles Scribner's Sons, 1928. 13 vols.

Federbusch, Simon. *World Jewry Today.* Jerusalem: Massada, 1959.

Finkelstein, Louis. *The Jews: Their History, Culture and Religion.* Philadelphia: Jewish Publication Society, 1949. 4 vols.

Fox, Len. *Australia and the Jews.* Melbourne: International Book Shop, 1943.

Fried, Jacob, ed. *Jews in the Modern World.* New York: Twayne, 1962.

Furnas, Joseph Chamberlain. *Anatomy of Paradise: Hawaii and the Islands of the South Seas.* New York: W. Sloane Associates, 1948.

Galanté, Abraham. *Histoire des Juifs D'Anatolie.* Istanbul: Babok, 1937.

Godbey, Allen H. *The Lost Tribes, A Myth.* Durham: Duke University Press, 1930.

Goldberg, Israel and Samson Benderly. *Outline of Jewish Knowledge.* 3 vols. New York: Bureau of Jewish Education, 1929.

Goldman, Lazarus Morris. *The History of the Jews in New Zealand.* Wellington: A.H. Reed, 1958.

Goodblatt, Morris S. *Jewish Life in Turkey in the 16th Century.* New York: Jewish Theological Seminary of America, 1952.

Goodman, Philip. *Purim Anthology.* Philadelphia: Jewish Publication Society, 1949.

Goodman, Philip and Hanna. *Jewish Marriage Anthology.* Philadelphia: Jewish Publication Society, 1965.

Gordon, Max. *Jews in Van Diemen's Land.* Sydney: Ponsford, Newman & Benson, 1965.

———. *Sir Isaac Isaacs, A Life of Service.* Melbourne: Heinemann, 1963.

Graetz, Heinrich. *History of the Jews.* Philadelphia: Jewish Publication Society, 1891. 6 vols.

Great Synagogue, The. *Jubilee History of the Great Synagogue, And Records of the Earlier Jewish Community of New South Wales.* Sydney 1928.

Harlow, Vincent T., ed. *Voyages of Great Pioneers.* London: Oxford University Press, 1929.

Harris, Maurice. *History of the Mediaeval Jews from the Moslem Conquest of Spain to the Discovery of America.* New York: Block, 1916.

Hart, Henry H. *Sea Road to the Indies.* New York: Macmillan, 1950.

Hertz, Joseph Herman. *The First Pastoral Tour to the Jewish Communities of the British Dominions by the Chief Rabbi.* London: H. Milford, 1924.

Hughes, Richard. *Hong Kong.* New York: F.A. Praeger, 1968.

Ibn Batutah, Abu Ullah Mohammad. *Travels in Asia and Africa.* London: George Routledge & Sons, 1929.

Isaac, I.A. *A Short Account of the Calcutta Jews.* Calcutta: The author, 1917.

Israel, Benjamin J. *Khan Bahadur Jacob Bapuji Israel.* Bombay: G.G. Pathere, 1960.

Japheth, M.D. *The Jews of India-A Brief Survey.* Bombay: The author, 1960.

Jewish Encyclopedia. New York: Funk & Wagnalls, 1901. 12 vols.

Kastein, Josef. *History and Destiny of the Jews.* New York: Garden City Publishing Co., 1936.

———. *The Messiah of Izmir.* New York: Viking Press, 1931.

Kayserling, Meyer. *Christopher Columbus and the Participation of the Jews in the Spanish and Portuguese Discoveries.* New York: Longmans, Green, 1894.

Kehimkar, Haeem Samuel. *History of the Bene Israel in India.* Tel Aviv: Dayag Press, 1937.

Kessel, Joseph. *The Valley of Rubies.* New York: David McKay, 1961.

Klass, Rosanne. *Land of the High Flags.* New York: Random House, 1964.

Komroff, Manuel, ed. *Contemporaries of Marco Polo.* New York: Liveright, 1928.

Kotsuji, Abraham. *From Tokyo to Jerusalem.* New York: Bernard Geiss Associates, 1964.

Landshut, S. *Jewish Communities in the Muslim Countries of the Middle East.* London: The Jewish Chronicle, 1950.

Learsi, Rufus. *Israel: A Short History of the Jewish People.* New York: World Publishing Co., 1949.

Lewis, Geoffrey L. *Turkey.* New York: F.A. Praeger, 1965.

Lord, Rev. J. Henry. *The Jewish Mission Field in the Bombay Diocese.* Bombay: Education Society's Press, 1894.

————. *The Jews in India and the Far East.* Bombay: Mission Press, 1907.

Luke, Sir Harry Charles Joseph. *Islands of the South Pacific.* London: George G. Harrap & Co., 1962.

Luzzatto, Rola, ed. *Hong Kong Who's Who 1958–60.* Hong Kong: Luzzatto, 1960.

Marcus, Jacob R. *The Jew in the Mediaeval World.* New York: Atheneum, 1969.

Margolis, Max L. and Alexander Marx. *A History of the Jewish People.* Philadelphia: Jewish Publication Society, 1927.

Marshall, Harry Ignatius. *The Karens of Burma.* London: Longmans, Green, 1945.

Mendelssohn, Sidney. *The Jews of Asia, Especially in the Sixteenth and Seventeenth Centuries.* London: Paul, Trench, Triebner, 1920.

Munz, Hirsch. *Jews in South Australia.* Adelaide: Thornquest Press, 1936.

Musleah, Ezekiel N. *Order of Service, on the occasion of the Seventy-Fifth Anniversary Celebration of the Maghen David Synagogue, incorporating a Brief History of the Synagogue.* Calcutta 1960.

Navy Records Society. *Naval Miscellany.* vol. 3. London 1928.

Prayers and Hymns for Special Occasions, According to the Rites of Shingli and the Cochin Congregation. Amsterdam: Salomons, 1757.

Price, Charles A. *Jewish Settlers in Australia.* Canberra: Australian National University, 1964.

Rabinowitz, Louis. *Far East Mission.* Johannesburg: Eagle Press, 1952.

Reuben, Rebecca. *The Bene Israel Annual and Year Book.* Bombay: The author, 1918.

Robinson, Nehemiah. *The Jewish Communities of the World.* New York: Institute of Jewish Affairs—World Jewish Congress, 1963.

Roth, Cecil. *The Sassoon Dynasty.* London: R. Hale, 1941.

Salem, Avraham Baruch. *Eternal Light or Jewtown Synagogue.* Ernakulam: S.D. Printing Works, 1929.

Salmon, Ernest. *Alexandre Salmon 1820–1866 et sa femme Ariitaimai 1821–1897 Deux figures de Tahiti à l'époque du Protectorat.* Paris: Publications de la Société des Océanistes, No. 11, 1964.

Schechtman, Joseph. *On Wings of Eagles, The Plight, Exodus and Homecoming of Oriental Jewry.* New York: T. Yoseloff, 1961.

Schwarzbart, Isaac. *Report of the World Jewish Congress.* New York: World Jewish Congress, 1951.

Simon, A.I. *Songs of the Jews of Cochin.* Cochin: Archaeological Society of South India, 1946.

Steinberg, Isaac N. *Australia—The Unpromised Land.* London: Gollancz, 1948.

Stevenson, H.N.C. *The Hill Peoples of Burma.* London: Longmans, Green, 1944.

Stone, Julius. *Stand Up and Be Counted, An Open Letter to the Rt. Hon. Sir Isaac Isaacs.* Sydney: Ponsford, Newman and Benson, 1944.

Strizower, Schifra. *Exotic Jewish Communities.* London: Yoseloff, 1962.

Thomson, William Campbell. *Fiji Past and Present.* Melbourne: Royal Geographical Society of Australia, 1899.

Universal Jewish Encyclopedia. 10 vols.

Victorian Jewish Board of Deputies. *Annual Report.* Melbourne: The author, 1965.

Werblowski, R.J. Zwi and Geoffrey Wigoder. *The Encyclopedia of the Jewish Religion.* Jerusalem: Massada, 1968.

Wilber, Donald N. *Contemporary Iran.* New York: F.A. Praeger, 1963.

Wolf, L., ed. *Menasseh ben Israel's mission to Oliver Cromwell.* London: Macmillan, 1901.

Wolff, Joseph. *Journal of the Rev. Joseph Wolff.* London: J. Burns, 1839.

PAMPHLETS—PERIODICALS—NEWSPAPERS

Alliance Review, The. New York

Anglo-Jewish Association. *Annual Reports.* London: The author.

Australian Israelite. Melbourne, 1871–1874.

Bougainville, Louis Antoine de. "La Decouverte de Tahiti." *La Revue de France,* September 1928.

Brauer, Erich. "The Jews of Afghanistan." *Jewish Social Studies,* April 1942.

Buchanan, Rev. Claudius. *Report of the London Society for Promoting Christianity amongst the Jews, with Dr. Buchanan's speech as to the state of the Jews in the East.* Brooklyn: T. Kirk, 1811.

Executive Council of Australian Jewry. *Annual Report–1965.* Sydney.

Fischel, Walter J. "Abraham Navarro—Jewish Interpreter and Diplomat in the Service of the English East India Company." *Proceedings of the American Academy for Jewish Research,* 1956.

———. "Cochin in Jewish History." ibid. 1962.

———. "Jews and Judaism at the Court of the Moghul Emperors in Mediaeval India." ibid. 1948–49.

———. "Secret Jews of Persia." *Commentary,* January 1949.

———. "The Jews of Persia—1795–1940." *Jewish Social Studies,* April 1950.

Fischer, Alfred J. "The Jews in Turkey." *Jewish Affairs,* March 1959.

Hill, Lionel. "Are Japanese Kin to the Jews?" *The American Hebrew,* August 16, 1929.

Hort, Abraham. "Letters." *Voice of Jacob,* September 16, 1842; July 21, 1843; December 8, 1843.

India and Israel. Bombay, July 1948–March 1953.

Indo-Israel Review. Bombay, September 1959–December 1963.

Israelite, The. Bombay

Jewish Chronicle. London

Jewish Ladies' Organization of Iran. *Brochure on the Occasion of the Twentieth Anniversary.* Teheran, July 1966.

Jewish Welfare Association, Delhi and Northern India. *Reports.* New Delhi, 1955–1957.

Kloetzel, Z.C. *Dokumento Judaica, Anjuvannam-Sonderhefte Judische Revue.* Munkacs: Nekuda Verlag, 1938.

Kopellowitz, Jehudah. "The Jews of Persia." *Menorah Journal,* January 1930.

Lippmann, Walter M. "Report from Overseas: Australia." *Congress Weekly,* March 14, 1949.

———. *Demography of Australian Jewry.* Sydney: Executive Council of Australian Jewry, 1961.

Mandelbaum, David G. "The Jewish Way of Life in Cochin." *Jewish Social Studies,* October 1939.

Marks, Percy J. *The First Synagogue in Australia.* Sydney: Ford, 1925.

Nathan, Naphtali. "Notes on the Jews of Turkey." *Jewish Journal of Sociology,* December 1964.

New Zealand Official Yearbook. *History, Constitution and Government.* Wellington: Government Printer, 1967.

Ort Federation, American. *ORT Yearbook.* New York, 1969.

Paiva, Moses Pereyra de. *Notisias dos Judeos de Cochim.* Amsterdam: Caza de Vry Levy, 1687.

———. *News of the Jews of Cochin.* Lisbon: Museu Comercial, 1923.

Philippines Herald. Manila, August 9, 1960.

Reissner, H.G. "Indian-Jewish Statistics (1837–1941)." *Jewish Social Studies,* October 1950.

Reuben, Rebecca. *The Bene Israel of Bombay.* London: Cambridge University Press, 1913.

Robinson, Nehemiah. *Persia and Afghanistan and Their Jewish Communities.* New York: Institute of Jewish Affairs-World Jewish Congress, 1953.

Samuel, Samuel R. "The Bene Israel of India." *Jewish Literary Annual* 1905.

Schwarzbart, Isaac. *The rise and decline of Jewish communities in the Far East and Southeast Asia.* New York: World Jewish Congress, 1957.

Shema. Calcutta.

Steinberg, Isaac N. *Report on the Kimberleys.* New York: Freeland League for Jewish Territorial Colonization, 1939.

Strizower, Schifra. "Jews as an Indian Caste." *Jewish Journal of Sociology,* 1959.

Temple Sinai Bulletin. Wellington.

Truth. Rishon L'Zion, Bene Israel Action Committee.

Werblowski, Zwi. "Bene Israel Battle." *And Ye Shall Teach Them,* New Delhi, June 1962.

Williams, Maynard O. "The Turkish Republic Comes of Age." *National Geographic,* May 1945.

World Jewry. London.